HEARING SECRET HARMONIES

The recipient of the Magnus Donners Prize was given dinner at the expense of the Company. A selection of writers, publishers, literary editors, columnists, anyone else deemed helpful to publicity in the circumstances, was invited. Speeches were made. It was not an evening-dress affair. Convened in a suite of rooms on the upper floor of a restaurant much used for such occasions, the party was usually held in the early months of the year following that for which the book had been chosen. As a function, the Magnus Donners Memorial Prize dinner was just what might be expected, a business gathering, rather than a social one. Delavacquerie, who had its arranging, saw that food and drink were never less than tolerable. When he and I next met for one of our luncheons together I asked what had been Widmerpool's condition for showing so easygoing an attitude.

'That he should himself be invited to the dinner.'

'Did he make the request ironically?'

'Not in the least.'

As a public figure of a sort, although one fallen into comparative obscurity, issue of an invitation to Widmerpool would in no way run counter to the general pattern of guests; even if his presence, owing to the particular circumstances, might strike a bizarre note. It was likely that a large proportion of those present would be too young to have heard – anyway too young to take much interest in – the scandals of ten years before.

A Dance to the Music of Time

All the books in the series
are available from Mandarin Paperbacks

ANTHONY POWELL

Hearing
Secret Harmonies

Mandarin

A Mandarin Paperback
HEARING SECRET HARMONIES

First published in Great Britain 1975
by William Heinemann Ltd
This edition published 1991
by Mandarin Paperbacks
Michelin House, 81 Fulham Road, London SW3 6RB

Mandarin is an imprint of the Octopus Publishing Group,
a division of Reed International Books Limited

Copyright © 1975 by Anthony Powell

A CIP catalogue record for this title
is available from the British Library

ISBN 0 7493 0646 7

Printed and bound in Great Britain
by Cox & Wyman Ltd, Reading, Berkshire

For Robert Conquest

A DANCE TO THE MUSIC OF TIME

★ ★ ★ ★ ★ ★ ★ ★ ★ ★ ★ ★

HEARING SECRET HARMONIES

1

DUCK, FLYING IN FROM THE south, ignored four or five ponderous explosions over at the quarry. The limestone cliff, dominant oblong foreground structure, lateral storeyed platforms, all coral-pink in evening sunlight, projected towards the higher ground on misty mornings a fading mirage of Babylonian terraces suspended in haze above the mere; the palace, with its hanging gardens, distantly outlined behind a group of rather woodenly posed young Medes (possibly young Persians) in Mr Deacon's *Boyhood of Cyrus*, the picture's recession equally nebulous in the shadows of the Walpole-Wilsons' hall. Within this hollow bed of the stream the whole range of the quarry was out of sight, except for where the just visible peak of an escarpment of spoil shelved up to the horizon's mountainous coagulations of floating cottonwool, a density of white cloud perforated here and there by slowly opening and closing loopholes of the palest blue light. It was a warm windy afternoon. Midday thunder had not brought back rain. Echoes of the blasting, counterfeiting a return of the storm, stirred faintly smouldering wartime embers; in conjunction with the duck, recalling an argument between General Bobrowski and General Philidor about shooting wildfowl. The angular formation taken by the birds (mimed by Pole and Frenchman with ferocious gestures) was now neatly exhibited, as the flight spiralled down deliberately, almost vertically, settling among reeds and waterlilies at the far end of the pool. Two columns of smoke rose above a line of blue-black trees thickly concentrated together beyond the dusty water, scrawling slate-coloured diagonals across the ceiling of powdered grit, inert and translucent, that swam above the screened workings. Metallic odours, like those of a laboratory, drifted down from a westerly direction, over-laying a nearer-by scent of fox.

'Here's one,' said Isobel. 'At least he's considering the matter.'

After the dredging of crevices lower down the brook, expectation was almost at an end. The single crayfish emerging from under the stones was at once followed by two more. Luck had come at last. The three crayfish, swart miniature lobsters of macabrely knowing demeanour, hung about doubtfully in a basin of mud below the surface. The decision was taken by the crayfish second to enter. He led the way with fussy self-importance, the other two bustling along behind. The three of them clawed a hold on to opposite sides of the outer edge of the iron rim supporting the trap's circle of wire-netting submerged at the water's edge, all at the same moment hurrying across the expanse of mesh towards a morsel of flyblown meat fastened at the centre.

'Do you want to hold the string, Fiona?' asked Isobel. 'Wait a second. A fourth has appeared.'

'Give it to me.'

The dark young man spoke with authority. Presented under the name of Scorpio Murtlock, he was by definition established as bossing the other three. As Fiona made no attempt, either as woman or niece, to assert prior right, Isobel handed him the lengths of twine from which the trap dangled. His status, known on arrival, required observation to take in fully. The age was hard to estimate. He could be younger than Barnabas Henderson, the other young man, thought to be in his later twenties. Fiona herself was twenty-one, so far as I could remember. The girl introduced as Rusty (no surname attached) looked a battered nineteen. I felt relieved that crayfish, as such, had not proved illusory, a mere crazy fancy, recognizable from the start as typical of those figments of a superannuated imagination older people used to put forward when one was oneself young. Four cray-fish had undeniably presented themselves, whether caught or not hardly mattered. In any case the occasion had been elevated, by what had been said earlier, to a level above that of a simple sporting event. This higher meaning had to be taken into consideration too.

'The trap must be hauled up gently, or they walk off again,' said Isobel. 'The frustration of the Old Man and the Sea is nothing to it.'

Murtlock, still holding the strings, gathered round him the three-quarter-length bluish robe he wore, a kind of smock or kaftan, not too well adapted to country pursuits. He went down on one knee by the bank. Sweeping out of his eyes handfuls of uncared-for black hair, he leant forward at a steep angle to inspect the crustaceans below, somehow conveying the posture of a priest engaged in the devotions of a recondite creed. He was small in stature, but impressive. The shining amulet, embossed with a hieroglyph, that hung round his throat from a necklace of beads, splashed into the water. He allowed it to remain for a second below the surface, while he gazed fixedly into the depths. Then, having waited for the fourth crayfish to become radically committed to the decomposing snack, he carefully lifted the circle of wire, outward and upward as instructed, from where it rested among pebbles and weed under the projecting lip of the bank.

'The bucket, Barnabas—the gloves, one of you.'

The order was sternly given, like all Murtlock's biddings.

3

Barnabas Henderson fumbled with the bucket. Fiona held out the gardening gloves. Rusty, grinning to herself uneasily, writhed her body about in undulating motions and hummed. Murtlock snatched a glove. Fitting on the fingers adroitly, without setting down the trap, by now dripping over his vestment-like smock, he picked a crayfish off the wire, dropping the four of them one by one into a pail already prepared quarter-full with water. His gestures were deft, ritualistic. He was totally in charge.

This gift of authority, ability to handle people, was the characteristic attributed by hearsay. At first the outward trappings, suggesting no more than a contemporary romantic vagabondage, had put that reputation in doubt. Now one saw the truth of some at least of what had been reported of him; that the vagabond style could include ability to control companions—notably Fiona—as well as crayfish and horses; the last skill demonstrated when they had arrived earlier that day in a small horse-drawn caravan. Murtlock's rather run-of-the-mill outlandishness certainly comprised something perceptibly priestly about it. That was over and above the genuflexion at the water's edge. There was an essentially un-sacerdotal side, one that suggested behaviour dubious, if not actively criminal. That aspect, too, was allied to a kind of fanaticism. Such distinguishing features, more or less, were to be expected after stories about him. A novice in a monastery of robber monks might offer not too exaggerated a definition. His eyes, pale, cold, unblinking, could not be denied a certain degree of magnetism.

Barnabas Henderson was another matter. He was similarly dressed in a blue robe, somewhat more ultramarine in shade, a coin-like object hanging from his neck too, hair in ringlets to the shoulder, with the addition of a Chinese magician's moustache. His spectacles, large and square, were in yellow plastic. The combination of moustache and spectacles created an effect not unlike those one-piece cardboard

4

contraptions to be bought in toyshops, moustache and spectacles held together by a false nose. That was unfair. Henderson was not a badlooking young man, if lacking Murtlock's venturesome bearing, as well as his tactile competence. Henderson's garments, no less eclectically chosen, were newer, a trifle cleaner, less convincingly part of himself. The genre was carried off pretty well by Murtlock, justly heralded as handsome. Henderson's milder features remained a trifle apologetic, his personality, in contrast, not by nature suited to the apparent intent. He was alleged to have abandoned a promising career as an art-dealer to follow this less circumscribed way of life. Perhaps that was a wrong identification, the new life desirable because additionally circumscribed, rather than less so. There could be little doubt that Henderson owned the caravan, painted yellow, its woodwork dilapidated, but drawn by a sound pair of greys. Probably Henderson was paying for the whole jaunt.

The girls, too, were dressed predominantly in blue. Rusty, whose air was that of a young prostitute, had a thick crop of dark red hair and deep liquid eyes. These were her good points. She was tall, sallow-skinned, hands large and coarse, her collar-bones projecting. Having maintained total silence since arrival, except for intermittent humming, she could be assessed only by looks, which certainly suggested extensive sexual experience.

Fiona, daughter of Isobel's sister Susan and Roddy Cutts, was a pretty girl ('Fiona has a touch of glamour,' her first-cousin, Jeremy Warminster, had said), small, fair-skinned, baby-faced, with her father's sandy hair. Otherwise she more resembled her mother, without the high spirits (an asset throughout her husband's now closed political career) brought out in Susan by any gathering that showed signs of developing into a party. Susan Cutts's occasional bouts of melancholy seemed latterly to have descended on her

5

daughter in the form of an innate lugubriousness, which had taken the place of Fiona's earlier tomboy streak.

The upper halves of both girls were sheathed in T-shirts, inscribed with the single word HARMONY. Rusty wore jeans, Fiona a long skirt that swept the ground. Dragging its flounces across the damp grass, she looked like a mediaeval lady from the rubric of an illuminated Book of Hours, a remote princess engaged in some now obsolete pastime. The appearance seemed to demand the addition of a wimple and pointed cap. This antique air of Fiona's could have played a part in typecasting Murtlock as a reprobate boy-monk. Equally viewed as whimsical figures in a Tennysonian-type Middle Age, the rôles of Rusty and Henderson were indeterminate; Rusty perhaps a recreant knight's runaway mistress disguised as a page; Henderson, an unsuccessful troubadour, who had mislaid his lute. This fanciful imagery was not entirely disavowed by the single word motto each girl bore on her breast, a lettered humour that could well have featured in the rubric of a mediaeval manuscript, inscribed on banner or shield of a small figure in the margin. The feet of all four were bare, and—another mediaeval touch—long unwashed.

Fiona (whose birth commemorated her parents' reconciliation after Roddy Cutts's misadventure with the cipherine during war service in Persia) had given a fair amount of trouble since her earliest years. This was in contrast with her two elder brothers: Jonathan, married, several children, rising rapidly in a celebrated firm of fine arts auctioneers; Sebastian, still unmarried, much addicted to girlfriends, though no less ambitious than his brother, 'in computers'. Both the Cutts sons were tireless conversationalists in their father's manner, uncheckable, informative, sagacious, on the subject of their respective jobs. Fiona, who had run away from several schools (been required to leave at least one), had strengthened her status as a difficult subject by catching typhoid abroad when aged fourteen or fifteen, greatly alarming everyone by her state. Abandonment of boisterous forms of rebellion, in favour of melancholic opposition, dated from the unhappy incident with the electrician, handsome and good-natured, but married and not particularly young. Since then nothing had gone at all well. Fiona's educational dislodgements had not impaired education sufficiently to prevent her from getting a living on the outskirts of 'glossy' journalism.

No one seemed to know where exactly Fiona had run across Scorpio Murtlock, nor the precise nature of this most recent association. It was assumed—anyway by her parents —to include cohabitation. Her uncle, Isobel's brother, Hugo Tolland, cast doubts on that. Hugo's opinions on that sort of subject were often less than reliable, a taste for exaggeration marring the accuracy that is always more interesting than fantasy. In this case, Hugo coming down on the side of scepticism—on grounds that, if Murtlock liked sex at all, he preferred his own—the view had to be taken into consideration. How Murtlock lived seemed as unknowable as his sexual proclivities. The Cutts parents, Roddy and Susan, always very 'good' about their daughter's vagaries, continued to be so, accepting the Murtlock régime with accustomed resignation.

The member of the family best equipped to speak with anything like authority of Fiona, and her friends, was Isobel's unmarried sister, Blanche Tolland, who had, in fact, rung up to ask if we were prepared to harbour a small caravan in our field for one night, its destination unspecified. The easygoing unambitious nature that had caused Blanche, in early days, to be regarded—not wholly without reason—as rather dotty, had latterly given her a certain status in dealing with a generation considerably younger than her own; Blanche's unemphatic personality providing a diplomatic contact, an agency through which dealings

7

could be negotiated by either side without prejudice or loss of face. This good nature, allied to a deep-seated taste for taking trouble in often uncomfortable circumstances, led to employment in an animal sanctuary, a job that had occupied Blanche for a long time by now.

'Blanchie meets the animals on their own terms,' said her sister, Norah, also unmarried. 'The young people too. She really runs a sanctuary for both.'

'Do you mean the young people think of Blanchie as an animal, or as another young person?' asked her brother.

'Which do you suppose, Hugo?' said Norah sharply. 'It's true they might easily mistake you for an ape.'

Hugo, rather a sad figure after the death of his partner, Sam, could still arouse the mood in Norah that had caused her to observe he would 'never find a place for himself in the contemporary world'. Working harder than ever in the antique shop, now he was on his own, Hugo's career could be regarded, in general, as no less contemporary than anyone else's. Sam (said to have begun life as a seaman) had remained surnameless (like Rusty) to the end, so far as most of the family were concerned. It was during this exchange in Norah's Battersea flat that I first heard the name of Scorpio Murtlock.

'Blanchie says Fiona's turned over a new leaf under the influence of this new young man, Scorp Murtlock. Sober, honest, and an early riser, not to mention meditations. No hint of a drug. It's a kind of cult. Religious almost. Harmony's the great thing. They have a special greeting they give one another. I can't remember the exact words. Quite impressive. They don't wash much, but then none of the Cutts family ever did much washing.'

'How did he come to be christened Scorp?' I asked.

'Short for Scorpio, his Zodiac sign.'

'What's he like?'

'Blanche says attractive, but spooky.'

At this point Hugo showed unexpected knowledge.

'I didn't know Fiona's latest was Scorpio Murtlock. I've never met him, but I used to hear about him several years ago, when he was working in the antique business. Two fellow antique dealers told me they had engaged a very charming young assistant.'

Norah was not prepared for Hugo to take over entirely in the Murtlock field.

'Blanchie says he has a creepy side too.'

'You can be creepy and attractive. There are different forms of creepiness, just as there are different forms of attractiveness.'

'The antique dealers are presumably queers?'

'Even so, that's hardly the point. Murtlock made himself immensely useful in the business—which ranges from garden furniture to vintage cars—so useful that the owners suddenly found they were being relegated to a back place themselves. Murtlock was slowly but surely elbowing them out.'

'Did their passion remain unsatisfied?'

'I'm not sure.'

'Unlike you, Hugo, not to be sure about that sort of thing.'

'One of them implied he'd brought off something. That was not the rather nervy one. The nervy one complained he had begun to feel like a man bewitched. Those were his own words. The unnervy one agreed after a while that there was something uncomfortable about Murtlock. They were wondering how best to solve their problem, when Murtlock himself gave notice. He'd found someone more profitable to work over. His new patron—a man of some age, even older than oneself, if that can be imagined—was apparently more interested in what Blanchie calls Murtlock's spooky side than in his sex appeal. They met during some business deal.'

9

'Murtlock doesn't sound a particularly desirable friend for Fiona.'

'Blanche says he makes her behave herself.'

'Even so.'

'Susan and Roddy are thankful for small mercies.'

'Taking exercise, meditation, no alcohol, sound quite large ones.'

'They sound to me like the good old Simple Life,' said Hugo. 'Still it's a relief one won't catch one's foot in a hypodermic when next at Blanchie's cottage.'

'You always talk about your nephews and nieces in the way Aunt Molly used to talk about you,' said Norah.

Hugo was not at all discomposed by the comparison.

'And you, Norah dear—and you. Think how Aunt Molly used to go on about you and Eleanor Walpole-Wilson. As a matter of fact, I quite agree I've turned into Aunt Molly. I'd noticed it myself. Old age might have transformed one into something much worse. Everybody liked her. I flatter myself I'm much what she'd have been had she remained unmarried.'

'I shall begin to howl, Hugo, if you talk like that about poor Eleanor.'

The Norah Tolland/Eleanor Walpole-Wilson ménage had not been revived after the war, their ways dividing, though they remained friends. Norah, never so fulfilled as during her years as driver in one of the women's services, had taken a job with a small car-hire firm, where she continued to wear a peaked cap and khaki uniform. Later she became one of the directors of the business, which considerably enlarged itself in scope, Norah always remaining available to drive, especially if a long continental trip were promised. Eleanor Walpole-Wilson, for her part, securing a seat on the Urban District Council, became immersed in local politics. Of late years she had embarked on a close relationship with a Swedish woman-doctor. Staying with this friend in Stockholm, Eleanor had been taken ill and died, bequeathing to Norah, with a small legacy, a pair of short-tempered pugs. Sensing mention of their former mistress, this couple now began to rush about the flat, snuffling and barking.

'Oh, shut up, pugs,' said Norah.

The commendation accorded to Scorpio Murtlock—that he could keep Fiona in order—limited in compass, was not to be lightly regarded, if valid. It was reiterated by Blanche, when she rang up about the caravan party. Never very capable of painting word pictures, she was unable to add much additional information about Murtlock, nor did she know anything, beyond her name, of the girl Rusty. Barnabas Henderson, on the other hand, possessed certain conventional aspects, notably a father killed in the war, who had left enough money for his son to buy a partnership in a small picture-dealing business; a commercial venture abandoned to follow Murtlock into the wilderness.

Blanche's assurance of comparatively austere behaviour—what Hugo called the good old Simple Life—had been to some extent borne out, on the arrival of Fiona and her friends, by refusal of all offers of food and drink. Provided with a bivouac under some trees, on the side of the field away from the house, they at once set about various minor tasks relative to settling in caravan and horses, behaviour that seemed to confirm the ascription of a severe standard of living. When, early in the afternoon, Isobel and I went to see how they were getting on, they had come to the end of these dispositions. Earlier negotiations about siting the caravan had been carried out with Fiona, Murtlock standing in silence with folded arms. Now he showed more sign of emerging as the strong personality he had been billed.

'Is there anything you'd all like to do?'

Fiona had been addressed. Murtlock took it upon himself to answer.

'Too late in the year to leap the fires.'

He spoke thoughtfully, without any touch of jocularity. This was evidently the line Blanche had denominated as spooky. Since we had agreed to put up the caravan, there was no reason, if kept within bounds, why Beltane should not be celebrated, or whatever it was he had in mind.

'We could make a bonfire.'

'Too near the solstice.'

'Something else then?'

'A sacrifice.'

'What sort?'

'One in Harmony.'

'Like Fiona's shirt?'

'Yes.'

He did not laugh. He did not even smile. This affirmative somehow inhibited further comment in a frivolous tone, imposing acquiescence in not treating things lightly, even Fiona's shirt. At the same time I was uncertain whether he was not simply teasing. On the face of it teasing seemed much more likely than all this assumed gravity. Nevertheless uncertainty remained, ambivalence of manner leaving one guessing. No doubt that was intended, after all a fairly well recognized method of establishing one sort of supremacy. The expressed aim—that things should be in Harmony—could not in itself be regarded as objectionable. It supported the contention that Fiona's latest set of friends held to stringent moral values of one sort or another. How best to achieve an act of Harmony was another matter.

'Harmony is not easy to define.'

'Harmony is Power—Power is Harmony.'

'That's how you see it?'

'That's how it is.'

He smiled. When Murtlock smiled the charm was revealed. He was a boy again, making a joke, not a fanatical young mystic. At the same time he was a boy with whom it was better to remain on one's guard.

'How are we going to bring off an act of Harmony on a Saturday afternoon?'

'Through the Elements.'

'What elements?'

'Fire, Air, Earth, Water.'

The question had been a foolish one. He smiled again. We discussed various possibilities, none of them very sparkling. The other three were silent throughout all this. Murtlock seemed to have transformed them into mere shadows of himself.

'Is there water near here? I think so. There is the feel of water.'

'A largish pond within walking distance.'

'We could make a water sacrifice.'

'Drown somebody?'

He did not answer.

'We could go crayfishing,' said Isobel.

Since demands made by improvisation at a moment's notice of the necessary tackle for this sport were relatively onerous, the proposal marked out Isobel, too, as not entirely uninfluenced by Murtlock's spell.

'The crayfish are in the pond?'

'In the pools of the brook that runs out of it.'

He considered.

'It can't be exactly described as a blood sport,' I added.

I don't know why inserting that lame qualification seemed required, except that prejudice against blood sports could easily accord with an outlook to be inferred from people dressed in their particular style. If asked to rationalize the comment, that would have been my pretext. Aggressive activities against crayfish might be, by definition, excluded from an afternoon's programme devoted to Harmony. Who could tell? Harmony was also Power, he said. Power would be exercised over crayfish, if caught, but possibly the wrong sort of Power. He pretended to be puzzled.

'You mean that without blood there is no vehicle for the spirit?'

'I mean that you might not like killing.'

'I do not kill, if not killed.'

He seemed glad to have an opportunity to make that statement, gnomic to say the least. It sounded like a favourite apophthegm of a luminary of the cult to which they all belonged, the familiar ring of Shortcuts to the Infinite, Wisdom of the East, Analects of the Sages. For some reason the pronouncement seemed also one recently brought to notice. Had I read it not long before in print? The Murtlock standpoint, his domination over Fiona and the others, was becoming a little clearer in a certain sense, if remaining obscure in many others.

'I don't think we'll be killed. Deaths crayfishing are comparatively rare.'

'You spoke not of death, but of killing.'

'The latter is surely apt to lead to the former?'

'There is killing—death is an illusion.'

This was no help so far as deciding how the afternoon was to be spent.

'The point is whether or not you would consider the killing of crayfish to be in Harmony?'

Once more his smile made me feel that it was I, rather than he, who was being silly.

'Not all killing is opposed to Harmony.'

'Let's kill crayfish then.'

The odd thing was that he managed never to be exactly discourteous, nor even embarrassing, when he talked in this way. It was always close to a joke, though a joke not quite brought to birth. At least you did not laugh. You accepted on its own merits what he said, unintelligible or the reverse. I wondered—had not some forty years stretched between us—

whether, as a contemporary, I should have been friends with Scorpio Murtlock. Indications were at best doubtful. That negative surmise was uninfluenced by his manner of talking, mystic and imperative, still less the style of dress. Both might have been acceptable at that age in a contemporary. In any case fashions of one generation, moral or physical, are scarcely at all assessable in terms of another. They cannot be properly equated. So far as they could be equated, the obstacles set up against getting on with Murtlock were in themselves negligible.

The objection to him, if objection there were, was the sense that he brought of something ominous. He would have been ominous—perhaps more ominous—in a City suit, the ominous side of him positively mitigated by a blue robe. His accents, liturgical, enigmatic, were also consciously rough, uncultivated. The roughness was imitated by Fiona and Henderson, when they remembered to do so. Rusty never uttered. No doubt Murtlock's chief attraction was owed to this ominousness, something more sexually persuasive than good looks, spectacular trappings, even sententious observations. Certainly Fiona was showing an altogether uncharacteristic docility in allowing, without any sign of dispute or passive disapproval, someone else to make all the going. It might be assumed that she and Rusty were 'in love' with Murtlock. Probably Henderson shared that passion. Murtlock himself showed no sign of being emotionally drawn to any of them. In the light of what had been reported, it would have been surprising had he done so.

'What do we need?'

He spoke this time in a tone of practical enquiry.

'A circle of wire mesh kept together by a piece of iron. Something like the rim of an old saucepan or fryingpan does well.'

'The circle, figure of perfection—iron, abhorred by demons.'

15

'Those aspects may help too.'

'They will.'

'Then a piece of preferably rotting meat.'

'Nothing far different from a sacrifice for a summoning.'

'In this case summoning crayfish.'

'Crayfish our sacrifice, rather.'

The requirements took a little time to get into order. A morsel of doubtful freshness was found among bones set aside for stock. The four of them joined in these preparations usefully, shaping the wire-netting, measuring out cords, fixing the tainted bait. When the trap was assembled Murtlock swung it gently through the air. Even in undertaking this trial of weight, which showed grasp of the sport, there was something of the swaying of a priest's censer.

'And now?'

'The crayfish beds, such as they are, lie about a quarter of a mile away.'

The brook flowed through fields of poorish pasture, tangled with undergrowth as they sloped down more steeply to the line of the stream. Once the trap was slung among its stones Murtlock seemed satisfied. If the others were bored, they did not dare show it during the long period when there was no sign of a catch. Conversation altogether flagged. Murtlock himself possessed to a marked degree that characteristic—perhaps owing something to hypnotic powers—which attaches to certain individuals; an ability to impose on others present the duty of gratifying his own whims. It seemed to matter that Murtlock should get what he wanted—in this case crayfish—while, if the others were bored, that was their affair. No particular obligation was laid on oneself to prevent it. When at last the circle of iron showed signs of possessing the supposedly magical properties he had attributed, four crayfish caught, this modest final success, obviously pleasing to Murtlock, was for some reason exceptionally pleasing to oneself too. By then afternoon was turning to evening. Again he took the initiative.

'We'll go back now. There are things to do at the caravan. Barnabas must water the horses.'

'Sure you won't dine?'

'Yes.'

'I can easily run up something,' said Isobel.

'The day is one of limited fast.'

Fiona had not explained that when the dinner invitation had been issued some hours earlier.

'Nothing else you want?'

'No.'

'A bottle of wine?'

Then I remembered that they abstained from alcohol.

'No—have you a candle?'

'We can lend you an electric torch.'

'Only for a simple fire ritual.'

'Come back to the house. We'll look for candles.'

'Barnabas can fetch it, if needed. It may not be.'

'Don't start a forest fire, will you?'

He smiled at that.

'Only the suffusion of a few laurel leaves.'

'As you see, laurel is available.'

'Pine-cones?'

'There are one or two conifers up the road to the right.'

'We'll go back then. Take the bucket, Barnabas. The gloves are on the ground, Fiona. Rusty, carry the trap—no, Rusty will carry it.'

None of them was allowed to forget for a moment that he or she was under orders. When the crayfishing paraphernalia had been brought together we climbed the banks that enclosed this length of the stream. After crossing the fields the path led through trees, the ground underfoot thick with wild garlic. At one point, above this Soho restaurant smell,

17

the fox's scent briefly reasserted itself. Here Murtlock stopped. Gazing towards a gap between the branches of two tall oaks, he put up a hand to shade his eyes. The others imitated his attitude. In his company they seemed to have little or no volition of their own. Murtlock's control was absolute. The oak boughs formed a frame for one of the blue patches of sky set among clouds, now here and there flecked with pink. Against this irregular quadrilateral of light, over the meadows lying in the direction of Gauntlett's farm a hawk hovered; then, likely to have marked down a prey, swooped off towards the pond. Murtlock lowered his arm. The others copied him.

'The bird of Horus.'

'Certainly.'

'Do you often see hawks round here?'

He asked the question impatiently, almost angrily.

'This particular one is always hanging about. He was near the house yesterday, and the day before. He's a well-known local personality. Perhaps a retired kestrel from a 'Thirties poem.'

The allusion might be obscure to one of his age. So much the better. Obscurity could be met with obscurity. A second later, either on the hawk's account, or from some other disturbing factor in their vicinity—the quarry end of the pond—the duck flew out again. Rising at an angle acute as their former descent, the flight took on at once the disciplined wedge-shaped configuration used in all duck transit, leader at apex, main body following behind in semblance of a fan. Mounting higher, still higher, soaring over copper and green beechwoods, the birds achieved considerable altitude before a newly communicated command wheeled them off again in a fresh direction. Adjusting again to pattern, they receded into creamy cavernous billows of distant cloud, beyond which the evening sun drooped. Into this opaque glow of fire they disappeared. To the initiated, I reflected—to ancient soothsayers—the sight would have been vaticinatory.

'What message do the birds foretell?'

Even allowing for that sort of thing being in his line, Murtlock's question, put just at the moment when the thought was in my own mind, brought a slight sense of shock. He uttered the words softly, as if now gratified at being able to accept my train of thought as coherent, in contrast with earlier demur on the subject of death and killing. Even with intimates that sort of implied knowledge of what is going on in one's head, recognition of unspoken thoughts passing through the mind—in its way common enough—can be a little disconcerting, much more so to be thought-read by this strange young man. The ducks' coalescence into the muffled crimsons of sunset had been dramatic enough to invoke reflection on mysterious things, and such a subject as ornithomancy was evidently of the realm to which he aspired. The process was perhaps comparable with the intercommunication practised by the birds themselves, their unanimous change of direction, well ordered regrouping, rapid new advance, disciplined as troops drilling on the square; more appositely, aircraft obeying a radioed command.

This well disciplined aspect of duck behaviour must have been partly what entranced the generals, when with such fervour both of them had demonstrated the triangular formation. The evening came back vividly. Duties of the day over—I had been conducting officer with a group of Allied military attachés—we had been sitting in the bar of the little Normandy auberge where we were billeted. Bobrowski had almost upset his beer in demonstrating the precise shape of the flight. Philidor was calmer. Some years after the war—he was in exile, of course, from his own country—Bobrowski had been knocked down by a taxi, and killed. Oddly enough Philidor, too, had died in a car accident—so a Frenchman at their Embassy said—having by then attained quite high rank. Perhaps such deaths were appropriate to men of action, better than a slow decline. Aware that a more than usually acute consciousness of human mortality had descended, I wondered for a moment whether Murtlock was responsible for that sensation. It was not impossible.

'I was thinking of the Roman augurs too.'

'They also scrutinized the entrails of animals for prophecy.'

He added that with a certain relish.

'Sometimes—as the Bard remarks—the sad augurs mocked their own presage.'

One had to fight back. Murtlock made no comment. I hoped the quotation had floored him. The rest of the walk back to where the caravan was parked took place in silence and without incident. At the caravan our ways would divide, if the four of them were not to enter the house. Separation was delayed by the appearance of Mr Gauntlett advancing towards us.

'Good afternoon, Mr Gauntlett.'

Mr Gauntlett, wearing a cowslip in his buttonhole, greeted us. He showed no sign whatever of thinking our guests at all unusually dressed, nodding to them in a friendly manner, without the least curiosity as to why the males should be wearing blue robes.

'Happen you've seen my old bitch, Daisy, this way, Mr Jenkins? Been gone these forty-eight hours, and I don't know where she's to.'

'We haven't, Mr Gauntlett.'

A farmer, now retired as close on eighty, Mr Gauntlett lived in an ancient tumbledown farmhouse not far away, where—widower, childless, sole survivor of a large family —he 'did for himself', a life that seemed to suit him, unless rheumatics caused trouble. His house, associated by local legend with a seventeenth-century murder, was said to be haunted. Mr Gauntlett himself, though he possessed a keen sense of the past, and liked to discuss such subjects as whether the Romans brought the chestnut to Britain, always asserted that the ghosts had never inconvenienced him. This taste for history could account for a habit of allowing himself archaisms of speech, regional turns of phrase, otherwise going out of circulation. In not at all disregarding the importance of style in facing life—even consciously histrionic style—Mr Gauntlett a little resembled General Conyers. They both shared the same air of distinction, firmness, good looks that resisted age, but above all this sense of style. Mr. Gauntlett had once told me that during service (in the first war) with the Yeomanry, he had found himself riding through the Khyber Pass, a background of vast mountains, bare rocks, fierce tribesmen, that seemed for some reason not at all out of accord with his own mild manner.

'Maybe Daisy's littered in the woods round here, as she did three years gone. Then she came home again, and made a great fuss, for to bring me to a dingle down by the water, where she'd had her pups. The dogs round about knew of it. They'd been barking all night for nigh on a week to drive foxes and the like away, but I haven't heard 'em barking o' nights this time.'

'We'll keep an eye out for Daisy, Mr Gauntlett. Tell her to go home if we find her, report to you if we run across a nest of her pups. We've all been crayfishing.'

I said that defensively, speaking as if everyone under thirty always wore blue robes for that sport. I felt a little diminished by being caught with such a crew by Mr Gauntlett.

'Ah?'

'We landed four.'

Mr Gauntlett laughed.

'Many a year since I went out after crayfish. Used to as a boy. Good eating they make. Well, I must go on to be looking for the old girl.'

He was already moving off when Murtlock addressed him.

'Seek the spinney by the ruined mill.'

He spoke in an odd toneless voice. Mr Gauntlett, rare with him, showed surprise. He looked more closely at Murtlock, evidently struck not so much by eccentricity of dress as knowledge of the neighbourhood.

'Ah?'

'Go now.'

Murtlock gave one of his smiles. Immediately after speaking those two short sentences a subtle change in him had taken place. It was as if he had fallen into—then emerged from—an almost instantaneous trance. Mr Gauntlett was greatly pleased with this advice.

'I'll be off to the spinney, instead of the way I was going. That's just where Daisy might be. And my thanks to you, if I find her.'

'If you find her, make an offering.'

'Ah?'

'It would be well to burn laurel and alder in a chafing dish.'

Mr Gauntlett laughed heartily. The suggestion seemed not to surprise him so much as might be expected.

'I'll put something extra in the plate at church on Sunday. That's quite right. It's what I ought to do.'

'Appease the shades of your dwelling.'

Mr Gauntlett laughed again. I do not know whether he took that as an allusion to his haunted house, or even if such were indeed Murtlock's meaning. Whatever intended, he certainly conveyed the impression that he was familiar with the neighbourhood. Perhaps he had already made enquiries about haunted houses round about, the spinney by the old mill entering into some piece of information given. Murtlock would have been capable of that. Mr Gauntlett turned again to continue his search for Daisy. Then, suddenly thinking of another matter, he paused a moment.

'Is there more news of the quarry and The Fingers, Mr Jenkins?'

'They're still hoping to develop in that direction,' said Isobel.

'Ah?'

'We mustn't take our eye off them.'

'No, for sure, that's true.'

Mr Gauntlett repeated his farewells, and set off again, this time in the direction of the old mill.

'How on earth did you know about Daisy being at the spinney?'

'The words came.'

Murtlock spoke this time almost modestly. He seemed to attach no great importance to the advice given, in fact almost to have forgotten the fact that he had given it. He was clearly thinking now of quite other matters. This was where we should leave them. Henderson had set down the bucket containing the crayfish. Rusty was sitting on the grass beside the trap. When Fiona handed over the gardening gloves she allowed a faint gesture in the direction of humdrum usage to escape her.

'Thanks for letting us put up the caravan.'

She looked at Murtlock quickly to make sure this was not too cringing a surrender, too despicable a retreat down the road of conventionality. He nodded with indifference. There was apparently no harm in conceding that amount in the circumstances. Henderson, blinking through the yellow specs, simpered faintly under his Fu Manchu moustache. Rusty, rising from the ground, scratched under her armpit thoughtfully.

'Why not take the crayfish as hors d'oeuvres for supper—or would they be too substantial for your limited fast?'

Fiona glanced at Murtlock. Again he nodded.

'All right.'

'They have to be gutted.'

Murtlock seemed pleased at the thought of that.

'Fiona can do the gutting. That will be good for you, Fiona.'

She agreed humbly.

'You'll be able to prophesy from the entrails,' I said.

No one laughed.

'Bring the bucket back before you leave in the morning,' said Isobel. 'I expect we shall see you in any case before you go, Fiona?'

The matter was once more referred to Murtlock for a ruling. He shook his head. The answer was negative. We should not see them the following day.

'No.'

Murtlock gruffly expanded Fiona's reply.

'We take the road at first light.'

'Early as that?'

'Our journey is long.'

'Where are you making for?'

Instead of mentioning a town or village he gave the name of a prehistoric monument, a Stone Age site, not specially famous, though likely to be known to people interested in those things. Aware vaguely that such spots were the object of pilgrimage on the part of cults of the kind to which Fiona and her friends appeared to belong, I was not greatly surprised by the answer. I supposed the caravan did about twenty miles a day, but was not at all sure of that. If so, the group of megaliths would take several days to reach.

'We were there some years ago, coming home from that

part of the world. Are you planning to park near the Stones?'

It was a characteristic 'long barrow', set on the edge of a valley, two uprights supporting a capstone, entrance to a chambered tomb. The place had been thoroughly excavated.

'As near as sanctity allows.'

Murtlock answered curtly.

'Sanctity was being disturbed a good deal by tourists when we were there.'

A look of anger passed over his face, either at the comment, or thought of the tourists. He was quite formidable when he looked angry.

'If you're interested in archaeological sites, we've a minor one just over the hill from here. You probably know about it. The Devil's Fingers—The Fingers, as Mr Gauntlett calls it.'

If he knew something of Mr Gauntlett's house being haunted, he might well have heard of The Devil's Fingers. The name seemed new to him. He became at once more attentive.

'It's worth a visit, if you like that sort of thing. Only a short detour from the road you'll probably be taking in any case.'

'A prehistoric grave?'

'No doubt once, though that's been disputed.'

'What remains?'

'Two worn pillars about five foot high, and the same distance apart.'

'No portal?'

'Only the supports survive, if that's what they are.'

'The Threshold.'

'If a tomb, the burial chamber has long disappeared through ploughing. The general consensus of archaeological opinion accepts the place as a neolithic grave. There have been dissentient theories—boundary stones in the Dark Ages, and so on. They don't amount to much. Local patriotism naturally makes one want the place to be as ancient as possible. The lintel probably went for building purposes in one of the farms round about. The uprights may have been too hard to extract. In any case there's usually a superstition that you can't draw such stones from the earth. Even if you do, they walk back again.'

'Why the name?'

'One Midsummer night, long ago, a girl and her lover were lying naked on the grass. The sight of the girl's body tempted the Devil. He put out his hand towards her. Owing to the night also being the Vigil of St John, the couple invoked the Saint, and just managed to escape. When the Devil tried to withdraw his hand, two of his fingers got caught in the outcrop of rock you find in these quarrying areas. There they remain in a petrified condition.'

Murtlock was silent. He seemed suddenly excited.

'Any other legends about the place?'

'The couple are sometimes seen dancing there. They were saved from the Devil, but purge their sin by eternal association with its scene.'

'They dance naked?'

'I presume.'

'On Midsummer Night?'

'I don't know whether only on the anniversary, or all the year round. In rather another spirit, rickety children used to be passed between the Stones to effect a cure.'

That was one of Mr Gauntlett's stories.

'Is the stag-mask dance known to have been performed there?'

'I've never heard that. In fact I've never heard of the stag-mask dance.'

Murtlock was certainly well up in these things.

'Do the Stones bleed if a dagger is thrust in them at the Solstices?'

26

'I've never heard that either. There's the usual tale that at certain times—when the cock crows at midnight, I think —the Stones go down to the brook below to drink.'

Murtlock made no comment.

'Covetous people have sometimes taken that opportunity for seeking treasure in the empty sockets, and been crushed on the unexpected return of the Stones. The Stones' drinking habits are threatened. They will have to remain thirsty, unless the efforts of various people are successful. One of the quarries is trying to extend in that direction. They want to fill up the stream. Local opposition is being rallied. Where else will the Stones be able to quench their thirst? That was what the old farmer who talked to us was referring to.'

This time Murtlock showed no interest. The threat to The Devil's Fingers might have been judged something to shock anyone who had spoken of the sanctity of another prehistoric site, but he seemed altogether unmoved. At least he enquired no further as to the conservation problem as presented to him. He did, however, ask how the place could be reached, showing close attention when Isobel explained. He discarded all his elaborately mystical façade while listening to instructions of that sort.

'Is it a secluded spot?'

'About half-a-dozen fields from the road.'

'On high ground?'

'I'd guess about five or six hundred feet.'

'Surrounded by grass?'

'Plough, when we were last there, but the farmer may have gone back to grass.'

'Trees?'

'The Stones stand in an elder thicket on the top of a ridge. It's one of those characteristic settings. The land the other side slopes down to the stream.'

Murtlock thought for a moment or two. His face was

27

pallid now. He seemed quite agitated at what he had been told. This physical reaction on his part suggested in him something more than the mere calculating ambition implied by Hugo's story. Forces perhaps stronger than himself dominating him, made it possible for him also to dominate by the strength of his own feelings. He turned abruptly on the others, standing passively by while his interrogation was taking place.

'Tomorrow we'll go first to The Devil's Fingers. We'll reach there by dawn.'

They concurred.

'You'll find it of interest.'

He made an odd gesture, indicative of impatience, amazement, contempt, at the inadequacy of such a comment in the context. Then his more mundane half-amused air returned.

'Barnabas will leave the bucket by the kitchen door when we set out in the morning.'

'That would be kind.'

'Don't forget, Barnabas.'

Henderson's lip trembled slightly. He muttered that it would be done.

'Then we'll bid you goodbye,' said Isobel.

Fiona, assuming the expression of one taking medicine, allowed herself to be kissed. Henderson rather uneasily offered a hand, keeping an eye on Murtlock in case he was doing wrong. Rusty gave a grin, and a sort of wave. Murtlock himself raised his right hand. The gesture was not far short of benediction. There was a feeling in the air that, to be wholly correct, Isobel and I should have intoned some already acquired formula to convey that gratitude as to the caravan's visit was something owed only by ourselves. There was a short pause while this antiphon remained unvoiced. Then, since nothing further seemed forthcoming on either side, each party turned away from the other. The four visitors moved towards the caravan, there to perform what-ever rites or duties, propitiatory or culinary, might lie before them. We returned to the house.

'I agree with whoever it was thought the dark young man creepy,' said Isobel.

'Just a bit.'

Departure the following morning must have taken place as early as announced. No one heard them go. A candle had apparently proved superfluous, because Henderson never arrived to demand one. His own responsibilities, material and moral, must have turned out too onerous for him to have remembered about the bucket. It was found, not by the kitchen door, but on its side in the grass among the tracks of the caravan. The crayfish were gone. Traces of a glutinous substance, later rather a business to clean out, adhered to the bucket's sides, which gave off an incense-like smell. Isobel thought there was a suggestion of cam-phor. A few charred laurel leaves also remained in an empty tomato juice tin. Whatever the scents left behind, they were agreed to possess no narcotic connotations. This visit, well defined in the mind at the time, did not make any very lasting impression, Fiona and her companions manifesting themselves as no more than transient representa-tives of a form of life bound, sooner or later, to move into closer view. Their orientation might be worth attention, according to mood; meanwhile other things took precedence.

2

TWO COMPENSATIONS FOR GROWING OLD are worth putting on record as the condition asserts itself. The first is a vantage point gained for acquiring embellishments to narratives that have been unfolding for years beside one's own, trimmings that can even appear to supply the conclusion of a given story, though finality is never certain, a dimension always possible to add. The other mild advantage endorses a keener perception for the authenticities of mythology, not only of the traditional sort, but—when such are any good— the latterday mythologies of poetry and the novel. One such fragment, offering a gloss on the crayfishing afternoon, cropped up during the summer months of the same year, when I was reading one night after dinner.

The book, Harington's translation of *Orlando Furioso*— bedside romance of every tolerably well-educated girl of Byron's day—now requires, if not excuse, at least some sort of explanation. Twenty years before, writing a book about Robert Burton and his *Anatomy of Melancholy*, I had need to glance at Ariosto's epic, Burton being something of an Ariosto fan. Harington's version (lively, but inaccurate) was then hard to come by; another (less racy, more exact), just as suitable for the purpose. Although by no means all equally readable, certain passages of the poem left a strong impression. Accordingly, when a new edition of Harington's *Orlando Furioso* appeared, I got hold of it. I was turning the pages that evening with the sense—essential to mature enjoyment of any classic—of being entirely free from responsibility to pause for a second over anything that threatened the least sign of tedium.

In spite of the title, Orlando's madness plays a comparatively small part in the narrative's many convolutions. This does not mean Ariosto himself lacked interest in that facet of his story. On the contrary, he is profoundly concerned with the cause—and cure—of Orlando's mental breakdown. What happened? Orlando (Charlemagne's Roland), a hero, paladin, great man, had gone off his head because his girl, Angelica, beautiful, intelligent, compassionate, everything a nice girl should be—so to speak female counterpart of Orlando himself—had abandoned him for a nonentity. She had eloped with a good-looking utterly boring young man. Ariosto allows the reader to remain in absolutely no doubt as to the young man's total insignificance. The situation is clearly one that fascinates him. He emphasizes the vacuity of mind shown by Angelica's lover in a passage describing the young man's carving of their intertwined names on the trunks of trees, a whimsicality that first reveals to Orlando himself his own banal predicament.

Orlando's ego (his personal myth, as General Conyers would have said) was murderously wounded. He found himself altogether incapable of making the interior adjustment required to continue his normal routine of living the Heroic Life. His temperament allowing no half measures, he chose, therefore, the complete negation of that life. Discarding his clothes, he lived henceforth in deserts and waste places, roaming hills and woods, gaining such sustenance as he might, while waging war against a society he had renounced. In short, Orlando dropped out.

Ariosto describes how one of Orlando's friends, an

English duke named Astolpho, came to the rescue. Riding a hippogryph (an intermediate beast Harington calls his 'Griffith Horse', like the name of an obscure poet), Astolpho undertook a journey to the Moon. There, in one of its valleys, he was shown all things lost on Earth: lost kingdoms: lost riches: lost reputations: lost vows: lost hours: lost love. Only lost foolishness was missing from this vast stratospheric Lost Property Office, where by far the largest accretion was lost sense. Although he had already discovered in this store some of his lost days and lost deeds, Astolpho was surprised to come across a few of his own lost wits, simply because he had never in the least missed them. He had a duty to perform here, which was to bring back from his spacetrip the wits (mislaid on an immeasurably larger scale than his own) of his old friend and comrade-in-arms, Orlando. It was Astolpho's achievement—if so to be regarded—to restore to Orlando his former lifestyle, make feasible for him the resumption of the Heroic Life.

Journeys to the Moon were in the news at that moment (about a year before the astronauts actually landed there) because Pennistone had just published his book on Cyrano de Bergerac, whose *Histoire comique des états et empires de la lune* he used to discuss, when we were in the War Office together. Pennistone was more interested in his subject as philosopher and heresiarch than space-traveller, but, all the same, Cyrano had to be admitted as an example of a remark once made by X. Trapnel: 'A novelist writes what he is. That is equally true of authors who deal with mediaeval romance or journeys to the Moon.' I don't think Trapnel had ever read Ariosto, feel pretty sure he had never attempted Cyrano—though he could surprise by unexpected authors dipped into—but, oddly enough, *Orlando Furioso* does treat of both Trapnel's off-the-cuff fictional categories, mediaeval romance and an interplanetary journey.

Among other adventures on the Moon, during this expedition, Astolpho sees Time at work. Ariosto's Time—as you might say, Time the Man—was, anthropomorphically speaking, not necessarily everybody's Time. Although equally hoary and naked, he was not Poussin's Time, for example, in the picture where the Seasons dance, while Time plucks his lyre to provide the music. Poussin's Time (a painter's Time) is shown in a sufficiently unhurried frame of mind to be sitting down while he strums his instrument. The smile might be thought a trifle sinister, nevertheless the mood is genial, composed.

Ariosto's Time (a writer's Time) is far less relaxed, indeed appallingly restless. The English duke watched Ariosto's Time at work. The naked ancient, in an eternally breathless scramble with himself, collected from the Fates small metal tablets (one pictured them like the trinkets hanging from the necks of Murtlock and Henderson), then moved off at the double to dump these identity discs in the waters of Oblivion. A few of them (like Murtlock's medallion at the pond) were only momentarily submerged, being fished out, and borne away to the Temple of Fame, by a pair of well disposed swans. The rest sank to the bottom, where they were likely to remain.

On the strength of this not too obscure allegory, I decided to go to bed. Just before I closed the book, my eye was caught by a stanza in an earlier sequence.

> And as we see straunge cranes are woont to do,
> First stalke a while er they their wings can find,
> Then soare from ground not past a yard or two,
> Till in their wings they gather'd have the wind,
> At last they mount the very clouds unto,
> Triangle wise according to their kind:
> So by degrees this Mage begins to flye,
> The bird of *Jove* can hardly mount so hye;

And when he sees his time and thinks it best,
He falleth downe like lead in fearfull guise,
Even as the fawlcon doth the foule arrest,
The ducke and mallard from the brooke that rise.

The warm windy afternoon, cottonwool clouds, ankle-deep wild garlic, rankness of fox, laboratory exhalations from the quarry, parade ground evolutions of the duck, hawk's precipitate flight towards the pool, all were suddenly recreated. Duck, of course, rather than cranes, had risen 'triangle wise', but the hawk, as in Ariosto's lines (or rather Harington's), had hung pensively in the air, then swooped to strike. I tried to rationalize to myself this coincidental passage. There was nothing at all unusual in mallard getting up from the water at that time of day, nor a kestrel hovering over the neighbouring meadows. For that matter, reference to falconry in a Renaissance poem was far from remarkable. Something in addition to all that held the attention. It was the word Mage. Mage carried matters a stage further.

Mage summoned up the image of Dr Trelawney, a mage if ever there was one. I thought of the days when, as a child, I used to watch the Doctor and his young disciples, some of them no more than children themselves, trotting past the Stonehurst gate on their way to rhythmical callis-thenics—whatever the exercises were—on the adjacent expanse of heather. In those days (brink of the first war) Dr Trelawney was still building up a career. He had not yet fully transformed himself into the man of mystery, the thaumaturge, he was in due course to become. The true surname was always in doubt (Grubb or Tibbs, put forward by Moreland), anyway something with less body to it than Trelawney. In his avatar of the Stonehurst period he had been less concerned with the predominantly occult engage-ment of later years; then seeking The Way (to use his own phrase) through appropriate meditations, exercises, diet, apparel.

Once a week Dr Trelawney and his neophytes would jog down the pine-bordered lane from which our Indian-type bungalow was set a short distance back. The situation was remote, a wide deserted common next door. Dr Trelawney himself would be leading, dark locks flowing to the shoulder, biblical beard, grecian tunic, thonged sandals. The Doctor's robe (like the undefiled of Sardis) was white, somewhat longer and less diaphanous than the single garment—identical for both sexes and all weathers—worn by the disciples, tunics tinted in the pastel shades fashionable at that epoch. People who encountered Dr Trelawney by chance in the village post-office received an invariable greeting:

'The Essence of the All is the Godhead of the True.'

The appropriate response can have been rarely returned.

'The Vision of Visions heals the Blindness of Sight.'

One of the firmest tenets—so Moreland always said—in the later teachings of Dr Trelawney was that coincidence was no more than 'magic in action'. There had just been an example of that. *Orlando Furioso* had not only produced that evening a magical reconstruction of considerable force, it had also brought to mind the reason why such activities as Dr Trelawney's were already much in the air. A recent newspaper colour supplement article, dealing with contemporary cults, had mentioned that—with much of what Hugo Tolland called the good old Simple Life—a revival of Trelawneyism had come about among young people. That was probably where Murtlock had acquired the phrases about killing, and no death in Nature. It was Dr Trelawney's view—also that of his old friend and fellow occultist, Mrs Erdleigh—that death was no more than transition, blending, synthesis, mutation. To be fair to them both, they seemed to some extent to have made their point. However much the uninstructed might regard them both as 'dead', there were still those for whom they were very much alive. Mrs Erdleigh (quoting the alchemist, Thomas Vaughan) had spoken of how the 'liberated soul ascends, looking at the sunset towards the west wind, and hearing secret harmonies'. Perhaps Vaughan's words, filtered through a kind of Neo-Trelawneyism, explained the girls' T-shirts.

In any case it was impossible to disregard the fact that, while a dismantling process steadily curtails members of the cast, items of the scenery, airs played by the orchestra, in the performance that has included one's own walk-on part for more than a few decades, simultaneous derequisition-ings are also to be observed. Mummers return, who might have been supposed to have made their final exit, even if—like Dr Trelawney and Mrs Erdleigh—somewhat in the rôle of Hamlet's father. The touching up of time-expired sets, reshaping of derelict props, updating of old refrains, are none of them uncommon. An event some days later again brought forcibly to mind these lunar rescues from the Valley of Lost Things. This was a television programme devoted to the subject of the all-but-forgotten novelist, St John Clarke.

Above all others, St John Clarke might be judged, criti-cally speaking, as gone for good. Not a bit of it. Here was a consummate instance of a lost reputation—in this case a literary one—salvaged from the Moon, St John Clarke's Astolpho being Ada Leintwardine. Keen on transvestism, Ariosto would have found nothing incongruous in a woman playing the part of the English duke. Maidens clad in armour abound throughout the poem. Ada Leintwardine, as a successful novelist married to the well-known publisher, J. G. Quiggin, could be accepted as a perfectly concordant Ariosto character. In any case she had latterly been taking an increasingly executive part in forming the policy of the firm of which her husband was chairman. Quiggin used to complain that St John Clarke's novels (all come finally to rest under his firm's imprint) sold 'just the wrong amount', too steady a trickle to be ruthlessly disregarded, not enough comfortably to cover production costs. Nor was there compensatory prestige—rather the reverse—in having a name in the list unknown to a younger generation. In fact Quiggin himself did not deny that he was prepared to allow such backnumbers to fall out of print. Ada, on the other hand, would not countenance that. Her reasons were not wholly commercial; not commercial, that is, on the short-term basis of her husband's approach.

Ada's goal was to have a St John Clarke novel turned into a film. This had become almost an obsession with her. Ten years before she had failed—she alleged by a hair's breadth—to persuade Louis Glober to make a picture of *Match Me Such Marvel*, and, after Glober's death, vigorous canvassing of other film producers, American or British, had been no less fruitless. Meanwhile, St John Clarke's literary shares continued to slump. Ada, though she made fairly frequent appearances on television, had not herself produced a novel for some years. Remaining preoccupied with the St John Clarke project, she at last achieved the small advance in her plans that a television programme should be made about the novelist's life and work. This she regarded as a start, something to prepare the ground for later adaptation of one of the books.

Even their old friend, Mark Members, agreed that the Quiggins' marriage, whatever its ups and downs, had been on the whole a success. Members, who had no children himself, used to laugh at the disparity between Quiggin's former views on rebellion, and present attitude towards his twin daughters, Amanda and Belinda, now of university age and troublemakers. Quiggin's grumbling on that subject usually took place when Ada was not about. One of the twins had recently been concerned (only as a witness) in a drug prosecution; the other, about the same time, charged (later acquitted) with kicking a policeman. Quiggin was less reconciled to that sort of thing than, say, Roddy Cutts in relation to Fiona's caprices. In business matters the Quiggins got on well together too, showed a united front. It was the exception that there should be disagreement about St John Clarke.

Quiggin was doubtful as to the wisdom of propagating the novelist's name at this late stage. He feared that a small temporary increase in demand for the books would merely add to his own embarrassments as their publisher. His objection did not hold out very long. In due course Ada had her way. She seems to have brought about her husband's conversion to the idea by pointing out that he himself, as former secretary of St John Clarke, would play a comparatively prominent part in any documentary produced. Quiggin finally gave in at one of their literary dinner parties, choosing the moment after his wife had produced an aphorism.

'The television of the body brings the sales everlasting.'

Quiggin bowed his head.

'Amen, then. I resign St John Clarke to the makers of all things televisible.'

As a fellow ex-secretary of St John Clarke, Members would also have to be included in any programme about the novelist. That was no great matter. Members and Quiggin had been on goodish terms now for years, even admitting the kinship (second-cousins apparently), always alleged by Sillery, nowadays disputing with each other only who had enjoyed the more modest home. Both had come to look rather distinguished, Quiggin's dome-like forehead, sparse hair, huge ears, gave him a touch of grotesquerie, not out of place in a prominent publisher. Members, his white hair worn long, face pale and lined, had returned to the

Romantic Movement overtones of undergraduate days. His air was that of an eighteenth-century sage too highminded to wear a wig—Blake, Benjamin Franklin, one of the Encyclopaedists—suitable image for a figure of his eminence in the cultural world. When in London, his American wife, Lenore, fell in with this historical mood, doing so with easy assurance. They remained married, though Lenore spent increasingly long spells in her own country, an arrangement that seemed to suit both of them.

A graver problem than Members, in relation to the St John Clarke programme, was Vernon Gainsborough—now generally styled Dr Gainsborough, as holding an academic post in political theory—who (under his original name of Wernher Guggenbühl) had as a young man, finally displaced both Members and Quiggin in St John Clarke's employment. Quiggin (in those days writing letters to the papers in defence of the Stalinist purges) used to complain that Guggenbühl (as he then was) had perverted St John Clarke to Trotskyism. Some sort of a rapprochement had taken place after the war, when the firm of Quiggin & Craggs had published the recantation of Gainsborough (as he had become) in his study *Bronstein: Marxist or Mystagogue?* Gainsborough could not, therefore, be omitted from the programme. The only other performer who had known St John Clarke in the flesh was L. O. Salvidge, the critic. In his early days, when in low water, Salvidge had done some devilling, when St John Clarke was without a secretary, collecting French Revolution material for *Dust Thou Art*. The cast was made up with several self-constituted friends of the deceased novelist, professional extras, who appeared in all such literary resuscitations on the TV screen.

Isobel and I watched this rescue job from the Valley of Lost Things, to which another small item was added by the opening shot, St John Clarke's portrait (butterfly collar,

39

floppy bow tie), painted by his old friend, Horace Isbister, RA. A few minutes later, Isbister's name appeared again, this time in an altogether unexpected connexion, only indirectly related to painting.

For some years now fashion had inclined to emphasize, rather than overlook, the sexual habits of the dead. To unearth anything about a man so discreet as St John Clarke had proved impossible, but Salvidge ventured to put forward the possibility that the novelist's 'fabulous parsimony' had its origins in repressed homosexuality. Members then let off a mild bombshell. He suggested that the friendship with Isbister had been a homosexual one. The contention of Members was that the central figure in an early genre picture of Isbister's—*Clergyman eating an apple*—was not at all unlike St John Clarke himself as a young man, Members advancing the theory that Isbister could have possessed a fetishist taste for male lovers dressed in ecclesiastical costume.

Quiggin questioned this possibility on grounds that Isbister had finally married his often painted model, Morwenna. Members replied that Morwenna was a lesbian. Gainsborough—who had never heard of Morwenna, and found some difficulty with the name—attempted to shift the discussion to St John Clarke's politics. He was unsuccessful. Something of an argument ensued, Gainsborough's German accent thickening, as he became more irritable. St John Clarke, rather a prudish man in conversation, would have been startled to hear much surmised, before so large an audience, on the subject of his sexual tastes. It was not a very exciting forty minutes, of which Ada was to be judged the star. Isbister's portrait of his friend—perhaps more than friend—flashed on the screen again as finale.

'Shall we stay for the News?'

'All right.'

There was some routine stuff: the Prime Minister in a

safety helmet at a smelting plant; royalty launching a ship; strike pickets; tornado damage. Then, from out of the announcer's patter, a name brought attention—'...Lord Widmerpool, where he was recently appointed the university's chancellor...'

The last time I had seen Widmerpool, nearly ten years before, was soon after the troubles in which he had been involved: his wife's grim end; official enquiries into his own clandestine dealings with an East European power. We had met in Parliament Square. He said he was making for the House of Lords. He looked in poor shape, his manner wandering, distracted. We had talked for a minute or two, then parted. Whatever business he had been about that morning, must have been the last transacted by him for a longish period. The following week he disappeared for the best part of a year. He was probably on his way to wind up for the time being his House of Lords affairs.

Pamela Widmerpool's death, in itself, had caused less stir than might be supposed. Apart from the bare fact that she had taken an overdose in an hotel bedroom, nothing specially scandalous had come to light. Admittedly the hotel—as Widmerpool had complained in Parliament Square—had been a sordid one. Russell Gwinnett, the man with whom Pamela was believed to be in love, was staying there, but Gwinnett had an explicable reason for doing so, the place being a haunt of the novelist, X. Trapnel, whose biography he was writing. Pamela had occupied a room of her own. In any case her behaviour had long burst the sound barrier of normal gossip. It was thought even possible that, having heard of the hotel through Gwinnett, she had booked a room there as a suitably anonymous setting to close her final act. Sympathetic comment gave Pamela credit for that.

From the point of view of 'news', Gwinnett's scholarly affiliations, adding a touch of drabness, detracted from such public interest as the story possessed. The suicide of a life peer's wife obviously called for some coverage. That was likely to be diminished by the addition of professorial research work on a novelist unknown to the general public. The coroner went out of his way to express regret that a young American academic's visit to London should have been clouded by such a mishap. Gwinnett had apparently made an excellent impression at the inquest. In short, the whole business was consigned to the ragbag of memories too vague to remain at all clear in the mind. That was equally true of Widmerpool's dubious international dealings, regarding which, by now, no one could remember whether he was the villain or the hero.

'People say he was framed by the CIA,' said Lenore Members. 'The CIA may have fixed his wife's death too.'

By the time that theory had been put forward—and largely accepted—Widmerpool himself had recovered sufficiently to have crossed the Atlantic, reappearing in the United States after his year's withdrawal from the world. Whether by luck, or astute manipulations, no one seemed to know, he had been offered an appointment of some kind at the Institute for Advanced Study of an Ivy League university; ideal post for making a dignified retreat for a further period from everyday life in London. His years of engagement on the Eastern Seaboard were succeeded by a Westward pilgrimage. He was next heard of established at a noted Californian centre for political research. That was where Lenore Members had come across him. Widmerpool had impressed her as a man who had 'been through' a great deal. That was now his own line about himself, she said, one that could not reasonably be denied. Lenore Members was a woman with considerable descriptive powers. She conveyed a picture of undoubted change. Among other things, Widmerpool had spoken with contempt of parliamentary institutions. In public addresses he had been very generally expressing his scorn for such a vehicle of government. In his opinion the remedy lay in the hands of the young.

'Lord Widmerpool said he was working on a book that puts forward his views. It's to be called *Pogrom of Youth*.'

'How does he go down in the States?'

'He has strong adherents—strong opponents too. There's a pressure group to put his name forward for the Nobel Prize. Others say he's crazy.'

'You mean actually mad?'

'Mentally disturbed.'

'How long is he going to stay in the US?'

'He said he might be taking out naturalization papers.'

Whatever the reason, Widmerpool's vision of American citizenship must have been abandoned. He had returned to England. How, in general, he had been occupying himself, I did not know. During the past two or three years since arriving back there had been fairly regular appearances on television. These were usually in connexion with the sort of subjects Lenore Members had indicated as his latest interest, his new axis for power focus. He had played no part in the Labour administration of 1964. He may not even have been back in England by then. I had not watched any of his TV appearances, nor heard about this appointment to a university chancellorship. The post would not be at all inconsistent with the latest line he seemed to be designing for himself. I had no idea what were its duties and powers, probably a job that was much what the holder made of it.

The university to which Widmerpool had been nominated was a newish one. Malcolm Crowding (main authority on the last hours of X. Trapnel) taught English there. Crowding was not to be observed in the procession of capped and gowned figures on the screen; nor, for that matter, was Widmerpool. They had just reached the foot of a flight of steps. In the background were buildings in a

43

contemporary style of scholastic architecture. The persons composing the crocodile of dons and recipients of honorary degrees were preceded by a man in uniform bearing a mace. The cortège was making its way across an open space, shut in by what were probably lecture-halls. A fairly large crowd, students of both sexes, parents, friends, onlookers of one sort or another, stood on either side of the route, watching the ceremony. It was probably a more grandiose affair than usual owing to the installation of the new chancellor. I did not pick out Widmerpool immediately, my attention being caught for a moment by a black notability in national dress of his country, walking between two academically gowned ladies, all three recipients of doctoral degrees. Then Widmerpool came into sight. As he did so there was scarcely time to take in more of him than that he was wearing a mortarboard and gold brocaded robe, its train held up by a page.

Widmerpool, advancing towards the camera, had turned to say a word to this small boy, apparently complaining that the hinder part of his official dress was being borne in a manner inconvenient to its wearer, when the scene suddenly took on a new and startling aspect. What followed was acted out so quickly that only afterwards was it possible to disentangle specific incident from overall confusion. On different sides of the path, at two points, the watching crowd seemed to part. From each of these gaps figures of indeterminate sex briefly emerged, then withdrew themselves again. Some sort of a scuffle arose. An object, perhaps two objects, shot up in the air. In the background a flimsy poster, inscribed with illegible words outlined in shaky capital letters, fluttered for a second in the air, hoisted on the end of a long pole, then appeared to collapse. All these things, flitting by too quickly to be taken into proper account, were accompanied by the sound of singing or chanting. By the time I had grasped the fact that some sort of a demonstration was afoot, Widmerpool was no longer in sight.

Before the scene changed—which it did in a flash—I had just time to recollect Moreland's words, uttered at Stourwater nearly thirty years before. It was the night we had all dressed up as the Seven Deadly Sins, and been photographed by Sir Magnus Donners, with whom we were dining—'One is never a student at all in England, except possibly a medical student or an art student. Undergraduates have nothing in common with what is understood abroad by a student—young men for ever rioting, undertaking political assassination, overturning governments.'

Moreland had offered that opinion about the time of 'Munich'. Sir Magnus Donners had not shown much interest. Perhaps the innate shrewdness of his own instincts in such matters already told him that, within a few decades, Moreland's conviction about students would fall badly out of date, an epoch not far distant when the sort of student Moreland adumbrated would be accepted as a matter of course. This Stourwater memory had scarcely time to formulate, dissolve, before the announcer's voice drew attention to a close-up of Widmerpool, now standing alone.

'Lord Widmerpool, newly installed chancellor, wishes to give his own comments on what happened.'

At first sight, so ghastly seemed Widmerpool's condition that it was a wonder he was alive, much less able to stand upright and address an audience. He had evidently been the victim of an atrocious assault. His wounds were appalling. Dark stains, apparently blood, covered the crown of his bald head (now capless), streaking down the side of his face, dripping from shoulder and sleeve of the gold embroidered robe. When he raised his hands, they too were smeared with the dark sticky marks of gore. Nevertheless, mangled as the fingers must have been to display this

45

condition, he removed his bespattered spectacles. It was amazing that he had the strength to do so.

'Not the smallest resentment. Even glad this has taken place. Let me congratulate those two girls on being such excellent shots with the paint pot . . .'

All was explained. There were no wounds. The dark clots, at first seeming to flow from dreadful gashes, were no more than paint. Widmerpool was covered with paint. Paint spread all over him, shining in the sun, dripping off face and clothes, since it was not yet dry. He ignored altogether the inconceivable mess he was in. Now the origin of his condition was revealed he looked like a clown, a clown upon whom divine afflatus had suddenly descended. He was in a state of uncontrolled excitement, gesticulating wildly in a manner quite uncharacteristic of himself. It was like revivalist frenzy. Face gaunt, eyes sunk into the back of his head, he had lost all his former fleshiness. What Lenore Members had tried to convey was now apparent. He said a few words more. They were barely intelligible owing to excitement. It was noticeable that his delivery had absorbed perceptibly American intonations and technique, superimposed on the old hearty unction that had formerly marked his style. Before more could be assimilated, the scene, like the previous one, was wiped away, the announcer's professional tones taking over again, as the News moved on to other topics.

'That was livelier than the St John Clarke programme.'
'It certainly was.'

Setting aside the occasion—a very different one—when Glober had hit him after the Stevenses' musical party, the last time Widmerpool had suffered physical assault at all comparable with the paint-throwing was, so far as I knew, forty years before, the night of the Huntercombes' dance, when Barbara Goring had poured sugar over his head. More was to be noted in this parallel than that, on the one hand, both assaults were at the hands of young women; on the other, paint created a far more injurious deluge than castor sugar. The measure of the latest incident seemed to be the extent to which the years had taught Widmerpool to cope with aggressions of that kind. In many other respects, of course, the circumstances were far from identical. Widmerpool had been in love with Barbara Goring; for the girls who had thrown the paint—he had spoken of them as girls —there was no reason to suppose that he felt more than general approval of a politico-social intention on their part. Possibly love would follow, rather than precede, persecution at their hands. Yet even if it were argued that all the two attacks possessed in common was personal protest against Widmerpool himself, the fact remained that, while he had endured the earlier onslaught with unconcealed wretchedness, he had now learnt to convert such occasions—possibly always sexually gratifying—to good purpose where other ends were concerned.

What would have been the result, I wondered, had he been equipped with that ability forty years before? Would he have won the heart of Barbara Goring, proposed to her, been accepted, married, produced children by her? On the whole such a train of events seemed unlikely, apart from objections the Goring parents might have raised in days before Widmerpool had launched himself on a career. Probably nothing would have altered the fates of either Widmerpool or Barbara (whose seventeen-year-old granddaughter had recently achieved some notoriety by marrying a celebrated Pop star), and the paint-throwing incident, like the cascade of sugar, was merely part of the pattern of Widmerpool's life. It was not considered of sufficient importance to be reported in any newspaper. On running across L. O. Salvidge in London, I heard more of its details.

'I enjoyed your appearance in the St John Clarke programme.'

47

Salvidge, who had a glass eye—always impossible to tell which—laughed about the occasion. He seemed well satisfied with the figure he had cut.

'I was glad to have an opportunity to say what I thought about the old fraud. Did you watch the News that night, see the Quiggin twins throw red paint over the chancellor of their university?'

'It was the Quiggin twins?'

'The famous Amanda and Belinda. What a couple. I was talking about it to JG yesterday. At least I tried to, but he would not discuss it. He changed the subject to the Magnus Donners Prize. He's got a grievance that no book published by his firm has ever won the award. Who are you giving it to this year?'

'Nothing suitable has turned up at present. Something may appear in the autumn. Has JG's firm got anything special? We'll see it, no doubt, if they have. It's my last year on the Magnus Donners panel. Do you want to take my place there?'

'Not me.'

Both Salvidge's eyes looked equally glassy at the suggestion. That was no surprise. Almost as veteran a figure on literary prize committees as Mark Members, Salvidge always had a dozen such commissions on hand. They took up more time than might be supposed. I was glad of my own approaching release from the board of the Magnus Donners judges. This was my fourth and final year.

The origins of the Magnus Donners Memorial Prize went back a long way, in fact to the days when Sillery used to speculate about a project of Sir Magnus Donners to endow certain university scholarships for overseas students, young men drawn from places where the Company's interests were paramount. They were to be called Donners-Brebner Fellowships. Such a possibility naturally opened up a legitimate field for academic intrigue, Sillery in the forefront, if the fellowships were to take practical shape. Sillery (in rivalry, he lamented, with at least three other dons) made no secret of his aim to control the patronage. He had entangled in this matter Prince Theodoric (lately deceased in Canada, where his business ventures, after exile, had been reasonably successful), in those days always anxious to draw his country into closer contacts with Great Britain.

The Donners-Brebner Fellowships were referred to in Sillery's obituary notices (highly laudatory in tone, as recording a sole survivor of his own genus, who had missed his century only by a year or two), where it appeared that the project had been to some extent implemented before the outbreak of war in 1939. Post-war changes in the international situation prevented much question of the fellowships' revival in anything like their original form. Sir Magnus himself, anxious to re-establish a benefaction of a similar kind, seems to have been uncertain how best it should be reconstituted, leaving behind several contradictory memoranda on the subject. In practice, this fund seems to have been administered in a rather haphazard fashion after his death, a kind of all-purposes charitable trust in Donners-Brebner gift. That, any rate, was the version of the story propagated by his widow, Matilda Donners, when she first asked me to sit as one of the judges at the initiation of the Prize. That was four years before. Now—as I had told Salvidge—my term on the Prize committee was drawing to an end.

In Matilda's early days of widowhood it looked as if the memory of Sir Magnus was to be allowed to fade. She continued to circulate for some years in the world of politics and big business to which he had introduced her, to give occasional parties in rivalry with Rosie Stevens, more musically, less politically inclined, than herself. Latterly Matilda had not only narrowed down her circle of friends, but begun to talk of Sir Magnus again. She also moved to smaller premises. Sir Magnus had left her comfortably off, if in command of far smaller resources than formerly, bequeathing most of his considerable fortune to relations, and certain public benefactions. No doubt such matters had been gone into at the time of their marriage, Matilda being a practical person, one of the qualities Sir Magnus had certainly admired in her. Moreland, too, had greatly depended on that practical side of Matilda as a wife. In short, disappointment at having received less than expected at the demise of Sir Magnus was unlikely to have played any part in earlier policy that seemed to consign him to oblivion.

Then there was a change. Matilda began, so to speak, to play the part of Ariosto's swans, bringing the name of Donners—she had always referred to him by his surname—into the conversation. A drawing of him, by Wyndham Lewis, was resurrected in her sitting-room. She was reported to play the music he liked—*Parsifal*, for instance, Norman Chandler said—and to laugh about the way he would speak of having shed tears over the sufferings of the Chinese slavegirl in *Turandot*, no less when watching Ida Rubinstein in *The Martyrdom of St Sebastian*. Chandler remarked that, at one time, Matilda would never have referred to 'that side' of Sir Magnus. No doubt this new mood drew Matilda's attention to the more or less quiescent fund lying at Donners-Brebner. On investigation it appeared to be entirely suitable, anyway a proportion of it, for consecration to a memorial that would bear the name of its originator. One of the papers left on the file seemed even to envisage something of the sort. Matilda went to the directors of Donners-Brebner, with whom she had always kept up. They made no difficulties, taking the view that an award of that nature was not at all to be disregarded in terms of publicity.

Why Matilda waited not much less than fifteen years to commemorate Sir Magnus was never clear. Perhaps it was simply a single aspect of the general reconstruction of her life, desire for new things to occupy her as she grew older. Regarded as a *jolie laide* when young, Matilda would now have passed as a former 'beauty'. That was not undeserved. Relentless discipline had preserved her appearance, especially her figure. Once fair hair had been dyed a darker colour, a tone that suited the green eyes—a feature shared with Sir Magnus, though his eyes lacked her sleepy power—which had once captivated Moreland. A touch of 'stageyness' in Matilda's clothes was not out of keeping with her personality.

Another change had been a new inclination towards female friends. Matilda had always been on good terms with Isobel, other wives of men Moreland had known, but in those days, anyway ostensibly, she seemed to possess no female circle of her own. Now she had begun to show a taste for ladies high-powered as herself. They did not exactly take the place of men in her life, but the sexes were more evenly balanced. With men she had always been discreet. There had been no stories circulated about her when married to Sir Magnus. In widowhood there had been the brief affair with Odo Stevens, before his marriage to Rosie Manasch; that affair thought more to tease Rosie than because she specially liked Stevens. Hardly any other adventure had even been lightly attributed.

Some people believed Gibson Delavacquerie had been for a short time Matilda's lover. That was not my own opinion, although a closer relationship than that of friends was not entirely to be ruled out as a possibility. Matilda was, of course, appreciably the elder of the two. If there were anything in such gossip, its truth would have suggested a continued preference for the sort of man with whom her earlier life had been spent, rather than those who had surrounded her in middle years. She had certainly known Delavacquerie quite well before the Magnus Donners Prize was instituted.

His job—Delavacquerie was employed on the public relations side of Donners-Brebner—offered a good listening-post for Matilda to keep in touch with the affairs of the Company. Undoubtedly she liked him. That could very well have been all there was to the association.

This Delavacquerie connexion may well have played a part in the eventual decision to raise a memorial in literary form. Books were by no means the first interest of Sir Magnus. Notwithstanding Moreland's story that, as a young man, believing himself on the brink of an early grave, 'Donners had spoken of steeping himself in all that was best in half-a-dozen literatures', his patronage had always been directed in the main towards painting and music. According to Matilda various alternative forms of remembrance were put forward, a literary prize thought best, as easiest to administer. Delavacquerie may not only have influenced that conclusion, but, once the principle was established, carried weight as to the type of book to be encouraged.

In the end it was settled that the Prize (quite a handsome sum) should be presented annually for a biographical study dealing with (not necessarily written by) a British subject, male or female, born not earlier than the date of Sir Magnus's own birth. I think discretion was allowed to the judges, if the birth was reasonably close, the aim being to begin with the generation to which Sir Magnus himself belonged. Just how this choice was arrived at I do not know. It is worth bearing in mind that an official 'life' of Sir Magnus himself had not yet appeared. Possibly Matilda— or the Company—hoped that a suitable biographer might come to light through this constitution of the Prize. Any such writer would have to be equal to dealing with formidable perplexities, if the biography was to be attempted during the lifetime of its subject's widow; especially in the light of new freedoms of expression, nowadays to be expected, in the manner of the St John Clarke TV programme.

The possibility that a Donners biographer might be sought was borne out by the additional condition that preference would be given to works dealing with a man of affairs, even though representatives of the arts and sciences were also specifically mentioned in the terms of reference.

Delavacquerie, known to me only casually when Matilda opened up the question of the Magnus Donners committee, was then in his middle forties. He was peculiarly fitted to the rôle in which he found himself—that is to say a sort of unofficial secretary to the board of judges—having been one of the few, possibly the sole candidate, to have benefited by a Donners-Brebner fellowship, when these first came into being. This had brought him to an English university (he had somehow slipped through Sillery's fingers) just before the outbreak of war. During the war he had served, in the Middle East and India, with the Royal Signals; after leaving the army, working for a time in a shipping firm. No doubt earlier connexion with the Company, through the fellowship, played a part in ultimately securing him a job at Donners-Brebner. Although a British subject, Delavacquerie was of French descent, a family settled in the Caribbean for several generations. He would speak of that in his characteristically dry manner.

'They've been there a century and a half. An established family. You understand there are no good families. The island does not run to good families. The Gibsons were an established family too.'

Small, very dark, still bearing marks of French origins, Delavacquerie talked in a quick, harsh, oddly attractive voice. Between bouts of almost crippling inertia—according to himself—he was immensely energetic in all he did. We had met before, on and off, but became friends through the Magnus Donners Prize committee. By that time Delavacquerie had achieved some fame as a poet; fame, that is, over and above what he himself always called his 'colonial'

53

affiliations. Matilda asserted, no doubt truly, that the Company was rather proud of employing in one of its departments a poet of Delavacquerie's distinction. She reported that a Donners-Brebner director had assured her that Delavacquerie displayed the same grasp of business matters that he certainly brought to literary criticism, on the comparatively rare occasions when he wrote articles or reviews, there being no easy means of measuring business ability against poetry. This same Donners-Brebner tycoon had added that Delavacquerie could have risen to a post of considerably greater responsibility in the Company had he wished. A relatively subordinate position, more congenial in the nature of its duties, tied him less to an office, allowing more time for his 'own work'. Moreland—not long before he died—had spoken appreciatively of Delavacquerie's poetry, in connexion with one of Moreland's favourite themes, the artist as businessman.

'I never pay my insurance policy,' Moreland said, 'without envisaging the documents going through the hands of Aubrey Beardsley and Kafka, before being laid on the desk of Wallace Stevens.'

Before we knew each other at all well, Delavacquerie mentioning army service in India, I asked whether he had ever come across Bagshaw or Trapnel, both of whom had served in the subcontinent in RAF public relations, Bagshaw as squadron-leader, Trapnel as orderly-room clerk. It was a long shot, no contacts had taken place, but Bagshaw, Delavacquerie said, had published one of his earlier poems in *Fission*, and Trapnel had been encountered in a London pub. Although I had read other Delavacquerie poems soon after that period, I had no recollection of that which had appeared when I had been 'doing the books' for the magazine. I had then liked his poetry in principle, without gaining more than a rough idea where he stood among the young emergent writers of the post-war era. Most of his early verse had been written in the army, most of it rhymed and scanned. Trapnel, prepared to lay down the law on poets and poetry, as much as any other branch of literature, a great commentator on his own contemporaries, had never mentioned Delavacquerie's name. At that period, before Delavacquerie's reputation began to take shape—kept busy earning a living—he was not often to be seen about. Trapnel, living in a kaleidoscope world of pub and party frequenters, must have forgotten their own meeting. Perhaps he had not taken in Delavacquerie's name.

'When I was working in the shipping firm I didn't know London at all well. I wanted to explore all its possibilities—and of course meet writers.'

Delavacquerie made a slight grimace when he said that.

'Somebody told me The Hero of Acre was a pub where you found artists and poets. I went along there one night. Trapnel was at the bar, with his beard, and swordstick mounted with the ivory skull. I thought him rather a Ninetyish figure, and was surprised when his work turned out to be good. He was about the only one in the pub to qualify as a writer at all. Even he had only published a few stories then. Still, to my colonial eyes, it was something that he looked the part, even the part as played fifty years before. I didn't talk to him that night, but on another occasion we discussed Apollinaire over a bitter, a drink I have never learned to like. Trapnel's dead, isn't he?'

'Died in the early nineteen-fifties.'

This conversation between Delavacquerie and myself had taken place several years before Matilda's invitation to join the Magnus Donners Prize committee, which at first I refused, on general grounds of reducing such commitments to a minimum. Matilda, explaining she wanted to start off with a panel known to her personally, was more pressing than expected. She added that she was determined to get as much fun out of the Prize as possible, one aspect of that being a committee made up of friends.

'One never knows how long one's going to last,' she said.

I still declined. Matilda added an inducement. It was a powerful one.

'I've found the photographs Donners took, when we all impersonated the Seven Deadly Sins at Stourwater in 1938. I'll show them to you, if you join the committee. Otherwise not.'

In supposing these documents from a bygone age would prove irresistible as the Sins themselves, Matilda was right. I accepted the bribe. With some people it might have been possible to refuse, then persuade them to produce the photographs in any case. Matilda was not one of those. The board met twice annually at a luncheon provided by the Company. The judges, as constituted in the first instance, were Dame Emily Brightman, Mark Members, and myself. Delavacquerie sat with us, representing the Company, supplying a link with Matilda, acting as secretary. He arranged for publishers to submit books (or proofs of forthcoming books), kept in touch with the press, undertook all the odd jobs required. These were the sort of duties in which he took comparative pleasure, carried out with notable efficiency. He did not himself vote on final decisions about works that came up for judgment, though he joined in discussions, his opinions always useful. He particularly enjoyed arguing with Emily Brightman (created DBE a couple of years before for her work on The Triads, and polemical study of Boethius), who would allow Delavacquerie more range of teasing than was her usual custom, though sometimes he might receive a sharp rebuke, if he went too far.

Members, on the other hand (once publicly admonished by Dame Emily for a slip about the Merovingians), was rather afraid of her. His inclusion was almost statutory in assembling a body of persons brought together to judge a literary award of any type, quite apart from his own long acquaintance with Matilda Donners. It was from this semi-official side of his life, rather than the verse and other writings, that he had come to know Matilda, whose interests had always been in the Theatre, rather than books. Members had been included in her parties when Sir Magnus was alive. Emily Brightman, in contrast, was a more recent acquisition, belonging to that sorority of distinguished ladies Matilda now seemed to seek out. It was clear, at the first of these Magnus Donners luncheons, that Emily Brightman (whom I had seen only once or twice since the Cultural Conference in Venice, where Pamela Widmerpool first met Gwinnett) had lost none of her energy. The unobtrusive smartness of her clothes also remained unaltered.

'I have a confession to make. It should be avowed in the Dostoevskian fashion on the knees. You will forgive me if I dispense with that. To kneel would cause too much stir in a restaurant of this type. During our Venetian experience, you will remember visiting Jacky Bragadin's palazzo—our host didn't long survive our visit, did he?—the incomparable Tiepolo ceiling? Candaules showing Gyges his naked wife? How it turned out that Lord Widmerpool—such an unattractive man—had done much the same thing, if not worse? You remember, of course. That poor little Lady Widmerpool. I took quite a fancy to her, in spite of her naughtinesses.'

Emily Brightman paused; at the thought of those perhaps.

'It turns out that I was scandalously misinformed, accordingly misleading, in supposing Gautier to have invented the name Nysia for Candaules's queen. The one he exhibited in so uncalled for a manner. Nysia was indeed the name of the nude lady in Tiepolo's picture. I came on the fact, quite by chance, last year, when I was reading in bed one night. She is categorically styled Nysia in the *New*

History of Ptolemy Chennus—first century, as you know, so respectably far back—and I was up half the night establishing the references. In fact I wandered about almost as lightly clad as Nysia herself. I hope there was no Gyges in the College at that hour. It was sweltering weather, I had not been able to sleep, and allowed myself a gin and tonic, with some ice in it, while I was doing so. I found that Nicholas of Damascus calls her Nysia, too, in his *Preparatory Exercises*. He also ridicules the notion of an oriental potentate of the Candaules type becoming enamoured of his own wife. I thought that showed the narrowness of Greek psychology in dealing with a subtle people like the Lydians. Another matter upon which Nicholas of Damascus —wasn't he Herod the Great's secretary?—throws doubt is the likelihood of the ladies of Sardis undressing before they went to bed. He may have a point there.'

'Perhaps the sheer originality of his queen undressing was what so enthralled Candaules,' said Members. 'I can never sufficiently regret having missed that Conference. Ada Leintwardine and Quentin Shuckerly talk of it to this day. What was the name of the American who got so involved with Kenneth Widmerpool's wife there?'

'Russell Gwinnett. An old friend of mine. He was put in an unfortunate position.'

Emily Brightman said that rather sharply. Members took the hint. I asked if she had seen anything of Gwinnett lately.

'Not a word from him personally. Another American friend, former colleague of both of us, said Russell was back in academic life again. The name of his college escapes me.

'Has he returned to the book he was writing about X. Trapnel?'

'There was no mention of what he was writing, if anything. I had myself always thought Trapnel, as a subject, a little lightweight. I hear, by the way, that Matilda Donners has some amusing photographs of the Seven Deadly Sins, in which you yourself figure. I must persuade her to produce them for me.'

Matilda had made good her promise by showing the photographs to Isobel and myself a few weeks before. The Eaton Square flat, where she lived (on the upper floors of a house next door to the former Walpole-Wilson residence, now an African embassy), was neither large, nor outstandingly luxurious, except for some of the drawings and small oil paintings. Matilda had sold the larger canvases bequeathed to herself. Apart from the high quality of what remained, the flat bore out that law which causes people to retain throughout life the same general characteristics in any place they inhabit. Matilda's Eaton Square flat at once called to mind the garret off the Gray's Inn Road, where she had lived when married to Moreland. The similarities of decoration may even have been deliberate. Moreland had certainly remained a little in love with Matilda until the end of his days. Something of the sort may have been reciprocally true of herself. Unlike Matilda's long silence about Sir Magnus, she had never been unwilling to speak of Moreland, often talking of their doings together, which seemed, some of them, happy in retrospect.

'Norman Chandler's coming to see the photographs. I thought he would enjoy the Sins. They belong to his period. Norman was always such a support to Hugh, when there was anything to do with the Theatre. The Theatre was never really Hugh's thing. He wasn't at all at ease there, even when he used to come round and see me after the performance. I particularly didn't want Norman to miss Hugh's splendid interpretation of Gluttony.'

'What's Norman directing now?'

'Polly Duport's new play. I haven't seen it yet. It sounds rather boring. Do you know her? She was here the other night. Polly's having a very worrying time. Her mother's married to a South American—more or less head of the government, I believe—and there are a lot of upheavals there. Here's Norman. Norman, my pet, how are you? We were just saying how famous you'd become. That new fringe makes you look younger than ever—like Claudette Colbert. And what a suit. Where did you get it?'

Chandler, whose air, even in later life, was of one dancing in a perpetual ballet, was not at all displeased by these comments on his personal appearance. He looked down critically at what he was wearing.

'This little number? It's from the Boutique of the Impenitent Bachelor—Vests & Transvests, we regular customers call the firm. The colour's named Pale Galilean. To tell the truth I can hardly sit down in these trousers.'

'Our brother-in-law, Dicky Umfraville, always refers to his tailor as Armpits & Crotch.'

'Their cutter must have moved over to the Boutique. How are you both? Oh, Isobel, I can't tell you how much I miss your uncle, Ted Jeavons. Watching the telly will never be the same without his comments. Still, with that piece of shrapnel, or whatever it was from the first war, inside him, he never thought he'd last as long as he did. Ted was always saying how surprised he was to be alive.'

Inhabiting flats, both of them, in what had formerly been the Jeavons house in South Kensington, Chandler and Jeavons had developed an odd friendship, one chiefly expressed in watching television together. Jeavons, who had always possessed romantic feelings about theatrical life, used to listen in silence, an expression of deep concentration on his face, while Chandler rattled on about actors, directors, producers, stage designers, most of whose names could have meant little or nothing to Jeavons. Umfraville—who always found Jeavons a bore—used to pretend there was a homosexual connexion between them, weaving elaborate fantasies in which they indulged in hair-raising orgies at the South Kensington house. Umfraville himself did not change much as the years advanced, spells of melancholy alternating with bursts of high spirits, the last latterly expressed by a rather good new impersonation of himself as an old-fashioned drug-fiend.

When Matilda spread out the photographs on a table the manner in which the actual photography 'dated' was immediately noticeable; their peculiarity partly due to the individual technique of Sir Magnus as photographer, efficient at everything he did, but altogether unversed in any approach to the camera prompted by art. This was especially true of his figure subjects. Painfully clear in outline (setting aside the superimposed exoticism of the actions portrayed), they might have been taken from the pages of a mail-order catalogue, the same suggestion of waxworks, in this case, rather sinister waxworks. Details of costume scrupulously distinct, the character of the models was scarcely at all transmitted. This method did not at all diminish the interest of the pictures themselves. Sir Magnus had remarked at the time that he had taken up photography with a view to depicting his own collections—china, furniture, armour—in the manner he himself wished them photographically recorded, something in which no professional photographer had ever satisfied him. One speculated whether—the Seven Deadly Sins pointing the way—he had later developed this hobby in a manner to include his own tastes as a voyeur. A certain harshness of technique would not necessarily have vitiated that sphere of interest. That Sir Magnus had actually introduced Widmerpool to the practices of which Pamela had so publicly accused her husband at Venice, was less likely, though there, too, photography, of a dubious intention, was alleged. Matilda set out the photographs, as if playing a game of Patience.

'So few of one's friends qualify for all the Sins. Quite a lot of people can offer six, then break down at the seventh.

They're full of Lust, Envy, Gluttony, Pride, Anger, Sloth—then fall down on Avarice. One knows plenty of good performers at Avarice, but they so often lack Gluttony or Sloth. Of course it helps if you're allowed to include drink, in place of food, for Gluttony.'

She picked up the picture of herself as Envy.

'It was unjust of Donners to make me take on Envy. I'm not at all an envious person.'

That was probably true, notwithstanding her green eyes. Matilda had never shown any strong signs of being envious. Then one thought of her rivalry with Rosie Stevens. Even that was scarcely Envy in the consuming sense that certain persons display the trait. It was competitive jealousy, something rather different, even if partaking of certain envious strains too. Matilda liked her friends to be successful, rather than the reverse. That in itself was a rare characteristic.

'I suppose Donners thought I was envious of that silly girl he was then having one of his fancies for. What is she called now? Her maiden name was Lady Anne Stepney. She's married to a Negro much younger than herself, rather a successful psychedelic painter. Donners knew at the time that Anne was conducting a romance with your friend Peter Templer. Do you remember? You and Isobel were staying at our cottage. This man, Peter Templer, picked us up in his car, and drove us over to Stourwater for dinner that night? There's Anne herself, as Anger, which wasn't bad. She had a filthy temper. Here she is again, with Isobel as Pride. That's not fair on Isobel either, anyway not the wrong sort of Pride. And Sloth's absurd for you, Nick. Look at all those books you've written.'

'Sloth means Accidie too. Feeling fed up with life. There are moments when I can put forward claims.'

'Hugh, too, I can assure you. Better ones than yours, I feel certain. But Hugh was so good as Gluttony, one wouldn't wish him doing anything else. Look at him.'

Even the lifeless renderings of Sir Magnus's photography had failed to lessen the magnificence of Moreland's Gluttony. He had climbed right on top of the dining-room table, where he was lying supported on one elbow, gripping the neck of a bottle of Kümmel. He had already upset a full glass of the liqueur—to the visible disquiet of Sir Magnus—the highlights of the sticky pool on the table's surface caught by the lens. Moreland, surrounded by fruit that had rolled from an overturned silver bowl, was laughing inordinately. The spilt liqueur glass recalled the story told by Mopsy Pontner (whom Moreland had himself a little fancied), her romp on another dining-room table with the American film producer, Louis Glober. That was a suitable inward reminiscence to lead on to the photographs of Templer as Lust; three in number, since he had insisted on representing the Sin's three ages, Youth, Middle Years, Senility.

'It was Senile Lust that so upset that unfortunate wife of his. She rushed out of the room. What was her name? Donners made her play Avarice. The poor little thing wasn't in the least avaricious. Probably very generous, if given a chance. Somebody had to do Avarice, as we were only seven all told. She might have seen that without kicking up such a to-do. Of course she was pretty well nuts by then. Peter Templer as a husband had sent her up the wall. Donners insisted she should go through with Avarice. That was Donners at his worst. He could be very sadistic, unless you stood up to him, then he might easily become masochistic. Betty—that's what she was called. She ought to have seen it was only a game, and numbers were short. I believe she had to be put away altogether for a time, but came out after her husband was killed, and had lots of proposals. You know how men adore mad women.'

'Women like mad men, too, Matty, you must admit that. Besides, she wasn't really mad. Did she accept any of the proposals?'

'She married a man in the Foreign Office, and became an ambassadress. They were very happy, I believe. He's retired now. Most of these pictures are pretty mediocre. Hugh's the only star.'

Chandler turned the pictures over.

'I think they're wonderful, Matty. What fun it all was in those days.'

Matilda made a face.

'Oh, it wasn't. Do you truly think that, Norman? I always felt it was dreadfully grim. I don't believe that was only because the war was going to happen. Do you remember that awful man Kenneth Widmerpool coming in wearing uniform? He ought to have played the eighth Sin— Humbug.'

I was a little surprised by the violence of Matilda's comment. So far as I knew Widmerpool had taken no particular part in her life, though she might have heard about him from Sir Magnus. She was, in any case, a woman who said —and did—unexpected things, a strangeness of character reflected by her marriages to Carolo, Moreland and Sir Magnus, even if the marriage to the violinist had been a very brief one.

'I think I rather like humbugs,' said Chandler. 'People like old Gossage, the music critic, he's always been quite a friend of mine.'

Matilda laughed.

'I mean something much above poor old Gossage's bumblings. I'm speaking of making claims to a degree of virtue, purity, anything you like to call it—morals, politics, the arts, any field you prefer—which the person concerned neither possesses, nor is seriously attempting to attain. They just flatter themselves they are like that. How solemn I'm getting. That sounds just like the speeches I used to make in my early days from behind the footlights. Tell Norman about the Magnus Donners Memorial Prize, Nick.'

She began to put the photographs away. I described the Prize to Chandler.

'My dear, you ought to link the Prize with the photographs. Do the Seven Deadly Sins in rotation. The book wins, which best enhances the Sin-of-the-Year.'

'Oh, Norman, I wish we could.'

That emendation would have added spice to the Magnus Donners Prize, which got off to an unspirited start, with a somewhat pedestrian biography of Sir Horrocks Rusby. A contemporary of Sir Magnus, this once celebrated advocate's life-story was the only book of that year falling within the terms required. The frontispiece, a florid portrait of Rusby in wig and gown, was from the brush of Isbister, foreshadowing the painter's later resurgence. The following year there were sufficient eligible candidates to make me regret ever having let myself in for so much additional reading of an unexciting kind. It was won with a lively study of a wartime commander, written by a military historian of repute. The third year's choice, reflecting a new mood of free expression, was of greater interest than its forerunners; a politician, public personality rather than statesman, chronicled by a journalist friend, who provided, in generous profusion, details of his subject's adventures (he had been homosexual), which would have remained unrecorded only a few years before. Emily Brightman made one of her pronouncements, when this book had been finally adopted for the Prize.

'In its vulgar way, a painstaking piece of work, although one must always remember—something often forgotten today—that because things are generally known, they are not necessarily the better for being written down, or publicly announced. Some are, some aren't. As in everything else, good sense, taste, art, all have their place. Saying you prefer to disregard art, taste, good sense, does not mean that those

65

elements do not exist—it merely means you lack them yourself.'

On the fourth and final year of the panel, the existing committee was confronted with much the same situation as that of the first presentation of the award, except that then there had been at least one eligible book, if no very inspiring one. This year, as I had told Salvidge, nothing at all seemed available. For one reason or another every biography to appear, or billed to appear within the publishing period required, fell outside the Magnus Donners category. When I arrived at the table for the second annual meeting, Emily Brightman and Mark Members were discussing procedure for announcing that, this year, the Prize would not be presented. A minute or two later Delavacquerie came into the restaurant. He held under his arm what looked like the proof copy of a book. When he sat down Emily Brightman tried to take it from him. Delavacquerie resisted. He would not even let her see the title, though admitting he had found a possible entrant for the Prize.

'The publishers got in touch with me yesterday.'

'Who's it about?'

'I'd like to speak of a few things first, before we get on to the actual merits of the book. There are complications. Other copies of this proof are in the post to the private addresses of all members of the Magnus Donners committee. If you decide in favour, the publishers can get the book out within the appointed time. Let's order luncheon before we go into the various problems.'

Delavacquerie kept the proof copy hidden on his knee. He always gave the impression of knowing exactly what he wanted to say, how he was going to behave. Emily Brightman, aware that to show impatience would undermine the strength of her position, displayed self-control. Delavacquerie possessed several of her own characteristics, firmness, directness, grasp of whatever subject had to be considered.

66

If they opposed each other, she was prepared to accept him on equal terms as an adversary, by no means true of everyone. When food and drink had been ordered, Delavacquerie began to make his statement. Even at the outset this was a sufficiently startling one.

'You remember, a long time ago, the name came up at one of these meetings of the novelist, X. Trapnel, author of *Camel Ride to the Tomb, Dogs Have No Uncles*, and other works? He died in the nineteen-fifties. You knew him quite well, I think, Nick?'

Members broke in.

'I knew Trapnel well too. We all knew him. Did he leave a posthumous biography of somebody, which has just been discovered?'

'I never knew Trapnel,' said Emily Brightman. 'Not personally, that is. I'm always promising myself to read his books, but this must be—'

'Please,' said Delavacquerie.

Smiling, he held Emily Brightman in check.

'I'm sorry, Gibson, but I'm sure I know more about this subject than you do.'

Delavacquerie, still smiling, shook his head. He continued. In relation to Trapnel he was determined to clarify his own position before anything else was said.

'I met Trapnel himself only once, and that not for long, more than twenty years ago, but I believe him to be a good writer. We have a life of Trapnel here. His career was not altogether uneventful. This book is by an American professor, a doctoral dissertation, none the worse for that. I have read the book. I think you will like it.'

Emily Brightman was not to be held in any longer. She raised a fork threateningly, as if about to stab Delavacquerie, if he did not come quickly to the point. Members, too, was showing signs of wanting to ventilate his own Trapnel experiences, before things went much further. I myself felt the same impelling urge.

'Gibson, this book must be written by Russell Gwinnett.'

Delavacquerie, who, reasonably enough, had forgotten that Emily Brightman once announced herself an old friend of Gwinnett's, looked a little surprised that she should know the name of the biographer.

'Have the publishers sent your proof copy already, Emily?'

'Not yet, but I knew Russell Gwinnett was writing a life of Trapnel. So did Nicholas. We could have told you at once, Gibson, had we been allowed to speak. Russell is an old friend of mine. Nicholas, too, met him when we were in Venice. We talked of it at the first meeting of this committee. You could not have been attending, Gibson. You see you sometimes underrate our capabilities.'

Delavacquerie laughed. Before he could defend himself, Members pegged out his own claim.

'I don't know Gwinnett, but I knew Trapnel. You count as knowing a man reasonably well after he's borrowed five pounds off you. Is that incident mentioned? I hope so.'

If Delavacquerie considered Gwinnett's book good, the judgment was likely to be sound. I was less surprised to hear that Gwinnett's biography of Trapnel was well done, than that it had ever been completed at all. If the work was accomplished, Gwinnett was likely to have brought to it the powers he certainly possessed. Personally, I had doubted that the study would ever see light. Emily Brightman must have thought the same. She was greatly excited by the news. When they had both been teaching at the same women's college in America, in a sense Gwinnett had been a protégé of hers. She had always supported a belief in his abilities as a writer. How much she was prepared to face another, more enigmatic, even more sinister, side of his character, was less easy to assess.

'I told you Russell was an industrious young man, Nicholas. A capable one too. I suppose he can't be spoken of as young any longer. He must be well into his forties. At last it looks as if we've found someone for the Prize. There is no writer to whom I would rather award it than Russell. It's just what he needs to give him self-assurance, and what the Prize itself needs, to lift it out of the rut of the commonplace. Show me the proof at once, Gibson.'

Delavacquerie continued to withhold the proof copy.

'Not yet, Emily.'

'Gibson, you are intolerable. Don't be absurd. Hand it over immediately.'

'I'm prepared to be magnanimous about the fiver,' said Members. 'I could ill afford forfeiture of five pounds at the time, but we were all penniless writers together, and bygones shall be bygones. The point is whether the book is good.'

'The merits of Gwinnett's book are not so much the issue,' said Delavacquerie. 'The difficulty is quite another matter.'

'I know what you're going to put forward,' said Emily Brightman. 'Libel. Am I right? I can see a book of that sort might be libellous, but that is surely the publisher's affair. We shall have given the Prize before the row starts.'

'That is not exactly the problem. At least the publishers are not worried in a general way on that ground. They think the possibility of anything of the sort very remote. The libel, if any, would be in connexion with Trapnel's love affair with Pamela Widmerpool. As you know, she destroyed the manuscript of his last novel. That business was largely responsible for Trapnel's final débâcle.'

'An interesting legal point,' said Members. 'Is it libellous to write that someone's deceased wife was unfaithful to him? I always understood, in days when I myself worked in a publisher's office, that you can't libel the dead. That was one of the firmest foundations of the publishing profession. On the other hand, I suppose the surviving partner might consider himself libelled, as being put on record as a trompé'd husband. At the time I was speaking of, my ancient publishing days, there also existed the element Emily brought up, rather severely, at one of our meetings—good taste—but fortunately we don't have to bother about that now—even if it does platonically exist, as Emily assures us. Don't say it's good taste that makes you waver, Gibson. I believe you're frightened of Emily's disapproval.'

Members and Delavacquerie, outwardly well disposed towards each other, anyway conversationally, were not much in sympathy at base. Delavacquerie, formal as always, may all the same have revealed on some occasion his own sense of mutual disharmony. If so, Members was now getting his own back. Delavacquerie, recognizing that, smiled.

'You may be right, Mark. At the same time you will agree, I think, when I state the problem, that it is a rather special one. Meanwhile, let me release these proofs.'

He handed the bundle to Emily Brightman, who almost snatched it from his hands. She turned at once to the title-page. I read the layout over her arm.

DEATH'S-HEAD SWORDSMAN
The Life and Works of
X. TRAPNEL
by
RUSSELL GWINNETT

In due course the proofs came my way. Gwinnett's academic appointment, named at the beginning of the book, was held at an American college to be judged of fairly obscure status, though lately in the news, owing to exceptionally severe student troubles on its campus. On the page where a dedication might have stood, an epigraph was set.

My study's ornament, thou shell of death,
Once the bright face of my betrothèd lady.

The Revenger's Tragedy.

For those who knew anything of Gwinnett, or of
Trapnel for that matter, the quotation was, to say the
least, ambiguous. The longer the lines were considered,
the more profuse in private meaning they seemed to
become. Moreland, too, had been keen on the plays of
Cyril Tourneur. He used often to quote a favourite image
from one of them: '... and how quaintly he died, like a
politician, in hugger-mugger, made no man acquainted
with it ...'

Tourneur, as Gwinnett himself, was obsessed with Death.
The skull, carried by the actor, his 'study's ornament', was
no doubt, in one sense, intended to strike the opening note
of Gwinnett's book, his own 'study'. The couplet drew
attention also to the melodramatic title (referring presumably to the death's-head, mentioned by Delavacquerie, on
the top of Trapnel's sword-stick); but had it deeper meaning as well? If so, who was intended? The lines could be
regarded as, say, dedication to the memory of Gwinnett's
earlier girlfriend (at whose death he had been involved in
some sort of scandal); alternatively, as allusion to Pamela
Widmerpool herself. If the latter, were the words conceived as spoken by Trapnel, by Gwinnett, by both—or,
indeed, by all Pamela's lovers? Even if ironical, they were
appropriate enough. At least they defined the tone of the
book. Then another thought came. Not only was the quotation about a skull, the title of Tourneur's play had also to
be considered. It was called *The Revenger's Tragedy*. Did
revenge play some part in writing the book? If so, Gwinnett's revenge on whom? Trapnel? Pamela? Widmerpool?
There were too many questions to sort out at that moment.
Delavacquerie allowed everyone to examine the proofs as

long as they wished, before he brought out the information he was holding in reserve.

'With regard to libel,' said Emily Brightman. 'I see that neither Lord Widmerpool, nor his late wife, is named in what is evidently a very full index. I am, by the way, hearing all sorts of strange stories about Lord Widmerpool's behaviour as a university chancellor. He seems to have the oddest ideas how the duties of that office should be carried out.'

I, too, had noticed the omission of the names of the Widmerpools, husband and wife, from the book's index. That did not mean that their identities were necessarily unrecognizable in the text. Members protested at all this talk about libel.

'I can't see that we need be punctilious about the susceptibilities of Lord Widmerpool, whatever Emily feels as to maintaining standards of good taste. Especially as she herself now draws attention to his much advertised broadmindedness, in various recent statements made by him, on the subject of students at his own university.'

This gave Delavacquerie the opportunity he was waiting for to produce an effective climax to what he had been saying.

'What you put forward, Mark, is quite true. Only last week I was watching a programme of Lord Widmerpool's dealing with protest, counterculture, alternative societies, all the things that he is now interested in. That does not entirely meet our problem, which is a rather more delicate one. The fact is that Lord Widmerpool acts as one of the trustees of the fund from which the Magnus Donners Memorial Prize derives.'

This piece of information naturally made a considerable impression. None of the committee came out with an immediate response. My own first thought was how on earth Widmerpool could have come to occupy such a position in relation to this literary prize, or any other. He might be planning to write a book, but, after all, he had been talking of doing that from his earliest days. More than this was needed as explanation. Who could have been insane enough to have made him trustee of the Magnus Donners Prize? Then, when Delavacquerie continued, the reason became plain.

'Lord Widmerpool, in his early business life, was for quite a long time associated with Donners-Brebner. He did many miscellaneous jobs for Sir Magnus himself. At one time he might almost have been called Sir Magnus's right-hand man, so I've been told, though I've never known Lord Widmerpool personally, only seen him at meetings.'

'The term jackal has been used,' said Members.

Delavacquerie ignored the comment. He was always determined that the formalities should be observed.

'Putting in work on organizing this fund for the Donners-Brebner Fellowships was one of the tasks allotted. In that capacity, as benefiting from them myself, I might even be considered in his debt. For some reason when the Prize was, so to speak, detached from the general sum, Lord Widmerpool's name remained as a trustee.'

Even Members agreed that a ticklish problem was posed. Any hypothetical question of libel sank into the background, compared with the propriety of awarding a substantial monetary prize, administered—at least in theory—by Widmerpool himself, to an author, who had been one of his wife's lovers, and written the biography of another man, of whom she had also been the mistress. Besides, Gwinnett had not merely been Pamela's lover, he was considered by some to be at least the indirect cause of her death; even if she herself had chosen that to be so. After quite a long pause, Emily Brightman spoke.

'I feel dreadfully sure that I am going to vote for Russell

73

getting the Prize, but I do agree that we are faced with a very delicate situation.'

Delavacquerie, who had no doubt given a good deal of thought to the perplexity which he knew would confront the panel, appeared quite prepared for its attitude to be one of irresolution.

'The first thing to do is for the committee to read the book, decide whether or not you want the Prize to be given to Professor Gwinnett. If you do, I am prepared to take the next step myself. I will approach Lord Widmerpool in person, and ask him where he stands on the matter. It will no doubt be necessary for him to read *Death's-head Swordsman* too, before he can make up his mind.'

Members showed uneasiness about that. I felt a little doubtful myself. It seemed going out of the way to meet trouble.

'But Kenneth Widmerpool may forbid publication. What shall we do then? Why should we be bullied by him? Surely it would be better to leave Widmerpool alone. What can he do?'

Delavacquerie was firm.

'The question to some extent involves the Company. The directors may not care tuppence what Widmerpool feels in the matter, but they would not wish attention to be drawn to the fact that he is still connected with the Company to that extent, and at the same time objects to publication. I should like to get Lord Widmerpool's attitude clearly stated, if I have to consult them. His name could be quietly removed. All sorts of things might be done. They can be gone into, when we know his own views. To remove his name right away, for instance, might induce trouble, rather than curtail it.'

That sounded reasonable. Members withdrew his objection. What had worried him, he said, was thought that the award could turn on Widmerpool's whim. In other respects, the idea that the committee's choice might cause a stir greatly pleased Members, who always enjoyed conflict.

'This is a courageous offer, Gibson,' said Emily Brightman.

Delavacquerie laughed.

'In not knowing Lord Widmerpool personally, I have the advantage of ignorance. That is sometimes a useful weapon. I am perhaps not so foolhardy as you all seem to think. There are aspects of the Trapnel story with which, in his latest frame of mind, Lord Widmerpool might even welcome association. I mean Trapnel the despised and rejected—insomuch as Trapnel was despised and rejected.'

I felt confidence in Delavacquerie's judgment, and could grasp some of what he meant. Nevertheless his train of thought was not wholly clear.

'But even the new Widmerpool will hardly stomach such an association with Gwinnett, will he?'

'We'll see. I may be wrong. It's worth a try.'

Delavacquerie was giving nothing away at this stage. During what remained of the meeting no matter of consequence was discussed. *Death's-head Swordsman* had first to be read. That was the next step. Luncheon came to an end. Emily Brightman said she was on her way to the British Museum. Members was going to his hairdresser, before attending another literary prize committee later that afternoon. After saying goodbye to the others, Delavacquerie and I set off for Fleet Street.

'How do you propose to tackle Widmerpool?'

Delavacquerie's manner changed a little from its carefully screened air employed at the table.

'Tell me, Nicholas, did not Pamela Widmerpool take an overdose that she might be available to the necrophilic professor?'

'That was how things looked at the time. She may have decided to do herself in anyway.'

'But it might be said that Gwinnett—by, perhaps only indirectly, being the cause of her end—avenged Trapnel for destruction of his novel, and consequent downfall?'

'You could look at it that way.'

'In a sense Gwinnett represents Widmerpool's revenge on Pamela too?'

'That also occurred to me. *The Revenger's Tragedy*. All the same, the point is surely not going to be easy to put, as man-to-man, when you confront Widmerpool?'

'Nevertheless, I shall bear it in mind.'

'I never thought Gwinnett would get the book finished. He gave up academic life when all the trouble happened. I last heard of him teaching water-skiing.'

'A promising profession for a man keen on Death?'

'I don't think Gwinnett does away with his girls. He is not a murderer. He just loves where Death is. The subject enraptures him. Emily Brightman says there was an earlier incident of his breaking into a mortuary, where a dead love of his lay.'

Delavacquerie thought for a moment.

'I can understand the obsession, like most others. People love where Beauty is, where Money is, where Power is—why not where Death is? An American poet said Death is the Mother of Beauty. No, I was being perhaps unduly secretive at lunch. I'll tell you. I have a special line on Lord Widmerpool. My son is at the university of which he is the chancellor.'

I knew Delavacquerie's wife had died ten or fifteen years before. I had never met her. They had come across each other in England, the marriage, so far as I knew, a happy one. Delavacquerie sometimes spoke of his wife. The son he had never before mentioned.

'In the ordinary way, of course, Etienne would scarcely know who was the chancellor of the university. Lord Widmerpool, as we were saying at lunch, has for some little time been laying stress on his own closeness to the younger generation, and its upheavals. You may have seen his letters —always signed nowadays "Ken Widmerpool", rather than just "Widmerpool", as a peer of the realm—a matey approach habitually brought into play so far as students of the university are concerned. He has made his house a centre for what might be called the more difficult cases.'

'Was your son involved in the Quiggin twins' paint-throwing?'

Delavacquerie laughed at the suggestion.

'On the contrary, Etienne is a hard-working boy, who wants to get a good economics degree, but naturally he does the things his own contemporaries do up to a point—knows all about them, I mean, even if he isn't the paint-throwing type. He has talked a lot about Lord Widmerpool. Quite a personality cult has been established there. Lord Widmerpool has made himself a powerful figure in the student world—which, I need hardly remind you, is by no means entirely made up of students.'

'You think your knowledge of Widmerpool's latest stance is such as to persuade him to create no difficulties about Gwinnett's book?'

'It is my own self-esteem that prompts me to attempt this. That is what I am like. I want to come back to the Magnus Donners Prize committee, and inform them that Lord Widmerpool is perfectly agreeable to *Death's-head Swordsman* receiving the award—that is, if you and the rest of the panel wish the book to be chosen.'

This statement of his own feelings in the matter was very typical of Delavacquerie; to admit ambitions of a kind not necessarily to be expected from a poet, anyway the poet of popular imagination. By the time we had this conversation the habit had grown up of our lunching together in London at fairly regular intervals (quite apart from the Magnus Donners meetings), so that I was already familiar with a side of him that was competitive in a manner he rather liked to emphasize. Then he came out with something for which I was not at all prepared.

'Isn't a girl called Fiona Cutts some sort of a relation of yours?'

'A niece.'

'She used to be a friend of Etienne's.'

'Lately?'

'A year or two ago. For a short time she and Etienne saw quite a lot of each other—I mean enough for me to have met her too. A nice girl. I think in the end she found Etienne too humdrum, though they got on well for a while.'

'Did they meet with the odd crowd Fiona is now going round with?'

'No, not at all. At some musical get-together, I think. The thing broke up when this other business started.'

Fiona's friendship with Etienne Delavacquerie had never percolated down through the family grapevine. There was no particular reason why it should. Even Fiona's parents were unlikely to keep track of all their daughter's current boyfriends. It was a pity Susan and Roddy Cutts had never known about this apparently reliable young man. They would have felt relieved, anyway for a short period of time. Delavacquerie, also regretting the termination of the relationship, was probably in ignorance of the extent to which Fiona could show herself a handful. I asked if he knew about Scorpio Murtlock.

'I knew she was now mixed up with some mystic cult. I didn't know Murtlock had anything to do with her. I thought he was a queer.'

'Hard to say.'

'All I know about Murtlock is that Quentin Shuckerly picked him up somewhere ages ago. Shuckerly, expecting an easy lay, put Murtlock up in his flat. Shuckerly can be quite tough in such matters—that former intellectual black boyfriend of his used to call him the Narcissus of the Nigger—but his toughness, or his narcissism, didn't stand up to Murtlock's. Shuckerly had to leave the country to get Murtlock out of his flat. A new book of Shuckerly poems was held up in publication in consequence. I wouldn't have thought Murtlock a wise young man to get mixed up with. Etienne never told me that.'

Delavacquerie looked quite disturbed. Here our ways had to part.

'I should like to bug your conversation with Widmerpool, anyway your opening gambit.'

Delavacquerie made a dramatic gesture.

'I shall take the bull by the horns—adopt the directness of the CIA man and the Cuban defector.'

'What was that?'

'He asked him a question.'

'Which was?'

'You know how it is in Havana in the Early Warning?'

Delavacquerie waved goodbye. I went on towards the paper, to get a book for review. In the anxiety he had shown about his son's abandoned love affair—and Fiona's own involvement with Murtlock—Delavacquerie had displayed more feeling than he usually revealed. It suggested that Etienne Delavacquerie had been fairly hard hit when Fiona went off. I was interested that Delavacquerie himself had met her, and would have liked to hear more of his views on that subject. There had been no opportunity. In any case the friendships of later life, in contrast with those negotiated before thirty, are apt to be burdened with reservations, constraints, inhibitions. Probably thirty was placing the watershed too late for the age when both parties begin more or less to know (at least think they know) what the other is talking about; as opposed to those earlier friendships—not unlike love affairs, with all sexual element

79

removed—which can exist with scarcely an interest in common, mutual misunderstanding of character and motive all but absolute.

In earlier days, given our comparative intellectual intimacy, there would have been no embarrassment in enquiring about Delavacquerie's own sexual arrangements. The question would have been an aspect of being friends. In fact, Delavacquerie himself would almost certainly have issued some sort of statement of his own on the matter, a handout likely to have been given early priority, when we were first getting to know one another. That was why the rumoured brush with Matilda remained altogether blurred in outline. There was no doubt that Delavacquerie liked women, got on well with them. His poetry showed that. If he possessed any steady company—hard to believe he did not—the lady herself never seemed to appear with him in public.

Thinking of the information now accumulating about Scorpio Murtlock, an incident that had taken place a few years before came to mind. It might or might not be Murtlock this time, the principle was the same. The occasion also marked the last time I had set eyes on an old acquaintance, Sunny Farebrother. I was in London only for the day. Entering a comparatively empty compartment on a tube train, I saw Farebrother sitting at the far end. Wearing a black overcoat and bowler hat, both ancient as his wartime uniforms, he was as usual holding himself very upright. He did not look like a man verging on eighty. White moustache neatly trimmed, he could have passed for middle sixties. In one sense a figure conspicuously of the past in turnout, there was also something about him that was extremely up-to-date, not to say brisk. He was smiling to himself. I took the vacant seat next to him.

'Hullo, Sunny.'

Farebrother's face at once lost its smile. Instead, it

assumed an expression of rueful compassion. It was the face he had put on when Widmerpool, then a major on the staff, seemed likely to be sacked from Divisional Headquarters. Farebrother, an old enemy, had dropped in to announce that fact.

'Nicholas, how splendid to meet again after all these years. You find me on my way back from a sad occasion. I am returning from Kensal Green Cemetery. The last tribute to an old friend. One of these fellows I'd known for a mighty long time. Life will never be quite the same again without him. We didn't always hit it off together—but, my goodness, Nicholas, he was someone known to you too. I've just been to Jimmy Stripling's funeral. Poor old Jimmy. You must remember him. You and I stayed at the Templers', a hundred years ago, when Jimmy was there. He was the old man's son-in-law in those days. Tall chap, hair parted in the middle, keen on motor-racing. I always remember how Jimmy, and some of the rest of the house-party, tried to play a trick on me, after we'd come back from a ball, and I had gone up to bed. Poor old Jimmy hoped to put a po in my hatbox. I was too sharp for him.'

Farebrother shook his head in sadness at the folly of human nature, folly so abjectly displayed by Jimmy Stripling in hoping to outwit Farebrother in a matter of that sort. I saw now that a black tie added to the sombre note struck by the rest of his clothes.

'Jimmy and I used to do a lot of business together in our early City days. He always pretended we didn't get on well. Then, poor old boy, he gave up the City—he was in Lloyd's, hadn't done too badly there, and elsewhere—gave up his motor-racing, got a divorce from Peter Templer's sister, and began mixing himself up with all sorts of strange goings-on that couldn't have been at all good for the nerves. Old Jimmy was a highly strung beggar in his way. Took up with a strange lady, who told fortunes. Occultism, all that.

Not a good thing. Bad thing, in fact. The last time I saw him, only a few years ago, he was driving along Piccadilly in a car that could have been fifty years old, if it was a day. Jimmy must have lost all his money. His cars were once his pride and joy. Always had the latest model before anyone else. Now he was grinding along in this old crock. I could have wept at seeing Jimmy reduced to an old tin can like that.'

Farebrother, a habit of his when he told almost any story, suddenly lowered his voice, at the same time looking round to see if we were likely to be overheard, though no one else was sitting at our end of the compartment.

'It was even worse than that, I fear. There weren't many at the funeral but those who were looked a rum lot, to say the least. I got into conversation with one of the few mourners who was respectably dressed. Turned out he was a member of Lloyd's, like Jimmy, though he hadn't seen him for a long time. Do you know what had happened? When that fortune-telling lady of Jimmy's was gathered in, he took up with a *boy*. Would you have believed it? Jimmy may have behaved like a crackpot at times, but no one ever guessed he had *those* tastes. This bloke I talked to told me he'd heard that a lot of undesirables used to live off Jimmy towards the end. I don't think he'd have invented the tale on account of the funny types at the funeral. Jimmy's boy was there. In fact he was more or less running the show. He wore a sort of coloured robe, hair not much short of his shoulders. Good-looking lad in his way, if you'd cleaned him up a bit. Funnily enough, I didn't at all take against him, little as I'm drawn to that type as a rule. Even something I rather liked, if you can believe that. He had an air of efficiency. That always gets me. It was a cremation, and this young fellow showed himself perfectly capable of taking charge. All these strange types in their robes sang a sort of dirge for Jimmy at the close of the proceedings.'

'Perhaps it was the efficiency Jimmy Stripling liked?'

'I hope you're right, Nicholas. I hadn't thought of that. Jimmy just needed somebody to look after him in his old age. I expect that was it. We all need that. I see I've been uncharitable. I'm glad I went to the funeral, all the same. I make a point of going to funerals and memorial services, sad as they are, because you always meet a lot of people at them you haven't seen for years, and that often comes in useful later. Jimmy's was the exception. I never expect to set eyes on mourners like his again, Kensal Green, or anywhere else.'

The train was approaching my station.

'How are you yourself, Sunny?'

'Top-hole form, top-hole. Saw my vet last week. Said he'd never inspected a fitter man of my age. As you probably know, Nicholas, I'm a widower now.'

'I didn't. I'm sorry to hear—'

'Three years ago. A wonderful woman, Geraldine. Marvellous manager. Knew just where to save. Never had any money of her own, left a sum small but by no means to be disregarded. A wonderful woman. Happy years together. Fragrant memories. Yes, I'm in the same little place in the country. I get along somehow. Everyone round about is very kind and helpful. You and your wife must come and see my roses. I can always manage a cup of tea. Bless you, Nicholas, bless you . . .'

As I walked along the platform towards the Exit staircase the train moved on past me. I saw Farebrother once more through the window as the pace increased. He was still sitting bolt upright, and had begun to smile again. On the visit to which he had himself referred, the time when Stripling's practical joke had fallen so flat, Peter Templer had pronounced a judgment on Farebrother. It remained a valid one.

'He's a downy old bird.'

3

IRRITATED BY WHAT HE JUDGED the 'impacted clichés' of some review, Trapnel had once spoken his own opinions on the art of biography.

'People think because a novel's invented, it isn't true. Exactly the reverse is the case. Because a novel's invented, it is true. Biography and memoirs can never be wholly true, since they can't include every conceivable circumstance of what happened. The novel can do that. The novelist himself lays it down. His decision is binding. The biographer, even at his highest and best, can be only tentative, empirical. The autobiographer, for his part, is imprisoned in his own egotism. He must always be suspect. In contrast with the other two, the novelist is a god, creating his man, making him breathe and walk. The man, created in his own image, provides information about the god. In a sense you know more about Balzac and Dickens from their novels, than Rousseau and Casanova from their Confessions.'

'But novelists can be as egotistical as any other sort of writer. Their sheer narcissism often makes them altogether unreadable. A novelist may inescapably create all his characters in his own image, but the reader can believe in them, without necessarily accepting their creator's judgment on them. You might see a sinister strain in Bob Cratchit, conventionality in Stavrogin, delicacy in Molly Bloom. Besides, the very concept of a character in a novel—in real life too—is under attack.'

'What you say, Nick, strengthens my contention that only a novel can imply certain truths impossible to state by exact definition. Biography and autobiography are forced to attempt exact definition. In doing so truth goes astray. The novelist is more serious—if that is the word.'

'Surely biographers and memoir-writers often do no more than imply things they chronicle, or put them forward as uncertain. A novelist is subjective, and selective, all the time. The others have certain facts forced on them, whether they like it or not. Besides, some of the very worst novelists are the most consciously serious ones.'

'Of course a novelist is *serious* only if he is a good novelist. You mention Molly Bloom. She offers an example of what I am saying. Obviously her sexual musings—and her husband's—derive from the author, to the extent that he invented them. Such descriptions would have been a thousand times less convincing, if attributed to Stephen Dedalus—let alone to Joyce himself. Their strength lies in existence within the imaginary personalities of the Blooms. That such traits are much diminished, when given to a hero, is even to some extent exemplified in *Ulysses*. It may be acceptable to read of Bloom tossing off. A blow by blow account of the author doing so is hardly conceivable as interesting. Perhaps, at the base of it all, is the popular confusion of self-pity with compassion. What is effective is art, not what is "true"—using the term in inverted commas.'

'Like Pilate.'

'Unfortunately Pilate wasn't a novelist.'

'Or even a memoir-writer.'

'Didn't Petronius serve as a magistrate in some distant

part of the Roman Empire? Think if the case had come up before him. Perhaps Petronius was a different period.'

The *Satyricon* was the only classical work ever freely quoted by Trapnel. He would often refer to it. I recalled his views on biography, reading Gwinnett's—found on return home—and wondered how far Trapnel would have regarded this example as proving his point. That a biography of Trapnel should have been written at all was surprising enough, an eventuality beyond all guessing for those to whom he had been no more than another necessitous phantom at the bar, to stand or be stood a half pint of bitter. Now, by a process every bit as magical as any mutations on the astral plane claimed by Dr Trelawney, there would be casual readers to find entertainment in the chronicle of Trapnel's days, professional critics adding to their reputation by analysis of his style, academics rummaging for nuggets among the Trapnel remains. It seemed unlikely that much was left over. Gwinnett had done a thorough job.

I had been friends with Trapnel only a few years, but in those years witnessed some of his most characteristic attitudes and performances. Here was a good instance of later trimmings that throw light on an already known story. Gwinnett had not only recorded the routine material well, he had dealt judiciously with much else of general interest at that immediately post-war period; one not specially easy to handle, especially for an American by no means steeped in English life. Prudently, Gwinnett had not always accepted Trapnel (given to self-fantasy) at his own estimation. The final disastrous spill (worse than any on the race-course by his jockey father)—that is to say Trapnel's infatuation with Pamela Widmerpool—had been treated with an altogether unexpected subtlety. Gwinnett had once implied that his own involvement with Pamela might impair objectivity, but only those who knew of that already were likely to recognize the extent to which author identified himself

86

with subject. I wrote to Delavacquerie recommending that *Death's-head Swordsman* should receive the year's Magnus Donners Memorial Prize. He replied that, Emily Brightman and Mark Members being in agreement, he himself would, as arranged, approach Widmerpool. If Widmerpool objected to our choice, we should have to think again. In due course, Delavacquerie reported back on this matter. His letters, like his speech, always possessed a touch of formality.

'There are to be no difficulties for the judges from that quarter. Lord Widmerpool's assurances justify me in my own eyes. You would laugh at the professional pleasure I take in being able to write this, the quiet satisfaction I find in my own skill at negotiation. To tell the truth no negotiation had to take place. Lord Widmerpool informed me straightaway that he did not care a fart—that was his unexpected phrase—what was said about him in Professor Gwinnett's book, either by name or anonymously. He gave no reason for this, but was evidently speaking without reservation of any kind. At first he said he did not even wish to see a copy of *Death's-head Swordsman*, as he held all conventional writings of our day in hearty contempt, but, thinking it best to do so, I persuaded him to accept a proof. It seemed to me that would put the committee of judges in a stronger position. Lord Widmerpool said that, if he had time, he would look at the book. Nothing he found there would make any difference to what he had already told me. That allays all fears as to the propriety of the award. Have you seen Lord Widmerpool lately? He is greatly altered from what I remember of him, though I only knew him by sight. Perhaps the American continent has had that effect. As you know, I regard the Western Hemisphere as a potent force on all who are brought in contact with its influences, whether or not they were born or live there—and of course I do not merely mean the US. Possibly I was right in my assessment of how Lord Widmerpool would react towards Professor Gwinnett's book. At present I cannot be sure whether my triumph—if it may so be called—was owed to that assessment. Lord Widmerpool made one small condition. It will amuse you. I will tell you about it when we next lunch together—next week, if you are in London. I have kept Matilda in touch with all these developments.'

The news of Widmerpool's indifference to whatever Gwinnett might have written, unanticipated in its comprehensive disdain of the whole Trapnel—and Gwinnett—story, certainly made the position of the Prize committee easier. It looked as if the publishers had already cleared the matter with Widmerpool. They seemed to have no fear of legal proceedings, and Delavacquerie's letter gave the impression that his interview might not have provided Widmerpool's first awareness of the book. Even so, without this sanction, there could have been embarrassments owed to the Donners-Brebner connexion. I wrote to Gwinnett (with whom I had not corresponded since his Spanish interlude), addressing the letter to the English Department of the American college named at the beginning of his book.

The recipient of the Magnus Donners Prize was given dinner at the expense of the Company. A selection of writers, publishers, literary editors, columnists, anyone else deemed helpful to publicity in the circumstances, was invited. Speeches were made. It was not an evening-dress affair. Convened in a suite of rooms on the upper floor of a restaurant much used for such occasions, the party was usually held in the early months of the year following that for which the book had been chosen. As a function, the Magnus Donners Memorial Prize dinner was just what might be expected, a business gathering, rather than a social one. Delavacquerie, who had its arranging, saw that food and drink were never less than tolerable. When he and I next met for one of our luncheons together I asked what had been Widmerpool's condition for showing so easygoing an attitude.

'That he should himself be invited to the dinner.'

'Did he make the request ironically?'

'Not in the least.'

As a public figure of a sort, although one fallen into comparative obscurity, issue of an invitation to Widmerpool would in no way run counter to the general pattern of guests; even if his presence, owing to the particular circumstances, might strike a bizarre note. It was likely that a large proportion of those present would be too young to have heard—anyway too young to take much interest in— the scandals of ten years before.

'No doubt Widmerpool can be sent a card. You were right in thinking the stipulation would amuse me.'

'You haven't heard it all yet.'

'What else?'

'He wants to bring two guests.'

'Donners-Brebner can presumably extend their hospitality that far.'

'Of course.'

'Who are to be Widmerpool's guests?'

'Whom do you think?'

The answer was not so easy as first appeared. Whom would Widmerpool ask? I made several guesses at personalities of rather his own kind, figures to be judged useful in one practical sphere or another. In putting forward these names, I became aware how little I now knew of Widmerpool's latest orientations and ambitions. Delavacquerie shook his head, smiling at the wrongness of such speculation.

'I told you Lord Widmerpool had greatly changed. Let me give you a clue. Two ladies.'

I put forward a life peeress and an actress, neither in their first youth.

'Not so elderly.'

'I give it up.'

'The Quiggin twins.'

'The girls who threw paint over him?'

'The same.'

'But—is he having an affair with both of them?'

Delavacquerie laughed. He was pleased with the effect of the information he had given.

'Not, I feel fairly sure, in any physical sense, although I gather he has no objection to girls who frequent his place—boys too, Etienne assures me—being good to look at. If the weather is warm, undressing is encouraged. I doubt if he contemplates sleeping with either sex. You know Widmerpool is not far from making himself into a Holy Man these days, certainly a much venerated one in his own circle.'

'What will Gwinnett think of this, if he comes to the dinner himself? I imagine it is quite possible he will. Have you heard from him about getting the Prize? I wrote a line of congratulation, but have had no reply.'

That Gwinnett had not replied was no surprise. It did not at all diverge from the accustomed Gwinnett manner of going on. If anything, lack of an answer suggested that Gwinnett's harassing London experiences had left him unchanged.

'Professor Gwinnett wrote to me, as secretary of the Prize committee, to say he would take pleasure in travelling over here to receive the Prize in person.'

'That will add to the drama of the dinner.'

'He said he was on the point of visiting this country in any case. He would speed up his plans.'

'Was Gwinnett pleased his book was chosen?'

'Pleased—far from overwhelmed. He wrote a few conventional phrases, saying he was gratified, adding that he would turn up for the dinner, if I would let him know time and place. No more. He was not at all effusive. In fact, from my own experience of Americans, his appreciation was restrained to the point of being brusque.'

'That's his line.'

The publishers issued *Death's-head Swordsman* just in time to be eligible for the Prize, though not at an advantageous moment to receive much attention from reviewers. That was inevitable in the circumstances. Such notices as appeared were favourable, but still few in number by the time of the Magnus Donners dinner, which took place, as usual, in the New Year.

'I'm asking the committee to come early,' said Delavacquerie. 'It's going to be rather an exceptional affair this year. Last-minute problems may arise.'

When I arrived he was moving about the dining-room, checking that seating was correct. Emily Brightman and Mark Members had not yet turned up.

'Professor Gwinnett is on Matilda's right, of course, and I've put Isobel on his other side. Emily Brightman thought it might look too much as if she had been set to keep an eye on him, if she were next door. Emily is sitting next to you, Nick, and a Donners-Brebner director's wife on the other side. Let me see, Mrs—'

The winner of the Prize was always beside Matilda Donners, at a long table, which included judges, representatives of the Company, and wives of these. At the end of dinner Delavacquerie's duty was to say a few words about the Prize itself. One of the judges' panel then introduced the recipient, and spoke of his book. Members, a compulsive public speaker, had been easily persuaded to undertake this duty. Brevity would not be attained, but it was more than possible that, having known Trapnel personally, he would in any case have risen to his feet. To tell the story of the borrowed five pounds would be tempting. Members had once before 'said a few words', after the scheduled speeches were at an end, followed by Alaric Kydd, who also felt that a speech was owed from him. Kydd had been expatriate for some years now, so there was no risk of that tonight. Delavacquerie took a last look round the tables.

'I've placed Lord Widmerpool and the Miss Quiggins out of the way of the winner of the Prize and the judges. In the far corner of the room by the other door. I think that is wise, don't you? A quiet table. Elderly reviewers and their wives or boyfriends. No young journalists. That's just being on the safe side.'

'I doubt if the present generation of young journalists remember about Gwinnett's connexion with Widmerpool. They may recall that the Quiggin twins threw paint over him. Even that's back last summer, and ancient history. What sort of form is Gwinnett himself in?'

'I haven't seen him.'

'Didn't he call you up on arrival?'

'I've heard nothing from him since his reply to my second letter. I suggested we should make contact before this dinner. He answered that he had all the information he needed. He would just turn up at the appointed time.'

'Where's he staying?'

'I don't even know that. I offered to fix him up with an hotel. He said he'd make his own arrangements.'

'He's being very Gwinnett-like. I hope he will turn up tonight. On second thoughts, it might be better if he did not appear. We can easily go through the motions of awarding the Prize *in absentia*. The presence of the author is not required for voicing correct sentiments about his book. Various potential embarrassments might be avoided without Gwinnett himself.'

'Gwinnett will be here all right. He writes the letter of a man of purpose.'

I agreed with that view. Gwinnett was, without doubt, a

man of purpose. Before we could discuss the matter further Emily Brightman came in, followed a moment later by Members. She was dressed with care for her rôle of judge, a long garment, whitish, tufted, a medal hanging from her neck that suggested a stylish parody of Murtlock's medallion. Delavacquerie fingered this ornament questioningly.

'Coptic, Gibson. I should have thought a person of your erudition would have recognized its provenance immediately. Is Lenore coming tonight, Mark?'

'Lenore was very sad at not being able to attend. She had to dash over to Boston again.'

'Congratulations on your own award.'

Members bowed. He was in a good humour. Emily Brightman referred to the poetry prize he had just received —nothing so liberal in amount as the Magnus Donners, but acceptable—for his *Collected Poems*, a volume which brought together all his verse from *Iron Aspidistra* (1923) to *H-Bomb Eclogue* (1966), the latter, one of the few poems Members had produced of late years.

'Thank you, Emily.'

'You have heard that the Quiggin twins are to be here tonight?'

'Rather hard on JG and Ada, who are also coming. They've done their best for those girls. The only reward is that they throw paint over Kenneth Widmerpool, and then turn up with him at their parents' parties.'

The disapproval with which Members spoke did not conceal a touch of excitement. If the Quiggin twins were to be present there was no knowing what might not happen. The room began to fill. L. O. Salvidge, an old supporter of Trapnel's (he had taken some trouble to give *Death's-head Swordsman* a send-off review), brought a new wife, his fourth. Wearing very long shiny black boots, much blue round the eyes, she was a good deal younger than her predecessors. They were followed by Bernard Shernmaker, who, in contrast with Salvidge, had always remained un-married. Shernmaker, by not reviewing Gwinnett's book had still avoided committing himself about Trapnel. He was in not at all a good temper, in fact seemed in the depths of rage and despair. If looks were anything to go by, he was never going to write a notice of *Death's-head Swordsman*. Members, as an old acquaintance, did not allow Shern-maker's joyless façade to modify his own consciously jocu-lar greeting.

'Hullo, Bernard. Have you heard the Quiggin twins are coming tonight? What do you think about that?'

Shernmaker's face contorted horribly. Nightmares of boredom and melancholy oozed from him, infecting all the social atmosphere round about. Somebody put a drink in his hand. Tension relaxed a little. A moment later the Quiggin parents appeared. Ada, as customary with her, was making the best of things. If she knew about her daughters attending the party with Widmerpool, she was determined to carry the situation off at this stage as natural enough. The probability was that she did not yet know the twins were to be present. Fifty in sight, Ada had kept her looks remark-ably well. She began to profess immense enthusiasm at the prospect of meeting Gwinnett again.

'Is he here yet? I scarcely took him in at all, when we were all in Venice that time. I long to have another look. Fancy Pamela, of all people, going to such lengths for a man.'

'Gwinnett hasn't arrived yet.'

'Now that he's won the Magnus Donners, JG is furious we never signed him up for the Trapnel biography. I sug-gested that at the time. JG wasn't in the least interested. He said books about recently dead writers were dead ducks. He's specially angry because L. O. Salvidge gave it such a good notice. I told him that was only because there's nothing about at this time of year. JG's not only cross on account of none of our books ever winning the Magnus Donners, but he's got a bad throat too. It makes him full of *Angst*, worries, regrets of all sorts. He mustn't stay late.'

Quiggin was certainly looking sorry for himself. Giving off an exhalation of cold-cures, he was wrinkling his high forehead irritably. Contrary to Ada's words, he showed little or no interest in who might, or might not, have won the Prize, brushing off Evadne Clapham, when she tried to get his opinion about the selection this time. Evadne Clapham herself had recently made something of a comeback with *Cain's Jawbone* (her thirty-fifth novel), a story that returned to the style which had first made her name.

'The title of Mr Gwinnett's book is curiously like that of my own last novel, JG. Do you think he could have had time to be influenced by reading it? I'm so anxious to meet him. There's something I *must* tell him in confidence about Trappy.'

Quiggin, offering no opinion on book-titles, restated his own position.

'I oughtn't to have come tonight. I'm feeling rotten.'

'Do you think Kenneth Widmerpool knows Mr Gwinnett is in London?' Ada remarked.

That gave Members his chance.

'Hadn't you heard Widmerpool's coming tonight, Ada? He's bringing Amanda and Belinda.'

Members could not conceal all surprise at his luck in being able to announce that to the twins' parents. Ada controlled herself, but looked extremely put out. The information was altogether too much for her husband. Quiggin and Members might be on good terms these days, even so, there were limits to what Quiggin was prepared to take from his old friend. He received this disclosure as if it were a simple display of spite on the part of Members, whose genial tone did not entirely discount that proposition. Quiggin, pasty-faced from his indisposition, went red. He gave way to a violent fit of coughing. When this seizure was at an end, he burst out, in the middle of the sentence his voice rising to a near screech.

'Amanda and Belinda are coming to this dinner?'

Members was not prepared for his words to have had so violent an effect. He now spoke soothingly.

'Kenneth Widmerpool simply asked if he could bring them. There seemed no objection.'

'But why the buggery is Widmerpool coming himself?'

'He was just invited.'

Members said that disingenuously, as if inviting Widmerpool was the most natural thing in the world. In one sense it might be, but not within existing circumstances. Quiggin was too cross to think that out.

'Why the bloody hell didn't you tell us before, Mark? I didn't realize all the thing with Widmerpool and the twins was still going on. Anyway why should they want to turn up at a party like this?'

Ada intervened. Even if the announcement were just as irritating for herself, she was better able to conceal annoyance.

'Oh, do shut up about the girls, JG. They're all right. We know about their seeing a lot of Widmerpool. No harm in that. They joke about it themselves. After all he's chancellor of their bloody university. If anybody's got a right to be friends with them, he has. They might easily have been sent down, even these days, if it hadn't been for him. Why shouldn't they come and hear who's won the Prize. Do have some sense. Why, hullo, Evadne. Congratulations on *Cain's Jawbone*. I haven't read it yet, but it's on my list. Hullo, Quentin. What news on the cultural front? I enjoyed your piece on Musil, Bernard. So did JG. Have you read the Gwinnett book?'

Isobel arrived. She and I were talking with Salvidge, and

his new wife, when Delavacquerie came up. He brought with him a smallish bald thick-set man, wearing a dark suit of international cut, and somewhat unEnglish tie.

'Here's Professor Gwinnett, Nick.'

Delavacquerie, rather justly, said that a little reprovingly, as if I might have been expected, if not to mark down Gwinnett's entry into the room, at least to show quicker reaction, when brought face to face with him in person. Whatever Delavacquerie's right to take that line, I should have been quite unaware who the man in the dark suit might be, without this specific statement of identity. It was lucky I had not been close to the door when Gwinnett entered the room. So far as I was concerned, he was un-recognizable. Since Venice, a drastic transformation had taken place. Gwinnett held out his hand. He did not speak or smile.

'Hullo, Russell.'

'Good to see you, Nicholas.'

'You got my letter?'

'Thanks for your letter, and congratulations. I didn't reply. I was pretty sure I'd be seeing you, after what Mr Delavacquerie told me.'

'It was only meant as a line to say how much I'd enjoyed the book, Russell. Delighted it won the Prize. Also glad to see you over here again. You haven't met Isobel. You're sitting next to each other at dinner.'

Giving her a long searching look, Gwinnett took Isobel's hand. He remained unsmiling. When I had last seen him, his appearance seemed young for his age, then middle thirties. Now, in middle forties, he might have been con-sidered older than that. He had also added to his personality some not at once definable characteristics, a greater com-pactness than before. Perhaps that impression was due only to a changed exterior. All physical slightness was gone. Gwinnett was positively heavy now in build. He had shaved off the thin line of moustache, and was totally bald. Such hair as might have remained above his ears had been rigorously clipped away. Below were allowed two short strips of whisker. The shaven skull—which made one think at once of his book's title—conferred a tougher look than formerly. He had always something of the professional gymnast. The additional fleshiness might have been that of a retired lightweight boxer or karate instructor. Pale blue lenses, once worn in his spectacles, had been exchanged for large rimless circles of glass girdered with steel.

'I've heard a lot about you, Mr Gwinnett.'

Gwinnett slightly inclined his head. He wholly accepted Isobel must have heard a lot about him, that others in the room might have heard a lot about him too. Such was what his manner suggested. It was surprising how little to be regarded as authentic was available even now. The Pamela Widmerpool episode apart, he was scarcely less enigmatic than when I had first sat next to him at one of the luncheons of the Venice conference, and we had talked of the Sleaford Veronese. Delavacquerie returned, bringing with him Emily Brightman and Members, the last of whom had not previously met Gwinnett. Old friend as she was, Emily Brightman had observed Gwinnett's arrival no more than myself. She, too, may have found him unrecognizable. If so, she covered that by the warmth of greeting when she took his hand. I think, in her way, she was much attached to him. If she felt doubts about some of the complexities of Gwinnett's nature, she put into practice her belief that certain matters, even if known to be true, are not necessarily the better for being said aloud.

'How are you, Russell? Why have you never written and told me about yourself for all these years? Wasn't it nice that we were able to give you the Prize? You have produced a work to deserve it. How long are you remaining in this country?'

'Just a week, Emily. I'll be back again next year. I've got research to do over here.'

'Another great work?'

'I guess so.'

'What's the subject. Or is that a secret?'

'No secret at all—*The Gothic Symbolism of Mortality in the Texture of Jacobean Stagecraft.*'

Gwinnett, always capable of bringing off a surprise, did so this time. Neither Emily Brightman nor I were quite prepared for the title of his new book.

'Some people—I think you among them, Emily—judged X. Trapnel a little lightweight as a theme. I do not think so myself, but that has been suggested. I decided to look around for a new focus. I see the Jacobean project as in some ways an extension, rather than change, of subject matter. Trapnel had much in common with those playwrights.'

This offered yet another reason for the epigraph introducing *Death's-head Swordsman*. Gwinnett had been speaking with the enthusiasm that would suddenly, though rarely, come into his voice. Members, who had no reason to be greatly interested in Gwinnett's academic enterprises, strayed off to examine the new Mrs Salvidge. There was a pause. Even Emily Brightman seemed to have no immediate comment to make on the Jacobean dramatists. Gwinnett had the characteristic of imposing silences. He did so now. I broke it with a piece of seventeenth-century pedantry that seemed at least an alternative to this speechlessness.

'Beaumont, the dramatist, was a kind of first-cousin of my own old friend, Robert Burton of the *Anatomy of Melancholy.*'

'Sure.'

Gwinnett spoke as if every schoolboy knew that. Emily Brightman, abandoning seventeenth-century scholarship, asked where he was staying in London. Gwinnett named an hotel.

'Wait, I'll write that down.'

She took an address-book from her bag. Either the name conveyed nothing, or Emily Brightman was showing more then ever her refusal to find human behaviour, notably Gwinnett's, at all out of the ordinary, anyway when his was removed from the purely academic sphere. I was not sure I should myself have been equally capable of concealing the least flicker of recognition at the name. Gwinnett had chosen to visit again the down-at-heel hostelry in the St Pancras neighbourhood, where he had spent the night—her last—with Pamela Widmerpool. He drawled the address in his usual slow unemphasized scarcely audible tone. Emily Brightman's impassivity in face of this taste for returning to old haunts, however gruesome their associations, could have been due as much to forgetfulness as to pride in accepting Gwinnett's peculiarities. Nevertheless, she changed the subject again.

'Now tell me of your other doings, Russell. I don't know much about your college, beyond reading in the papers that it had been suffering from campus disturbances. Sum up the root of the trouble. What is the teaching like there?'

Gwinnett began speaking of his academic life. Emily Brightman, listening with professional interest, made an occasional comment. Delavacquerie, who was now standing by in silence, drew me aside. He had perhaps been waiting for a suitable opportunity to do that.

'As soon as Professor Gwinnett arrived I informed him that Lord Widmerpool was attending the dinner.'

'How did he take that?'

'He just acknowledged the information.'

'There's no necessity for them to meet.'

'Unless one of them feels the challenge.'

'Widmerpool probably wants to do no more than re-examine Gwinnett. He barely met him when we were in Venice. Widmerpool is not at all observant where individuals are concerned. Also, he had plenty of other things to think about at the time. It would be reasonable to have developed a curiosity about Gwinnett, after what happened, even if this is not a particularly sensitive way of taking another look at him.'

'Didn't they see each other at the inquest?'

'How are such enquiries arranged? Perhaps they did. All I know is that Gwinnett was exonerated from all blame. I find it more extraordinary that Widmerpool should choose to bring the Quiggin twins, rather than that he should wish to gaze at Gwinnett.'

'Aren't the girls just a way of showing off?'

Delavacquerie put on an interrogative expression that was entirely French. He was probably right. Commonplace vanity was the explanation. Widmerpool felt satisfaction, as a man of his age, in appearing with a pair of girls, who, if no great beauties, were lively and notorious. They could be a spur to his own exhibitionism, if not his masochism.

'I see Evadne Clapham making towards us. She tells me she has something vital to convey to Professor Gwinnett about Trapnel. Can Trapnel have slept with her? One never knows. It might be best to get the introduction over before dinner.'

Delavacquerie went off. By now Matilda had arrived. As queen of the assembly, she had got herself up even more theatrically than usual, a sort of ruff, purple and transparent, making her look as if she were going to play Lady Macbeth; an appearance striking the right note in the light of Gwinnett's new literary preoccupations. When Delavacquerie presented him to her this seemed to go well. Matilda must often have visited New York and Washington with Sir Magnus, and Gwinnett showed none of the moodiness of which he could be capable, refusal to indulge in any conversational trivialities. By the time dinner was announced the two of them gave the appearance of chatting together quite amicably. There was no sign yet of Widmerpool, nor the Quiggin twins. They would presumably all arrive together. As Delavacquerie had said, I found myself between Emily Brightman, and the wife of a Donners-Brebner director; the latter, a rather worried middle-aged lady, had put on all her best clothes, and most of her jewellery, as protection, when venturing into what she evidently regarded as a world threatening perils of every kind. We did not make much contact until the soup plates were being cleared away.

'I'm afraid I haven't read any of your books. I believe you write books, don't you? I hope you won't mind that.'

I was in process of picking out one of the several routine replies designed to bridge this not at all uncommon conversational opening—a phrase that at once generously accepts the speaker's candour in confessing the omission, while emphasizing the infinite unimportance of any such solicitude on that particular point—when need to make any reply at all was averted by a matter of much greater interest to both of us. This was entry into the room of Widmerpool and the Quiggin twins. My neighbour's attention was caught simultaneously with my own, though no doubt for different reasons. Widmerpool led the party of three, Amanda and Belinda following a short distance behind. As they came up the room most of the talk at the tables died down, while people stopped eating to stare.

'Do tell me about that man and the two girls. I'm sure I ought to know who they are. Isn't it a famous author, and his two daughters? He's probably a close friend of yours, and you will laugh at my ignorance.'

In the circumstances the supposition of the director's lady was not altogether unreasonable. If you thought of authors as a grubby lot, a tenable standpoint, Widmerpool certainly filled the bill; while the age of his companions in relation to his own might well have been that even of grandfather and granddaughters. Since I had known him as a schoolboy, Widmerpool had been not much less than famous for looking ineptly dressed, a trait that remained with him throughout life, including his army uniforms. At the same time—whether too big, too small, oddly cut, strangely patterned—his garments had hitherto always represented, even at his most revolutionary period, the essence of stolid conventionality as their aim. They had never been chosen, in the first instance, with the object of calling attention to himself. Now all was altered. There had been a complete change of policy. He wore the same old dark grey suit—one felt sure it was the same one—but underneath was a scarlet high-necked sweater.

'As a matter of fact he's not an author, though I believe he's writing a book. He's called Lord Widmerpool.'

'Not *the* Lord Widmerpool?'

'There's only one, so far as I know.'

'But I've seen him on television. He didn't look like that.'

'Perhaps he was well made-up. In any case he's said to have changed a good deal lately. I haven't seen him for a long time myself. He's certainly changed since I last saw him.'

Her bewilderment was understandable.

'Are the girls his daughters?'

'No—he's never had any children.'

'Who are they then? They look rather sweet. Are they twins? I love their wearing dirty old jeans at this party.'

'They're the twin daughters of J. G. Quiggin, the publisher, and his novelist wife, Ada Leintwardine. Their parents are sitting over there at the table opposite. J. G. Quiggin's the bald man, helping himself to vegetables, his wife the lady with her hair piled up rather high.'

'I believe I've read something by Ada Leintwardine—*The Bitch—The Bitches*—something like that. I know bitches came into the title.'

'*The Bitch Pack meets on Wednesday.*'

'That's it. I don't remember much about it. Are the girls with Lord Widmerpool, or are they just joining their parents?'

'They're with him.'

'Are they his girlfriends?'

The party was evidently coming up to expectations.

'He's chancellor of their university. They threw paint over him last summer. I don't know how close the relationship is apart from that.'

'Those two little things threw paint over him?'

'Yes.'

'Didn't he mind?'

'Apparently not.'

'And now they're all friends?'

'That's what it looks like.'

'What do you think about the Permissive Society?'

Widmerpool had entered the dining-room with the air of Stonewall Jackson riding into Frederick, that is to say glaring round, as if on the alert for flags representing the Wrong Side. Amanda and Belinda, apart from looking as ready for a square meal as the rebel horde itself seemed otherwise less sure of their ground, sullen, even rather hangdog. Their getup, admired by my neighbour, was identical. As companions for Widmerpool they belonged, broadly speaking, to the tradition of Gypsy Jones, so far as physical appearance was concerned. (A couple of lines had announced, not long before, the death of 'Lady Craggs, widow of Sir Howard Craggs, suddenly in Czechoslovakia'; and I had made up my mind to ask Bagshaw, when next seen, if he knew anything of Gypsy's end.) This Gypsy Jones resemblance gave a certain authenticity to the twins' Widmerpool connexion. Their bearing that evening, on the other hand, had none of her aggressive self-confidence. It more approximated to that of Baby Wentworth (also deceased the previous year, at Montego Bay, having just married a relatively rich Greek), when, as his discontented mistress, Baby entered a room in the company of Sir Magnus Donners. In the case of the Quiggin twins, as Delavacquerie had observed, sexual relations with Widmerpool highly improbable, the girls may have been embarrassed by merely appearing in front of this sort of public as his guests. If so, why did they accompany him? Perhaps there was a small gratifying element of exhibitionism for them too; in that a meeting of true minds. Emily Brightman allowed a murmur to escape her.

'I hope those young ladies are going to behave.'

Delavacquerie, already on the look out and seeing action required, had risen at once from his seat, when the Widmerpool party came in. Now he led them to the table indicated earlier, where three chairs remained unoccupied. The Donners-Brebner lady lost interest after they disappeared.

'What do you think about Vietnam?'

Widmerpool and the twins once settled at their table, dinner passed off without further notable incident. Isobel reported later that Gwinnett had given no outward sign of noticing Widmerpool's arrival. Possibly he had not even penetrated the disguise of the red sweater. That would have been reasonable enough. Alternatively, Gwinnett's indifference could have been feigned, a line he chose to take, or, quite simply, expression of what he genuinely felt. Neither with Isobel, nor Matilda, did he display any of his occasional bouts of refusing to talk. He had, Isobel said, continued to abstain from alcohol.

'What do you think of Enoch?' asked the Donners-Brebner lady.

The time came for speeches. Delavacquerie said his usual short introductory word. He was followed by Members, who settled down to what sounded like the gist of an undelivered lecture on The Novel; English, French, Russian;

notably American, in compliment to Gwinnett, and recognition of the American Novel's influence on Trapnel's style. Members went on, also at some length, to consider Trapnel as an archetypal figure of our time. The final reference to his own gone-for-ever five pounds was received with much relieved laughter.

'Was the last speaker a famous writer too?'

'A famous poet.'

Members seemed owed this description, within the context of the question. Gwinnett followed. He did not speak for long. In fact, without almost impugning the compliment of the award, he could hardly have been more brief. He said that he had admired Trapnel's work since first reading a short story found in an American magazine, taken immediate steps to discover what else he had written, in due course formed the ambition to write about Trapnel himself. His great regret, Gwinnett said, was never to have met Trapnel in the flesh.

'I called my book *Death's-head Swordsman*, because X. Trapnel's sword-stick symbolized the way he faced the world. The book's epigraph—spoken as you will recall, by an actor holding a skull in his hands—emphasizes that Death, as well as Life, can have its beauty.

'Whether our death be good
Or bad, it is not death, but life that tries.
He lived well: therefore, questionless, well dies.'

Gwinnett stopped. He sat down. The audience, myself included, supposing he was going to elaborate the meaning of the quotation, draw some analogy, waited to clap. Whatever significance he attached to the lines, they remained unexpounded. After the moment of uncertainty some applause was given. Emily Brightman whispered approval.

'Good, didn't you think? I impressed on Russell not to be prosy.'

Conversation became general. In a minute or two people would begin to move from their seats—a few were doing so already—and the party break up. I turned over in my mind the question of seeing, or not seeing, Gwinnett, while he remained in England. Now that his work on Trapnel was at an end we had no special tie, although in an odd way I had always felt well disposed towards him, even if his presence imposed a certain strain. The matter was likely to lie in Gwinnett's hands rather than mine, and in any case, he was only to stay a week. It could be put off until research brought him over here again.

'In the end we decided against the Bahamas,' said the director's lady.

At the far end of the dining-room a guest at one of the tables had begun to talk in an unusually loud voice, probably some author, publisher or reviewer, who had taken too much to drink. There had been enough on supply, scarcely an amount to justify anything spectacular in the way of intoxication. Whoever was responsible for making so much row had probably arrived tipsy, or, during the time available, consumed an exceptional number of pre-dinner drinks. Members, for instance—who put away more than he used—was rather red in the face, no more than that. Conceivably, the noise was simply one of those penetrative conversational voices with devastating carrying power. Then a thumping on the table with a fork or spoon indicated a call for silence. Somebody else wanted to make a speech. There was going to be another unplanned oration, probably on the lines of Alaric Kydd's tribute to the memory of the homosexual politician, whose biography had received the Prize that year.

'Look—Lord Widmerpool is going to speak. He was awfully good when I heard him on telly. He talked of all sorts of things I didn't know about in the most interesting way. He's not at all conventional, you know. In fact he said he hated all conventions. The American was rather dull, wasn't he?'

The moment inevitably recalled that when, at a reunion dinner of Le Bas's Old Boys, Widmerpool had risen to give his views on the current financial situation. I had seen little or nothing of his later career as a public man, so this occasion could have been far from unique. Even if he made a practice nowadays of impromptu speaking, the present gathering was an extraordinary one to choose to draw attention to himself.

'Magnus Donners Prize winner, judges and guests, there is more than one reason why I am addressing you tonight without invitation.'

The parallel with the Old Boy dinner underlined the changes taken place in Widmerpool's oratory. In former days a basic self-assurance had been tempered with hesitancy of manner, partly due to thickness of utterance, partly to consciousness of being on uneasy terms with his contemporaries. All suggestion of unsureness, of irresolution, was gone. When a sentence was brought out too quickly, one word, rasping over the next in a torrent of excited assertion, the meaning might become blurred, but, on the whole, the diction had become more effective with practice, and a changed accentuation.

'I address you in the first place as the once old friend and business colleague of the late Magnus Donners himself, the man we commemorate tonight by the award of the Prize named after him, and by the dinner we have just eaten. In spite of this, no more than a few words have been spoken of Donners, as public man or private individual. In certain respects that is justified. Donners represented in his public life all that I most abhor. Let me at once go on record as expressing this sentiment towards him. All that I hold most pernicious characterized Donners, and his doings, in many different ways, and in many parts of the world. Nevertheless

Donners put me in charge, many years ago, of the sources from which the monies derive that make up the amount of the Prize, and pay for our dinner tonight. That, as I say, was many years ago. I do not wish to speak more of my own work than that. It was hard work, work scrupulously done. I make these introductory remarks only to convince you that I have strong claims to be given a hearing.'

Widmerpool paused. He gazed round. The room was quite silent, except for the Quiggin twins, who, paying no attention whatever to Widmerpool's words, were muttering and giggling together. No one could blame them for that. It looked as if we were in for a longish harangue. Quiggin, from a table over the way, kept an eye on his daughters. On the other hand, Ada seemed riveted by Widmerpool himself. Half smiling, she sat staring at him, possibly musing how extraordinary that Pamela Flitton, her old friend, should once have been his wife. Matilda was watching Widmerpool too. Her face had assumed a look of conventional stage surprise, one appropriate to an actress, no longer young, playing a quizzical rôle in comedy or farce. This expression remained unchanged throughout Widmerpool's strictures on Sir Magnus. The dark profile of Delavacquerie, grave, firm, rather sad in repose, gave nothing away. Nor did Gwinnett, either by look or movement, show any reaction. Gwinnett might have been listening to the most banal of congratulatory addresses, delivered by the official representative of some academic body. Widmerpool passed his hand inside the neck of his sweater. He was working himself up.

'We are often told we must establish with certainty the values of the society in which we live. That is a right and proper ambition, one to be laid down without reticence as to yea or nay. Let me say at once what I stand for myself. I stand for the dictatorship of free men, and the catalysis of social, physical and spiritual revolution. I claim the right to do so in the name of contemporary counterculture, no less than in my status as trustee of the fund of which I have already spoken. But—let me make this very plain—neither of these claims do I regard as paramount. I have yet another that altogether overrides the second, and expresses in an intrinsic and individual formula a point of contact to be looked upon as the veritable hub of the first.'

Widmerpool again stopped speaking. He was sweating hard, though the night was far from warm. He took a long drink of water. No one interrupted—as some of the more impatient had done in the course of Alaric Kydd's extempore harangue—probably kept silent from sheer surprise. Widmerpool also managed to give the impression he was coming on to something that might be worth hearing. In fact the Donners-Brebner director's wife had been to some extent justified in her assessment.

'There are persons here tonight aware that I am myself referred to—even if not by name—in the biography that has received this year's Magnus Donners Memorial award, the work we have come together to celebrate at this dinner. For the benefit of those not already in possession of that information—those who do not know that, under the cloak of a specious anonymity, the story of my own married life is there recorded—I take the opportunity to announce that fact. I was the husband of the woman who destroyed the wretched author Trapnel's manuscript book—or whatever it was of his literary work that she destroyed—one of the steps on the downfall of Trapnel, and of herself.'

To describe as somewhat horrified the silence that continued to exist throughout the dining-room would be no undue exaggeration. These words were far more than the committee had bargained for. Delavacquerie especially must at the moment be feeling that, I thought, though in a sense Widmerpool's line was the one Delavacquerie himself had predicted; even if infinitely more aggressive. There was no way of stopping Widmerpool. He would have to be heard to the end.

'Some of you—not, I hope, the younger section of my audience—may be surprised at my drawing attention to my own case in playing a part—that of the so-called betrayed husband—once looked upon as discreditable and derisory. I go further than merely proclaiming that fact to you all. I take pride in ridiculing what is—or rather was—absurdly called honour, respectability, law, order, obedience, custom, rule, hierarchy, precept, regulation, all that is insidiously imposed by the morally, ideologically, and spiritually naked, and politically bankrupt, on those they have oppressed and do oppress. I am grateful to the author of this book—the title of which for the moment escapes me—for bringing home to so large an audience the irrelevance of such concepts in this day and age, by giving me opportunity to express at a gathering like ours, the wrongness of the way we live, the wrongness of marriage, the wrongness of money, the wrongness of education, the wrongness of government, the wrongness of the manner we treat kids like these.'

Widmerpool extended his hand in the direction of Amanda and Belinda. They were still conferring together. Neither took any notice of this reference to themselves. Perhaps they were unaware of it.

'I have brought these two children tonight by special request on my own part, and for a good reason. They are the couple who threw paint over me in my capacity as university chancellor. It was the right thing to do. It was the only thing to do. I was taking part in a piece of pompous and meaningless ceremonial, which my own good sense, and social opinions, should have taught me to avoid. I am now eternally glad that I did not avoid that. I learnt a lesson. Even now there are marks of red paint on my body, that may remain until my dying day, as memorial to a weak spirit. The entirely commendable act of Amanda and

Belinda brought to the surface many half-formulated ideas already in my mind. Crystallized them. These children are right to have abandoned the idea that they can get somewhere without violence. Festering diseases need sharp surgery. These kids were articulate in their own way, and, in a different manner, the book by Professor—Professor—this book, the one that has won the Prize, has crystallized my views—'

Quiggin was not taking Widmerpool's speech at all well. If he had been looking in poor health at the start of the evening, he now appeared almost at the end of his tether with his cold, and the unlooked for imposition of this flow of revolutionary principles. Ada, too, had begun to show signs of stress. Then Quiggin's expression suddenly changed. From sourness, irritability, air of being out of sorts, the features became distorted with alarm. He had noticed something about Widmerpool, so it seemed, that disturbed him out of all proportion to the words spoken, many of which he must often have heard before, even if exceptional in the present circumstances. I turned towards Widmerpool's table to see what the cause of this anxiety might be. The movement was too late. Whatever preparations Quiggin apprehended had by then passed into the sphere of active operation. There was a loud crackling explosion, like fireworks going off in an enclosed space, followed by a terrific bang. Widmerpool's table was enveloped in a dark cloud that recalled 'laying down smoke' in army exercises. Within half a second all that end of the room was hidden in thick fumes, some of which reached as far as the judges' table. At the same time a perfectly awful smell descended.

'I knew it would be a mistake to allow those girls in. I have some experience.'

Emily Brightman's voice was calm. Academic administration had accustomed her to such things as were taking place.

The smell that swept through the room was of stupefying nastiness. When the smoke cleared away—which for some reason it did quite quickly, the smell, in contrast, dilating in volume and foulness—the Quiggin twins had disappeared. They must have made a quick exit through the door at that end of the dining-room. A few wisps of blue smoke hung round Widmerpool himself, like a penumbra, where he still stood upright at the table. He seemed as unprepared as anyone else present for these discharges. His mouth continued to open and close. Either no words came out, or they could be heard no longer at this distance on account of the general turmoil made by people rising from their seats in an effort to escape the nauseating reek. The last I saw of the Donners-Brebner lady was a backview hurrying down the room, handkerchief raised to face. Emily Brightman, puckering her nostrils, fanned herself with a menu.

'This compares with the Mutilation of the Hermae. Fortunately Russell is used to the antics of students. He is always self-possessed in trying situations. I told you that Lord Widmerpool had become very strange. No one showed much interest in that information at the time.'

Delavacquerie was the first to reach Gwinnett to make some sort of an apology for what had happened. He was followed by others, including the Quiggin parents. Gwinnett himself was behaving as if fire-crackers, artificial smoke, stinkbombs, were all normal adjuncts of any literary prizegiving, in London, or anywhere else. Matilda, too, was taking it all quietly. The scene may even have appealed a little to her own adventurous side.

'Here's the maître d'hotel,' she said. 'We shall probably be asked to hold the party in another restaurant next year.'

The origin of all this tumult—Widmerpool and his speech, more precisely, Widmerpool and his guests—had been for the moment forgotten in the general confusion.

Now Widmerpool himself appeared in the crowd clustering round Gwinnett. He was in a state of almost uncontrollable excitement, eyes gleaming through his spectacles, hands making spasmodic jerky movements.

'That was a Happening, if you like. Amanda and Belinda don't do things by halves. I wouldn't have missed that for a cool million—I mean had money meant anything to me these days.'

He made for Gwinnett, whom Evadne Clapham had at last managed to pin down; Delavacquerie having moved away to speak with Matilda. Widmerpool—something of a feat—elbowed Evadne Clapham aside. He faced Gwinnett. They did not shake hands.

'Professor Gwinnett—at last I recall the name—I hope you did not mind what I said in my speech.'

'No, Lord Widmerpool, I did not mind.'

'Not at all?'

'Not at all.'

'You are probably familiar with its trend.'

'I am.'

'You have heard some of those concepts ventilated in academic circles?'

'I have.'

'Are you staying in this country?'

'Just a week.'

'I should like to see you. Where are you staying?'

Gwinnett expressed no view as to whether or not he himself wished to renew such acquaintance as already experienced with Widmerpool. He simply gave the name of his hotel. Widmerpool, who had taken out a pencil, was about to write the address on the back of a menu picked up from the table. He showed immediate signs of recognizing the place, which he must almost certainly have been required to enter in the course of clearing up his wife's affairs. His mouth twitched. Having gone thus far in making overtures to Gwinnett, expressly stating that he would like to see more of him while he was in England, he firmly went through with noting down the information given. The hotel, macabre as the choice might be, was a minor matter, it might be supposed, compared with the general wish to consort with Gwinnett himself.

'Will you have time to visit me, Professor Gwinnett—I should like you, as an academic, to inspect my little community in the country? There are young people there you might enjoy meeting. I flatter myself I have bridged the age-gap with success—and in a manner that could be of interest in connexion with your own students. It was a problem to which I gave special attention when I was in the USA.'

Gwinnett said nothing. His silence was altogether uncommitted. It carried neither approval and acceptance, nor disapproval and rejection. His own position was absolutely neutral so far as outward gesture was concerned. It recalled a little his treatment in Venice of Glober, the film tycoon. Widmerpool tore off half the menu he held, and wrote on it his own address.

'Here you are. Let me know, if you have a moment to come down. I shall leave here now, as I do not propose to stay any longer than necessary at a bourgeois gathering of a sort deeply repugnant to me. I came only to state in public certain things I deeply feel, and this seemed an ideal occasion for stating. I did not guess my words would be reinforced by militant action. So much the better. Why it took place, I myself do not know. Perhaps because you yourself—the winner of the Prize—are of American nationality, a citizen of the United States. If so, you will understand, Professor, that it was called for by your country's policies, not your own book, and will recognize a gesture of cultural paranoia, from representatives of Youth, in which nothing the least personal is intended.'

Widmerpool grinned unpleasantly for a second, then turned away. He did not say goodbye to Matilda, Delavacquerie, myself, nor anyone else. In fact he now seemed not only unaware that other persons were present, but altogether insensible to the smell, hardly at all abated in frightfulness. The transcendent beauty of the performance put on by the Quiggin twins alone absorbed him; as it were, levitated him into a world of almost absolute moral and political bliss. Deep in thought, he walked slowly down the room, now rapidly emptying.

4

IN DAYS WHEN UNCLE GILES had been (to borrow the expressive idiom of Dr Trelawney) a restless soul wandering the vast surfaces of the Earth, it had seemed extraordinary that a man of his age—by no means what I now considered venerable—should apparently regard his life as full of incident, take his own doings with such desperate seriousness. These arbitrarily accepted conjectures of one's earlier years—to the effect that nothing of the slightest interest happens to people, who, for reasons best known to themselves, have chosen to grow old—were not wholly borne out by observation of one's contemporaries, nor even to some degree by personal experience. Widmerpool was certainly a case in point. The backwash of the Magnus Donners dinner tended, naturally enough, to emphasize the action of the Quiggin twins, rather than Widmerpool's own performance that night, but, after all, Amanda and Belinda would never have had opportunity to break up the party, if Widmerpool had not negotiated the invitation.

Widmerpool himself had explained in the clearest terms, at the time, his reasons for taking the course he had, including the wish to be accompanied by the Quiggin twins, but not everyone was able to comprehend his latest standpoint. There were even found those to echo the conclusion of Lenore Members that he had become 'mentally disturbed.'

Then the answer dawned on me. Widmerpool was Orlando. The parallel with Ariosto's story might not be exact at every point, its analogy even partake of parody, but here was Widmerpool, for years leading what he certainly regarded himself as the Heroic Life, deserted by his Angelica, not for one but a thousand (in Widmerpool's eyes) nonentities. If Pamela lacked some of Angelica's qualities, Angelica, too, had sometimes drunk at enchanted fountains that excited violent passions. It was the consequence of this situation that seemed so apposite; the signs Widmerpool was showing, at least morally speaking, of stripping himself naked like Orlando, taking to the woods, in the same manner dropping out. It remained to be seen whether Widmerpool would find an Astolpho.

Later that spring there was another small reminder of Ariosto, this time in connexion with the Mage beginning to fly; in short, Scorpio Murtlock—perhaps annually incarnate at this season as a vernal demigod—whose name appeared in a newspaper paragraph. It reported some sort of a row that had taken place in the neighbourhood of the megalithic site to which the caravan had been travelling just about a year before. Whether the same party, or other members of the cult, had been in that area all the time was not clear. Only Murtlock was mentioned by name. I did not know whether Fiona still belonged to his community, enquiries about her doings from her parents being a delicate matter. The local inhabitants seemed to have objected to ceremonies, performed in and about the neolithic site, by Murtlock and his followers. The police were reported as undertaking investigations. Murtlock himself was represented as making vigorous protest against alleged persecution of the group for their beliefs. That was the sole reference to the incident at the time, anyway the only one I saw.

In a writer's life, as time shortens, work tends to predominate, among other things resulting in a reduction of attendance at large conjunctions of people. In relation to work itself there are arguments against this change of rhythm. An affair like the Magnus Donners dinner might be exceptional in what it had provided, but even assemblages of a calmer nature staved off that reclusion which seems to offer increasing attractions, keeping one in some sort of circulation, in a position to hear the latest news. Such jaunts prevented a repletion of ideas, mulled over constantly in the mind, wholly taking the place of experience. Thinking —as General Conyers used to insist—damages feeling. No doubt he had got the idea from a book. That did not make it less valid. Something can get lost, especially in the arts, by thinking too much, which sometimes confuses the instinct for what ought to go down on paper.

These professional reflexions, at best subjective, at worst intolerably tedious, are pretext for inclusion of yet another public dinner; though my life was far from consisting in a succession of such functions. When an invitation arrived for the Royal Academy banquet the phrase conjured up a tempting vision of former days: forgotten Victorian RAs, their names once a household word; vast canvases in vaster gilt frames; 'society' portraits of famous beauties and eminent statesmen; enigmatic Problem Pictures: fashionable crowds; a whole aesthetic and social cosmos with a myth of its own. The institution that had welcomed Isbister, excluded Mr Deacon, had now undergone a deathbed conversion to Modernism. Yet was the Academy on its deathbed? The reality of the occasion—as opposed to such reveries—had by no means discarded all vestige of the old tradition. If the pictures hanging on the now whitewashed walls might be called temperately avant-garde in treatment, a reassuring suspicion remained that techniques, long sunk in oblivion, were to be found tucked away in obscure corners. The company, too, was no less traditional, minor royalty likely to be present, not to mention a member of the Cabinet—possibly the Prime Minister himself—making, at this relatively free and easy party, a speech that could touch on some grave matter of policy.

The suggestion thus given of a kind of carnival, devoted to the theme of Past and Present, was heightened by the contrasted attire of the guests. White ties and black tail-coats, orders and decorations, mingled with dinner-jackets, the intermittent everyday suit. The last were rare. Those who despised evening-dress usually adopted an out-and-out knock-about-the-studio garb, accompanied by beard and flowing hair. The odd thing was that the appearance of these rebels against convention—alienated against a back-ground of stiff white shirts, coloured ribands, sparkling stars and crosses—made the rebels themselves seem as much survivors from an early nineteenth-century romantic bo-hemianism, as swallow-tailed coats and medals recalled the glittering receptions of the same era.

The seating plan showed my own place between an actor and a clergyman, both professions to strike the right arche-typal note for an evening of that sort. The actor (who had performed a rather notable Shallow the previous year) was now playing in an Ibsen revival, of which Polly Duport was the star. The clergyman's name—the Revd Canon Paul Fenneau—familiar, was not immediately placeable. A likely guess would be that he was incumbent of a London parish, a parson known for active work in some charitable sphere, possibly even the preservation of ancient buildings. Celebrity in such fields could have brought him to the dinner that night. The last possibility might also explain the faintly scholarly associations, not necessarily theological, that the name set in motion.

A crowd of guests was already collected by the bar in the gallery beyond the circular central hall. Members was there, talking to Smethyck (recently retired from the directorship of his gallery), both of them, Members especially, giving the impression that they intended to make a mildly uproarious evening of it. The flushed cheeks of Members enclosed by fluffy white hair and thick whiskers, contrasted with Smethyck's longer thinner whiskers, and elegantly shaped grey corkscrew curls, increased the prevailing atmosphere of Victorian jollification. Both were wearing white ties, an order round the neck. I had not seen Members since the Magnus Donners dinner, nor should we meet in future in that connexion, the panel of judges having been reconstituted. He was still taking immense pleasure in the scenes there enacted.

'I've been telling Michael about the Quiggin twins. Do you know he had never heard of them? What do you think of that for an Ivory Tower?'

Smethyck smoothed his curls and smiled, gratified at the implications of existing in gloriously rarefied atmosphere.

'True, I live entirely out of the world these days, Mark. How should I know of such things as stinkbombs?'

'I may have done some indiscreet things in my time,' said Members. 'I've never fathered any children. That's notwithstanding a few false alarms. Poor old JG. The great apostle of revolt in the days of our youth. Do you remember Sillers calling him our young Marat? Marat never had to bring up twins. What a couple.

> Dids't thou give all to thy daughters?
> And art thou come to this?

It won't be long before JG's out on Hampstead Heath asking that of passers-by.'

Smethyck pedantically demurred, thereby somewhat impugning his claim to know nothing of contemporary life.

'In Lear's case it was the father seeking an alternative society. The girls supported the Establishment. They're my favourite heroines in literature, as a matter of fact.'

Members accepted correction.

'Lindsay Bagshaw told me the other day that he regarded himself as a satisfied Lear. Since his wife died, he divides his time between his daughters' households, and says their food is not at all bad.'

'Your friend Bagshaw must be temperamentally equipped to accept the compromises that Lear rejected,' said Smethyck. 'I do not know him—'

He had evidently heard as much as he wanted about the Magnus Donners dinner, and moved away to speak with a well-known cartoonist. Members continued to brood on the Quiggin twins and their activities.

'Do you think Widmerpool arranged it all, to get his own back on Gwinnett?'

'Widmerpool was as surprised as anyone when the bang went off.'

'That's what's being generally said. I wondered whether it was true. He's here tonight.'

'Widmerpool?'

'Looking even scruffier than at the Magnus Donners. What does it all mean dressing like that? Do you think he will make another speech off the cuff?'

Members, speaking as one in a position to deplore slovenliness of dress, fingered the cross at his throat. A life peeress, also connected with the world of culture, passed at that moment, and he buttonholed her. A moment later Widmerpool came into sight at the far end of the gallery. He was prowling about by himself, speaking to no one. Members had called him scruffy, but his disarray, such as it was, did not greatly differ from that of the Magnus Donners evening. He was still wearing the old suit and red polo jumper, though closer contact might have revealed the last as unwashed since the earlier occasion. Widmerpool's appearance afforded an example of the curiously absorbent nature of the RA party. At almost any other public dinner the getup would have looked out of place. Here, clothes and all, he was unified with fellow guests. Those who did not know him already might easily have supposed they saw before them a professional painter, old and seedy—Widmerpool looked decidedly more than his later sixties—who had emerged momentarily, from some dilapidated artists' colony, to make an annual appearance at a function to which countless years as an obscure contributor had earned him the prescriptive right of invitation. In this semi-disguise, seen at long range, he could be pictured pottering about with an easel, in front of a row of tumbledown whimsically painted shacks lying along the seashore. Widmerpool moved out of sight. I did not see him again until we went into dinner, when he reappeared sitting a short way up the table on the other side from my own.

The clergyman, Canon Fenneau, was already engaged in conversation with the Regius Professor on his left, when I sat down. The actor and I talked. I had not seen the Ibsen production in which he was playing, but I told him that I had met Polly Duport, and knew Norman Chandler, who had directed a play in which my neighbour had acted not long before. Talk about the Theatre took us through the first course. The actor spoke of Molnar, a dramatist known to me from reading, on the whole, rather than seeing on a stage.

'Molnar must be about due for a revival.'

The actor agreed.

'Somebody was saying that the other day. Who was it? I know. It was after the performance last week. Polly Duport's friend with the French name. He's a writer of some sort, I believe. He thought Molnar an undervalued playwright in this country. What is he called? I've met him once or twice, when he's come to pick her up.'

'I wouldn't know. I don't know her at all well.'

'A French name. De-la-something. Delavacquerie? Could it be that?'

'There's a poet called Gibson Delavacquerie.'

'That's the chap. I remember Polly calling him Gibson. Small and dark. They're two of the nicest people.'

I heard no more about this revelation—it graded as a revelation—because someone on the far side of the table distracted the actor's attention by saying how much he had enjoyed the Ibsen. Almost simultaneously a voice from my other flank, soft, carefully articulated, almost wheedling, spoke gently.

'We met a long time ago. You will not remember me. I'm Paul Fenneau.'

Smooth, plump, grey curls (rather like Smethyck's, in neat waves), pink cheeks, Canon Fenneau stretched out a hand below the level of the table. It seemed rather unnecessary to shake hands at this late juncture, but I took it. The palm surprised by its firm even rough surface, electric vibrations. I had to admit he was right about my not remembering him.

'At a tea-party of Sillery's. I should place it in the year 1924. I may be in error about the date. I am bad at dates. They are so meaningless.'

For some reason Canon Fenneau made me feel a little uneasy. His voice might be soft, it was also coercive. He had small eyes, a large loose mouth, the lips thick, a somewhat receding chin. The eyes were the main feature. They were unusual eyes, not only almost unnaturally small, but vague, moist, dreamy, the eyes of a medium. His cherubic side, increased by a long slightly uptilted nose, was a little too good to be true, with eyes like that. In the manner in which he gave you all his attention there was a taste for mastery.

'In those days I was a frightened freshman from an obscure college. I can't tell you how impressed I was by the august company gathered in Sillery's room—if I rightly remember the afternoon we met. I didn't dare open my mouth. There was Mark Members, for instance, whom I noticed you talking with before dinner. I'd never seen a large-as-life poet in the flesh before. How I envied Mark for the fuss Sillers made of him. I remember Sillers pinched his neck. I'd have given the world in those days to have my neck pinched by Sillers. Then there was the famous Bill Truscott. Truscott, already working London, so tall, so distinguished, a figure entirely beyond my purview in the undergraduate world I frequented.'

Fenneau sighed, and smiled. It was hard to believe he had ever been frightened of anybody. I still had no recollection of meeting him, even while he recalled that particular tea-party of Sillery's; which, for various reasons, had made a strong impression on myself too. Fenneau could easily have been one of several undergraduates present, who were—and remained—unknown to me; though no doubt introduced at the time, Sillery being keen on introductions. Subsequent silence about Fenneau on Sillery's part would indicate not so much Fenneau's own pretensions to obscurity—Sillery rather liked to glory in the obscurity of some of his favourites—as cause given that afternoon, or at a later period, for Sillerian disapproval. Fenneau was probably one of the young men passed briskly through the Sillery machine, and found wanting; tried out once, never repro-cessed. So far as being speechless went, Sillery did not necessarily mind that. The occasional speechless guest could be a useful foil. Some of his own pupils in that genre were quite often at the tea-parties. They set off more ebullient personalities. I hoped Fenneau would not produce embar-rassing reminiscences of my own undergraduate behaviour at Sillery's, or elsewhere in the University.

'Did you often go to Sillery's?'

'Very few times after the first visit. I was not encouraged to pay too frequent calls. Just the necessary tribute from time to time. Rendering unto Sillers the things which were Sillers'. My claims could not have been less high, even for pennies that bore, so to speak, Sillery's own image and superscription.'

He smiled again, making, with a morsel of bread, a gesture indicative of extreme humility.

'Claims on Sillers?'

'Rather his claims on myself. My late father was an English chaplain on the Riviera. For a number of reasons Sillers found useful a South of France contact of that kind. Besides, my father was a personal friend of the Bishop of Gibraltar, a prelacy to attract the regard of Sillers, owing to the farflung nature of the diocese.'

'I can see that.'

'But my manner of talking about Sillers sounds most ungenerous. I would not speak a word against him. He did me, as a poor student, kindnesses on more than one occasion, although he could never reconcile himself to some of my interests.'

'You mean Sillery did not like you going into the Church?'

Fenneau smiled discreetly.

'Sillery had no objection to the Church—no objection to any Church—as such. He liked to have friends of all sorts, even clergymen. He did not at all mind my living in an undergraduate underworld, the *bas fond* of the University. The underworld, too, had its uses for Sillers—witness J. G. Quiggin, who attended that same historic tea-party.'

'You know Quiggin?'

'I do not often see JG these days. For a time—after meeting at Sillery's—we became quite close friends.'

Canon Fenneau made a sound that was not much short of a giggle, then continued.

'Like Sillers, JG found some of my interests ill advised. Socially unacceptable to Sillers, they were politically decadent to JG. Hopelessly unprogressive. JG wanted everyone he knew to be interested in politics in those days. He was a keen Marxist, you may remember. I have never liked politics.'

'May I ask what are these interests of yours that arouse so much antipathy?'

Fenneau smiled, this time gravely. He did not speak for a moment. His small watery eyes gazed at me. There was a touch of melodrama in the look.

'Alchemy.'

'The Philosopher's Stone? Turning base metal into gold?'

'I prefer to say more in the sense of turning Man from earthly impurity to heavenly perfection. It is a conception that has always gripped me—naturally in a manner not to run counter to my cloth. Some knowledge of such matters can indeed stand a priest in good stead.'

He spoke the last sentence a little archly. The reason for his name's familiarity was now revealed. Fenneau's signature would appear from time to time under reviews of books about Hermetic Philosophy, the Rosicrucians, Witchcraft, works that dealt with what might be called the scholarly end of Magic. His own outward physical characteristics—not in themselves exceptional ones in priests of any creed—were, more than in most ecclesiastics, those to be associated with the practice of occultism; fleshiness of body allied to a misty look in the eye. Dr Trelawney and Mrs Erdleigh, hierophants of other mysteries, were both exemplars of that same physical type, in spite of what was no doubt a minor matter, difference of sex. These preoccupations of Fenneau's would explain the faintly uncomfortable sensations his proximity generated. He seemed to convey, especially when he fixed his stare, that he hoped, without making too much fuss about it, to hypnotize his interlocutor; at the very least to read what was in his mind. That, too, was a trait not unknown among conventional priests of all denominations. Canon Fenneau, clearly not at all conventional, possessed the characteristic in a marked degree.

'Do you still see Mark Members?'

'Not for a long time until this evening. We have never entirely lost touch, although Mark—unlike JG—considered me less than the dust beneath his chariot wheels, when we were undergraduates. Years ago I was able to help him. He carelessly wrote somewhere that Goethe mentions Paracelsus in *Faust*, a slip confusing Paracelsus with Nostradamus. Mark was attacked on that account by a rather unpleasant personage, of whom you will certainly have heard, who called himself Dr Trelawney.'

'I've even met him.'

'I assisted Mark in rebutting these aggressions by pointing out that Trelawney's long and abstruse letter on the subject darkened counsel. I added that, even if Paracelsus supposed every substance to be made up of mercury, sulphur, and salt, mercury was only one of the elements. Trelawney recognized the warning.'

'What was the warning?'

'Mercury is conceived in alchemy as hermaphroditic. Trelawney was at that time engaged in certain practices to which he did not wish attention to be drawn. He sheered off.'

Fenneau's features had taken on a menacing expression. Dr Trelawney had evidently found an adversary worthy of crossing swords; perhaps, more appropriately, crossing divining rods. I retailed some of my own Trelawney contacts, beginning with the Doctor and his disciples running past the Stonehurst gate.

'That too? How very interesting. May I say that you bear out a deeply held conviction of mine as to the repetitive contacts of certain individual souls in the earthly lives of other individual souls.'

Fenneau again fixed his eyes on me. He gave the impression of a scientist who has found a useful specimen, if not a noticeably rare one. His stare was preferably not to be endured for too long. He may have been aware of that himself, because he immediately dropped this disturbing inspection. Perhaps he had settled to his own satisfaction whatever was in his mind. I took the initiative.

'Nietzsche thought individual experiences were recurrent, though he put it rather differently. But what did you mean by saying "that too"?'

'I was astonished to hear that as a child you should have known Trelawney.'

'Only by sight. I did not meet him till years later. It is true that, as a child, he haunted my imagination—at times rather more than I liked. Haunting the imagination was the closest we came to acquaintance at that early period.'

'Haunters of the imagination have already come close to the imagination's owner. From that early intimacy would you give any credence to the claim of Scorpio Murtlock that in him—Scorpio—Trelawney has returned in the flesh? Some proclaim that as well as Scorpio himself.'

The question was asked this time very quietly, put forward in this unemphatic manner, I think, deliberately to startle. In fact there can be little doubt that Canon Fenneau had such a motive in view. I took the enquiry as matter-of-factly as possible, while accepting its unexpectedness as an impressive conversational broadside. It would have been bad manners to admit less.

'You know Murtlock too?'

'Since he was quite a little boy.'

Fenneau spoke reflectively, almost sentimentally.

'What was he like as a child?'

'A beautiful little boy. Quite exceptionally so. And *very* intelligent. He was called Leslie then.'

Fenneau smiled at the contrast between Murtlock's nomenclature, past and present.

'You still see him?'

'From time to time. I have been seeing something of him recently. That was why I was aware he would be known to you. You may have read about certain antagonisms Scorpio was encountering. I believe a good deal never got into the papers. In consequence of this rumpus there was some talk of a television programme about the cult—one of the series *After Strange Gods*, in which Lindsay Bagshaw recently made a comeback, but perhaps you don't watch television—and I was approached as a possible compère. I had to say that I had long been a friend of Scorpio's, but could not publicly associate myself, even as a commentator, with his system, if it can be so called. Mr Bagshaw himself came to see me. It transpired, in the course of conversation, that Scorpio had visited you in the country.'

'That was produced as a reference?

'Mr Bagshaw seemed to think it a good one.'

I did not often see Bagshaw these days, but made a mental note to take the matter up with him, if we ran across each other.

'Murtlock was one of your flock in his young days?'

That was an effort to set the helm, so far as Fenneau was concerned, in a more professionally clerical direction; not exactly a call to order, so much as a plea for better defined premises for discussion of Murtlock's goings-on. If I were to be brought in by Bagshaw as a sort of reference for Murtlock's respectability—on the strength of allowing the caravan to be put up for one night—I had a right to be told more about Murtlock. That he had been a pretty little boy might be a straightforward explanation for extending patronage to him, but, anyway as a clergyman, it seemed up to Fenneau to provide a less sensuous basis for their early association together. After further biographical background was given, enquiries could proceed as to whether Fenneau himself had set Murtlock on the path to become a mage. Fenneau was in no way unwilling to elaborate the picture.

'Scorpio once sang in my choir. That was when I was in south London. His parents kept a newspaper shop. As ever in these cases, there was an interesting heredity. Both mother and father belonged to a small fanatical religious sect, but I won't go into that now. It was with great difficulty that I secured their son for the choir. I should never have done so, had Leslie himself not insisted on joining. His will was stronger than theirs.'

'Did you yourself introduce him to what might, in general terms, be called alchemy?'

'On the contrary, Scorpio—Leslie as he was then— already possessed remarkable gifts of a kinetic kind. As you certainly know, there has been of late years a great revival of interest in what can only be called, in many cases, the Black Arts, I fear. It was quite by chance that Scorpio's natural leanings fell within a province with which I had long concerned myself. Mystical studies—my Bishop agrees —can be unexpectedly valuable in combating the undesirable in that field.'

Fenneau's mouth went a little tight again at mention of his Bishop, the eyes taking on a harder, less misty surface. It was permissible to feel that the Bishop himself—elements of exorcism perhaps out of easy reach at that moment— could have agreed, not least from trepidation at prospect of being transformed into a toad, or confined for a thousand years within a hollow oak.

'What happened to Murtlock after he left your choir?'

'A success story, even if a strange one. After singing so delightfully—I wish you could have heard his solo:

> Now we are come to the sun's hour of rest,
> The lights of evening round us shine.

—Leslie won a scholarship at a choir-school. He was doing splendidly there. Then a most unfortunate thing happened. It was quite out of the ordinary. He developed a most unhappy influence over the choirmaster. Influence is a weak word in the circumstances.'

'You mean—'

Fenneau smiled primly this time.

'That is certainly what one might expect. There had been trouble of that sort earlier. Leslie was quite a little boy then, hardly old enough to understand. The man was not convicted—I think rightly—as there was a possibility that Leslie had—well—invented the whole thing, but, as people said at the time, no smoke without fire. That unhappy possibility did not arise with the choirmaster. I knew him personally, a man of blameless life. There are, of course, men of blameless life, who yield to sudden temptation—lead us not into Thames Station, as the choirboys are said to have prayed—and there is no question but Leslie was an unusually handsome boy. No one could fail to notice that. Not that he wasn't a boy with remarkable qualities other than physical ones. At the same time I am satisfied that not a hint of improper conduct took place on the part of the choirmaster.'

The thought extended the smile of Fenneau's long mouth into ogreish proportions. He moved quickly from the prim to the blunt.

'Not even pawing. Leslie assured me himself.'

'Murtlock gave the impression of being tough when I met him. I should have thought he would be as tough about sex, as about anything else.'

'You are right. Let me speak plainly. Leslie—Scorpio by now—is tough. That does not mean he is necessarily badly behaved in matters of sex. I have always thought him not primarily interested in sex. What he seeks is moral authority.'

'Mightn't he use sex to gain moral authority?'

Fenneau gave me an odd look.

'That is another matter. Possibly he might. I can only say that all who had anything to do with the choirmaster affair agreed that sex—in any commonplace use of the word —did not come into it. At the same time, having known Leslie from his earliest years, I was not altogether surprised at what happened. I felt sure something of the sort would take place sooner or later. I knew it would grieve me.'

'Had he ever tried to impose his moral authority in your own case?'

I thought Fenneau deserved the question. He showed no disposition to resent or sidestep it. When he spoke he gazed into the distance beyond me.

'Fortunately I knew how to handle the gifts Leslie had been granted.'

'How did the choir-school story end?'

'Most tragically. The choirmaster was going to be a difficult man to replace. Good men are always at a premium, let alone good schoolmasters. Leslie—or should I already call him Scorpio?—was leaving at the end of the following term to take up another scholarship. He had done nothing against the rules. Every effort was made to persuade the choirmaster to exert his own will sufficiently to contend with the few months that remained. It was no good. His will had altogether gone. He was in too demoralized a state to stay on. He wished to be relieved of his appointment without delay.'

'The choirmaster left, Murtlock remained?'

'That was so. The unfortunate man took a job at another school, in quite a different part of the country. He was thought to be doing well there. Alas, just before the opening of the summer term, the poor fellow was found drowned in the swimming-pool.'

Fenneau sighed.

'What's Murtlock's present position, over and above people objecting to what he does at prehistoric monuments? How far does he model himself on Trelawney? When he stayed with us he appeared to have indulged in nothing worse than burning laurel leaves, and scenting a bucket with camphor.'

'Camphor? I am glad to hear of that. Camphor traditionally preserves chastity. With regard to Trelawney, I hope Scorpio has purged away the more unpleasant side. Harmony is the watchword. Harmony, as such, is not to be disapproved. I fear things are not always allowed to rest there. An element of Gnosticism emphasizes the duality of austerity and licence, abasement as a source of power, also elements akin to the worship of Mithras, where the initiate climbed through seven gates, or up seven ascending steps, imagery of the soul's ascent through the spheres of the Planets—as Eugenius Philalethes says—hearing secret harmonies.'

'I remember Trelawney's friend, Mrs Erdleigh, quoting that. Did you know her?'

'Myra Erdleigh was ubiquitous.'

Toasts and speeches began to take place. When these were over, lighting a cigar, Fenneau began to speak of Gnosticism, and the Mithraic mysteries. I was relating how Kipling's Song to Mithras had so much puzzled my former Company Commander, Rowland Gwatkin (whose obituary, recently printed in the Regimental Magazine, said he had taken an active interest in Territorial and ex-Service organizations to the end), when, several seats opposite having been vacated by guests rising to relieve themselves, or stroll round the pictures, Widmerpool moved down to one of these empty chairs. I had forgotten all about him, even the possibility put forward by Members that another unscheduled speech of Widmerpool's might take place. Close up, he looked even more like a down-at-heel artist than at a distance. The scarlet sweater was torn and dirty. Nodding to me, he addressed himself to Fenneau.

'Canon Fenneau, I think?'

'Your servant.'

Fenneau said that like a djinn rising vaporously from an unsealed bottle.

'May I introduce myself? My name is Widmerpool—Ken Widmerpool. I am called by some Lord Widmerpool. Don't bother about the Lord. It is irrelevant. We have never met, Canon. I am no churchgoer nowadays, though once I served my turn as a churchman.'

Hoping to disengage myself from whatever business Widmerpool had with Fenneau—impossible to imagine what that could be—I was about to make off, having myself planned to do a lightning tour of the pictures, in search of interesting specimens from the past. Widmerpool delayed this.

'Nick Jenkins here will vouch for my credentials. We've known each other more years than I like to think. Canon Fenneau, I have a request to make.'

Fenneau watched Widmerpool with the eye of a croupier, fixed on the spinning roulette wheel, ready to deal with any number that might turn up, in this case none endowed with power to break the bank, whatever sum put on, at whatever odds.

'Let me say at once, Lord Widmerpool, that it is supererogatory to tell me about yourself. You are, if I may say so, too famous for that to be necessary.'

Widmerpool accepted this definition without demur.

'All the same don't keep on Lord-Widmerpooling me, Canon. Ken will do.'

Fenneau smiled deprecatingly, making no reciprocal request that he should be called Paul. Widmerpool seemed a little uncertain how to proceed. He drummed on the tablecloth with his knuckles.

'I could not help hearing snatches of your conversation during dinner. You were speaking of someone in whom I am interested. I had, in fact, made enquiries, and learnt already that this personage was known to you, Canon.'

Fenneau raised his almost non-existent eyebrows, and set his hands together as if in prayer. Widmerpool had perhaps hoped to be helped out in what he wanted to say. If so, he was disappointed.

'This young man Scorp Murtlock.'

'Ah, yes?'

'I am interested in him.'

'Scorpio is an interesting young man.'

Widmerpool, seeing he was to get no assistance, became somewhat more hectoring in manner.

'I am not—to speak plainly—attracted by mumbo-jumbo. What concern me, on the contrary, are the social aspects of Murtlock's community, if so to be called. Its importance as a vehicle of dissent. I read about his persecution by the police. That set me to making enquiries. I found—from certain young people with whom I am already in touch— that there was a clear case of injustice that ought to be taken up in law.'

'If you listened to our conversation, Lord Widmerpool, you will by now be aware that I have already confessed my-self, at this very table, as something of an amateur of mumbo-jumbo. Believe me, Lord Widmerpool, mumbo-jumbo has its place in this world of ours. Make no mistake about that.'

Fenneau spoke mildly. Widmerpool recognized the underlying firmness. He modified his tone.

'You may be right, Canon. I was not thinking along quite those lines. What I mean is that mumbo-jumbo has never played any part in my own life. I am—even now with my greatly changed views—a man of affairs, somebody who wants to get things done, and, since I want to get things done, let us move to more concrete matters. Young Murtlock, living much of his time in a caravan, is not an altogether easy person to contact. My informant—who had himself had some truck with him—said that he, Murtlock, sometimes visited you. I thought that perhaps a meeting, or at least the forwarding of a letter, could be arranged through your good self. What struck me about Scorp Murtlock—as I understand he is usually called—was his vigorous sense of rebellion. He is a genuinely rebellious personality. They are rarer than you might think, even today. He seems to have been treated scandalously, indeed *ultra vires*. His way of life, in certain details, may not be my own, but I am in sympathy with his determination to revolt. Would you be with me, Canon?'

Fenneau was not committed so easily.

'If you meet Scorpio, Lord Widmerpool, you will find he holds no less strong views on laws that he himself regards as binding, than is his desire to break the bonds that he feels fetter those laws.'

'That is just what I mean. He seems the prototype of what has become a positive obsession with me, that is to say the necessity to uproot bourgeois values, more especially bourgeois values in connexion with legality. On top of that I am told that young Scorp has a most attractive personality.'

'Scorpio's personality can be very attractive.'

Fenneau showed a few teeth when he said that.

'As you may know, I hold a certain academic appointment. A number of the young people with whom I am brought in contact have made my house something of a centre. I might almost use the word commune. Do you think that Scorp Murtlock would pay me a visit?'

'That is something on which I cannot pronounce with certainty, Lord Widmerpool.'

Fenneau placed his fingers together again, this time the

hands a little apart, in a conventionally parsonic position. He repeated his statement.

'No. I cannot be sure of that. For one thing I am myself uncertain of Scorpio's precise whereabouts at the moment.'

'They could no doubt be ascertained.'

'I could make enquiries.'

'I am sure you could run him to earth.'

'Do you really wish me to do so? I should issue a warning. Charming as Scorpio can be in certain moods, he has what can only be called a darker side too. I cannot advise contact with him to anyone not well versed in the mysteries in which he traffics—not always then.'

Fenneau spoke the words with profound gravity. Widmerpool showed no sign whatever of noticing this change of tone. He did not laugh, because he rarely laughed, but he made little or no attempt to hide the fact that he found this warning absurd. For some reason he was absolutely set on getting Murtlock into his clutches.

'I think I can assert, by this time, that I am something of an expert on the ways of young people at least as tricky to handle as Master Murtlock. As I said earlier, I should like to add him and his followers—if only temporarily—to our own community, anyway persuade him to come and see us. There is something about him that I have greatly taken to. It may be his refusal to compromise. The question is only whether or not you yourself will be able to bring us together.'

'Was there any particular aspect, in the difficulties Scorpio was having with the local people, that you found of interest —ones that I could tell him about, if we were to meet in the near future?'

Widmerpool hesitated.

'I understand there was some rather absurd complaint about nudity, which Murtlock sensibly answered by pointing out that, in the past, stripping to the skin was accepted as a sign of humility and poverty.'

'That worship should take place unclothed—in the manner of Adam—was a familiar heresy in the Middle Ages. If Scorpio practised such rites, they are ones which I cannot approve.'

Fenneau spoke severely. Widmerpool must have felt that he had got on to the wrong tack. He quickly abandoned what seemed to have become a delicate subject.

'That was just one of the points, Canon, just one of the points. It may even have been untrue. May I assume then that, if I send a letter through your good self, young Murtlock will get it sooner or later?'

'If you really wish that, Lord Widmerpool, but I advise against.'

'In spite of your advice.'

'Then I will do my best.'

Widmerpool made a gesture of thanks. He withdrew. He rightly saw that further conversation might harm rather than forward his aims. Fenneau asked one of the waiters whether it would be possible to have another cigar. He sat back in his chair.

'That was interesting.'

'You dealt with Widmerpool almost as if you were prepared for his approach.'

'To those familiar with the rhythm of living there are few surprises in this world. Not only is Lord Widmerpool anxious to meet Scorpio, Scorpio has already spoken of his intention to make himself known to Lord Widmerpool.'

'You kept that dark.'

'For a number of reasons I judged it best. I am by no means satisfied that their conjunction is desirable. At the same time, what happened tonight convinces me that no purpose is served by refusal to collaborate in transmission of a message. Other more powerful forces are on the march. *Che sarà sarà.*

'Why should Murtlock wish to meet Widmerpool?'

'Scorpio's plans are not often crystal clear.'

'He can hardly hope to bring Widmerpool into his cult.'

'There may be more material considerations. Scorpio is not unpractical in worldly matters. You have probably noticed that.'

'You mean Widmerpool's place might provide a convenient temporary base?'

'That is possible.'

'Which would make putting up with Widmerpool himself worth while?'

'To gain mastery is also one of Scorpio's aims.'

'Power?'

'The goal of the Alchemists.'

'Perhaps a mutual attraction in those terms?'

'We live in a world in which much remains—and must remain—unrevealed.'

Fenneau looked at his watch.

'I think I shall have to be wending my way homeward. We have had a most pleasant talk. Ah, yes. Something else. I expect that, in your profession, a lot of books pass through your hands for which you have little or no use, review copies and the like. Books of all kinds flow into a writer's daily life. Do please remember some of them for my Christmas bazaar. I will send you a reminder nearer the season. Let me have your address. Write it down here. Goodnight, goodnight.'

5

To be told something that comes as a surprise, then find everyone has known about it for ages, is no uncommon experience. The remarks on the subject of Delavacquerie and Polly Duport, dropped by the actor at the Royal Academy dinner, were a case in point. Mere chance must have been the cause of having heard nothing of this close association. It had been going on for some little time, and there appeared to be no secret about their relationship. Mention of it cropped up again, not long after, in some quite other connexion. All the same, although we continued to meet at comparatively regular intervals, Delavacquerie himself never brought up the matter. When he did so, that was about a year later than this first indication that they even knew each other.

During that year, among many other events in one's life, two things happened that could have suggested achievement of the mutually desired meeting between Widmerpool and Murtlock. The month of both indications was roughly dated as December, by the arrival of Canon Fenneau's reminder about books for his bazaar, and the fact that, when Greening and I ran across each other in London, we were doing our Christmas shopping. Neither event positively brought home the Widmerpool/Murtlock alliance at the time. The first of these was the bare announcement in the paper that Widmerpool, having resigned the chancellor-ship of the university, was to be replaced by some other more or less appropriate figure. After his various public pronouncements there seemed nothing particularly notable in Widmerpool preferring to disembarrass himself of official duties of any sort whatsoever.

Greening's information was rather another matter. It should have given a clue. We met in the gift department of some big shop. Greening, who had been badly wounded in the Italian campaign, had a limp, but was otherwise going strong. He had been ADC to the General at the Divisional Headquarters on which we had both served in the early part of the war; later rejoined his regiment, and, it had been rumoured, died of wounds. He looked older, of course, but his habit of employing a kind of schoolboy slang that seemed to predate his own generation had not changed. He still blushed easily. He said he was a forestry consultant, married, with three children. We talked in a desultory way of the time when we had soldiered together.

'Do you remember the DAAG at that HQ?'

'Widmerpool?'

'That's the chap. Major Widmerpool. Rather a shit.'

'Of course I remember him.'

'He was always getting my goat, but what I thought was really bloody awful about him was the way he behaved to an old drunk called Bithel, who commanded the Mobile Laundry.'

'I remember Bithel too.'

'Bithel had to be shot out, the old boy had to go all right, but Widmerpool boasted in the Mess about his own efficiency in getting rid of Bithel, and how Bithel had broken down, when told he'd got to go. It may have happened, but we didn't all want to hear about it from Widmerpool.'

'If it's any consolation, Widmerpool's become very odd himself now.'

'You know that already? I was coming on to that. He's gone round the bend. Nothing less.'

'You've seen him?'

'I was looking at some timber—woodland off my usual beat—and was told an extraordinary story by the johnny I was dealing with. Widmerpool—it must be the same bugger, from what he said—runs a kind of—well, I don't know what the hell to call it—sort of colony for odds and sods, not far away from the property I was inspecting. Widmerpool's place has been going for a year or two—a kind of rest-home for layabouts—but lately things have considerably hotted up, my client said. A new lot had arrived who wore even stranger togs, and went in for even gaudier monkey-tricks. This chap talked of Widmerpool as having made himself a sort of Holy Man. Not bad going after starting as a DAAG.'

Greening, unable to paraphrase the narrative of the owner of the woodland, could produce no revelation beyond that. Nevertheless the account of Widmerpool had evidently made a strong impression on him. I don't think the possibility of the new arrivals being Murtlock's adherents occurred to me at the time. If that had been at all conveyed, the conclusion would have been that Murtlock had been absorbed into Widmerpool's larger organization. In short, what Greening spoke of seemed little more than what had been initially outlined some time before by Delavacquerie's son. Greening began to collect his parcels.

'Well, I must go on my way rejoicing. Nice to have had a chin-wag. Best for the Festive Season. I'm determined not to eat too much plum pudding this year.'

When, Christmas over, I next saw Delavacquerie, it was well into the New Year. He gave news of Gwinnett being in London again.

'I thought him rather standoffish when he was over here

before. This time he got in touch with me at once. In his own remote way he was very friendly.'

'Has he returned to that gruesome dump in St Pancras?'

'I picked him up there the other day, and we lunched at the buffet at King's Cross Station.'

'How's he getting on with *Gothic Symbols, etc*?'

'I think it will be rather good. The Elizabethan and Jacobean dramatists happen to be a subject of mine too. In fact I was able to assist in a minor way by taking him to a Jacobean play that's rarely staged. It's ascribed to Fletcher. *The Humorous Lieutenant,* not particularly gothic, nor full of mortality, but Gwinnett seemed glad to have an opportunity to see it.'

Without reading the notices very carefully, I had grasped that a play of that name was being given a limited run of a few weeks at a theatre where such productions once in a way found a home. An energetic young director (more influential in that line than Norman Chandler) had been responsible for the revival of this decidedly obscure comedy, interest in it, so Delavacquerie now said, having been to to some extent aroused by himself.

'I once toyed with the idea of calling my own collected war poems *The Humorous Lieutenant,* from this play. Then I thought the title would be misunderstood, even ironically.'

'Why was he humorous?'

'He wasn't, in the modern sense, not a jokey subaltern, but moody and melancholy in the Elizabethan meaning of humorous—one of your Robert Burton types. The Lieutenant had reason to be. He was suffering from a go of the pox. Having a dose made him unusually brave, fighting being less of a strain than sitting about in camp feeling like hell. One sees the point. When he was cured all the Lieutenant's courage left him.'

'How did you persuade them to put the play on?'

'I infiltrated the idea through Polly Duport, who is rather a friend of mine. She thought she'd like to play Celia, though a bit old for the part of a young girl.'

This was Delavacquerie's first mention of Polly Duport. There was some parallel with the way in which Moreland had first produced Matilda, when she had been playing in *The Duchess of Malfi*. I was quite unable to tell whether this casual method of introducing the name was deliberate, or Delavacquerie supposed I had always known about the association. Clinging to privacy was characteristic of both of them. Apparent secrecy might be partly explained by the shut-in nature of Polly Duport's life of the Theatre, scarcely at all cutting across Delavacquerie's two-fold existence, divided between poetry and public relations.

'I believe you've met Polly?'

'I haven't seen her for ages. I used to know her parents —who are divorced of course.'

I did not add that, when we were young, I had been in love with Polly Duport's mother. There seemed no moral obligation to reveal that, in the light of Delavacquerie having kept quiet for so long about her daughter; an example of the limitations, mentioned before, set round about the friendships of later life.

'You knew both Polly's parents? It is almost unprecedented to have met the two of them. I myself have never seen either, though Polly spends a lot of time looking after her father, who has been very ill. She's marvellously good about him. He never sounds very agreeable. Her mother— as you probably know—was married to that South American political figure who was murdered by terrorists the other day.'

'Poor Colonel Flores? Was he murdered?'

'Wasn't he a general? He was machine-gunned from behind an advertisement hoarding, so Polly told me. It wasn't given much space in the English papers. I didn't see it reported myself. He was retired by then. It was bad luck.'

I felt sorry about Colonel Flores, a master of charm, even if other qualities may have played a part in his rise to power. Delavacquerie returned to the subject of Gwinnett and the play.

'He seemed to enjoy it a great deal. I had never seen Gwinnett like that before. He became quite talkative afterwards, when we all had supper together.'

'What's it about?'

'A King falls in love with his son's girlfriend—that's Celia, played by Polly—while the son himself is away at the wars. When the son returns, his father says the girl is dead. The King has really hidden Celia, and is trying to seduce her. As he has no success, he decides to administer a love potion. Unfortunately the love potion is drunk by the Humorous Lieutenant. In consequence the Lieutenant falls in love with the King, instead of Celia doing so.'

'Did the Lieutenant's exaggerated sense of humour cause him to drink the love philtre?'

'It was accidental. He had been knocked out in a fight, and someone, thinking a bowl of wine was lying handy, gave him the love philtre as a pick-me-up. The incident is quite funny, but really has nothing to do with the play— like so many things that happen to oneself. As a neurotic figure, the Lieutenant is perhaps not altogether unlike Gwinnett.'

'Possibly Gwinnett too should drink a love philtre?'

'Gwinnett is going to risk much stronger treatment than that. Do you remember that Lord Widmerpool, after making that speech at the Magnus Donners, asked Gwinnett to come and see him? Widmerpool has returned to the charge, as to a visit, and Gwinnett is going to go.'

'That sounds a little grisly.'

'Precisely why Gwinnett is going to do it. He wishes to

have the experience. Widmerpool's situation has recently become more than ever extraordinary. From being, in a comparatively quiet way, an encourager of dissidents and dropouts, the recent addition to his community of Scorpio Murtlock, the young man we talked about some little time ago, has greatly developed its potential. Murtlock provides a charismatic element, and apparently Widmerpool thinks there are immense power possibilities in the cult. He's got enough money to back it, anyway for the moment.'

'But surely it's Murtlock's cult, not Widmerpool's.'

'We shall see. Gwinnett thinks that a struggle for power is taking place. That is one of the things that interests him. Gwinnett's angle on all this is that the cult, with its rites and hierarchies, is all as near as you can get nowadays to the gothicism of which he is himself writing. He has seen something of the semi-mystic dropout groups of his own country, but feels this one offers a more Jacobean setting, through certain of its special characteristics.'

'Does Gwinnett approve or disapprove? I expect he doesn't show his hand?'

'On the contrary, Gwinnett disapproves. He talked quite a lot about his disapproval. As I understand it, one of the tenets of the cult is that Harmony, Power, Death, are all more or less synonymous—not Desire and Death, like Shakespeare. Gwinnett disapproves of Death being, so to speak, removed from the romantic associations of Love—his own approach, with which his book deals—to be prostituted to the vulgar purposes of Power—pseudo-magical power at that. At the same time he wants to examine the processes as closely as possible.'

'Some might think it insensitive of Gwinnett, in the circumstances, to visit Widmerpool, even in the interests of seventeenth-century scholarship.'

'On that question Widmerpool himself has made his own standpoint unambiguously clear by going out of his way to invite Gwinnett to come and see him. You said that Gwinnett, when writing about Trapnel, saw himself as Trapnel. Now Gwinnett, writing about gothic Jacobean plays, sees himself as a character in one of them. I regret to say that I shall not be in England when Gwinnett pays his visit to Widmerpool, and therefore won't hear how things went—that is, if Gwinnett chooses to tell me.'

'You're taking a holiday?'

'Polly and I may be going to get married. We've known each other for a long time now. In the light of the way we both earn a living, neither of us liked the idea of being under the same roof. We might be changing that now. She's coming to have a look at my Creole relations.'

Delavacquerie raised his eyebrows, as if that were going to be an unpredictable undertaking. I said some of the things you say when a friend of Delavacquerie's age announces impending marriage. He laughed, and shook his head. All the same, he seemed very pleased with the prospect. So far as I knew anything of Polly Duport, she seemed a nice girl.

'We shall see, we shall see. That is why we are visiting the Antilles.'

During the next month or so I did not go to London. Over and above the claims of 'work'—put forward earlier as taking an increasing stranglehold—attention was required for various local matters; the chief of these—and most tedious—the quarry question.

One of the neighbouring quarries (not that recalling the outlines of Mr Deacon's picture) was attempting encroachment, as mentioned earlier, in the area of The Devil's Fingers. The matter at issue had begun with the quarrying firm (using a farmer as 'front', at purchase of the land) acquiring about seventy agricultural acres along the line of the ridge on which the archaeological site stood. The firm was seeking permission from the Planning Authority to extend in the direction of the monument. Among other projects, if this were allowed, was creation of a 'tip', for quarry waste, above the stream near The Devil's Fingers; the waters of the brook to be channelled beneath by means of a culvert. If local opposition to workings being allowed so near the remains of the Stone Age sepulchre could be shown to be sufficiently strong, a Government Enquiry was likely to be held, to settle a matter now come to a head, after dragging on for three if not four years.

The quarry-owners were offering undertakings as to 'landscaping' and 'shelter belts', to demonstrate which an outdoor meeting had been arranged. Men carrying flags would be posted at various spots round about, indicating both the proposed extension of the workings, and related localities of tree-plantation. The assembly point for those concerned, timed at nine o'clock in the morning in order to minimize dislocation of the day's work, was a gap in the hedge running along a side road, not far from the scene of action. A stile led across the fields to the rising ground on which The Devil's Fingers stood, within a copse of elder trees.

'Quite a good turnout of people,' said Isobel. 'I'm glad to see Mrs Salter has shown up. She won't stand any non-sense from anyone.'

The previous night had been hot and muggy, a feeling of electricity in the atmosphere. The day, still loaded with electrical currents, warm, was uncertain in weather, bright and cloudy in patches. Cars were parked against gates, or up narrow grass lanes. All sorts were present, representa-tives of the quarry, officials from local authorities, members of one or two societies devoted to historical research or nature preservation, a respectable handful of private in-dividuals, who were there only because they took an interest in the neighbourhood. Mrs Salter, noted by Isobel, was in charge of the Nature Trust. A vigorous middle-aged lady in sweater and trousers, whitehaired and weatherbeaten, she carried a specially designed pruning-hook, a badge of office from which she was never parted.

'Who are the three by the stile?'

'Quarry directors. Mr Aldredge and Mr Gollop. I don't know who the midget is.'

The small energetic henchman with Mr Aldredge and Mr Gollop, almost as if he were shouting the odds, began to pour out a flow of technicalities on the subject of landscaping and arboriculture. Mr Aldredge, pinched in feature, with a pious expression, seemed at pains to prove that no mere hatred of the human race as such—so he gave the impression of feeling himself accused—caused him to pursue a policy of wholesale erosion and pollution. He denied those imputations pathetically. Mr Gollop, younger, aggressive, would have none of this need to justify himself or his firm. Instead, he spoke in a harsh rasping voice about the nation's need for nonskid surfacing on its motorways and arterial roads.

'I shall not make for Mr Todman immediately,' said Isobel. 'I shall choose my moment.'

Mr Todman was from the Planning Authority. Upstanding and hearty, he had not entirely relinquished a military bearing that dated from employment during the war on some aspect of constructing The Mulberry. That had been the vital experience of his life. He had never forgotten it. He had the air of a general, and brought a young aide-de-camp with him. Mr Todman was talking to another key figure in the operation, Mr Tudor, Clerk of the Rural District Council. Mr Tudor's appearance and demeanour were in complete contrast with Mr Todman's. Mr Tudor, appropriately enough, possessed a profile that recalled his shared surname with Henry VII, the same thoughtful shrewdness, if necessary, ruthlessness; the latter, should the interests of the RDC be threatened.

'I can't remember the name of the suntanned, rather sad figure, who looks like a Twenties film star making a comeback.'

'Mr Goldney. He's retired from the Political Service in Africa, now secretary of the archaeological society.'

There were quite a lot of others, too, most of whom I did not know by sight. The thicket of The Devil's Fingers was not to be seen from the stile. We set off across the first field. It was plough, rather heavy going. Mr Aldredge, the quarryman putting up a policy of appeasement, addressed himself to Mrs Salter, with whom he had probably had passages of arms before.

'Looks like being a nice Midsummer's Day. We deserve some decent weather at this time of year. We haven't seen much so far.'

Mrs Salter shook her head. She was not to be lulled into an optimistic approach to the weather, least of all by an adversary in the cause of conservation.

'It will turn to rain in the afternoon, if not before. Mark my words. It always does in these parts at this time of year.'

Mr Gollop, the pugnacious quarryman, took the opportunity, a good one, to draw attention to rural imperfections unconnected with his own industry.

'We quarry people get shot at sometimes for the fumes we're said to cause. It strikes me that's nothing to what's being inflicted on us all at this moment by the factory farms.'

The smell through which we were advancing certainly rivalled anything perpetrated by the Quiggin twins. Mrs Salter, brushing away this side issue, went into action.

'It's not so much the fumes you people cause as the dust. The rain doesn't wash it away. The leaves are covered with a white paste all the year round. After they've had a lot of that, the trees die.'

Mr Tudor, a man of finesse, must have thought this conversation too acrimonious in tone for good diplomacy. He had steered the Council through troubled waters before, was determined to do so this time.

'We do receive occasional complaints about intensive farming odours, Mr Gollop, just like those we get from time to time regarding your own industry. The Council looks on animal by-products as the worst offenders, even if poultry and pig-keepers cannot be held altogether blameless, and some of the silage too can be unpleasing to the nostrils. The air will be fresher, I hope, when we are over the next field. There's a lovely view, by the way, from the top of the ridge.'

Individual members of the party being concerned with different aspects of what was proposed, the group began to string out in all directions. Isobel, discussing with Mr Goldney the contrasted advantages of stone walls and hedges, a tactical feint, would quickly disengage herself, when opportunity arose, to obtain a good position to command the ear of Mr Todman, the figure likely to be most influential in the outcome of the morning's doings. Somebody, who had not joined the party at its point of departure by the stile, was now coming across the fields from the west. When he drew level this turned out to be Mr Gauntlett. He would usually appear on any occasion of this kind. Today he was wearing an orchid in his buttonhole.

'Good morning, Mr Gauntlett.'

'Morning, Mr Jenkins. Beautiful one too just now, tho' t'won't last.'

'That's what Mrs Salter says.'

'Not where the clouds do lie, nor the manner the rooks be flying.'

Mr Gauntlett's professional rusticity did not entirely cloak his faintly military air, which was in complete contrast with Mr Todman's soldierliness. Mr Todman suggested modern scientific warfare; Mr Gauntlett, military levies of Shakespearean days, or earlier.

'How are you keeping, Mr Gauntlett? Haven't seen you for a long while.'

'Ah, I can't grumble. There was a sad thing last week. Old Daisy died. She was a bad old girl, but she'd been with me a long time. I'll miss her.'

'I remember you were looking for her—it must have been two years ago or more—when those strange young people came to see us in their caravan.'

Still feeling rather self-conscious about being caught by Mr Gauntlett with the caravan party, I said that with implied apology. Mr Gauntlett brushed anything of the sort aside.

'Daisy was just where your young friend said. She'd whelped, and there was one pup left alive. It were a good guess on his part.'

'So he was right?'

'It were a good guess. A very good guess. He must know the ways o' dogs. Well, what are we going to be shown this morning, Mr Jenkins?'

'I wonder. There's quite a fair lot of people have come to see. It means local interest in preventing what the quarry want to do.'

Mr Gauntlett laughed at some amusing thought of his own in this connexion. When he voiced that thought the meaning was not immediately clear.

'Ernie Dunch won't be joining us today.'

'He won't?'

There was nothing very surprising about this piece of information. It looked as if Mr Gauntlett had cut across the fields from Dunch's farm, which was out to the west from where we were walking. Mr Dunch farmed the meadow on which The Devil's Fingers stood. He was not the farmer who had acted as figurehead in purchase by the quarry of the neighbouring fields, his land running only to the summit of the ridge, but his own attitude to quarry development was looked upon as unreliable by those who preferred some restriction to be set on the spread of quarry workings. Dunch was unlikely to bother much about what infringements might be taking place on territory with scenic or historical claims. Idle curiosity could have brought him to the meeting, nothing more. He would be no great loss. For some reason Mr Gauntlett found the fact immensely droll that Mr Dunch would not be present.

'Ernie Dunch didn't feel up to coming,' he repeated.

'I don't expect Mr Dunch cares much, one way or the other, what the quarry does.'

'Nay, I don't think 'tis that. Last Tuesday I heard Ernie saying he'd be out with us all today, to know what was happening nextdoor to him. I said I'd drop in, and we'd go together. I thought I'd see, that way, Ernie did come.'

Mr Gauntlett laughed to himself.

'That's natural enough, since the quarry would extend quite close to his own land. I'm glad he feels himself concerned. What's wrong with Mr Dunch?'

Obviously, from Mr Gauntlett's manner, that question was meant to be asked. He had a story he wanted to tell. I was not particularly interested myself why Dunch had made his decision to stay away.

'Ernie's quite a young fellow.'

'So I've been told. I don't know him personally.'

'Two-and-thirty. Three-and-thirty maybe.'

Mr Gauntlett pondered. We plodded on through the heavy furrows. Mr Gauntlett, having presumably settled in his own mind, within a few days, the date of Ernie Dunch's birth, changed his tone to the rather special one in which he would relate local history and legend.

'I'll warrant you've heard tell stories of The Fingers, Mr Jenkins?'

'You've told me quite a few yourself, Mr Gauntlett—the Stones going down to the brook to drink. That's what we want to make sure they're still able to do. Not be forced to burrow under a lot of quarry waste, before they can quench their thirst. I should think the Stones would revenge themselves on the quarry if anything of the sort is allowed to happen.'

'Aye, I shouldn't wonder. I shouldn't wonder.'

'Smash up the culvert, when the cock crows at midnight.'

'Ah.'

I hoped for a new legend from Mr Gauntlett. He seemed in the mood. They always came out unexpectedly. That was part of Mr Gauntlett's technique as a story-teller. He cleared his throat.

'I've heard tales o' The Fingers since I was a nipper. All the same, it comes like a surprise when young folks believe such things, now they're glued to the television all day long.'

Mr Gauntlett watched television a good deal himself. At least he seemed always familiar with every programme.

'I'm pleased to hear young people do still believe in such stories.'

'Ah, so am I, Mr Jenkins, so am I. That's true. It's a surprise all the same.'

I thought perhaps Mr Gauntlett needed a little encouragement.

'I was asked by a young man—the one who told you where to find Daisy—if the Stones bled when a knife was thrust in them at Hallowe'en, or some such season of the year.

'I've heard tell the elder trees round about The Fingers do bleed, and other strange tales. I can promise you one thing, Mr Jenkins, in Ernie Dunch's grandfather's day, old Seth Dunch, a cow calved in the dusk o' the evening up there one spring. Old Seth Dunch wouldn't venture into The Fingers thicket after dark, nor send a man up there neither—for no one o' the men for that matter would ha' gone—until it were plain daylight the following morning. Grandson's the same as grandfather, so t'appears.'

'If Ernie Dunch is afraid of The Fingers, he ought to take more trouble about seeing they're preserved in decent surroundings.'

Mr Gauntlett laughed again. He did not comment on the conservational aspect. Instead, he returned to young Mr Dunch's health.

'Ernie's not himself today. He's staying indoors. Going to do his accounts, he says.'

'Accounts make a bad day for all of us. You've just been seeing him, Mr Gauntlett, have you?'

I could not make out what Mr Gauntlett was driving at.

'Looked in on the farm, as I said I would, on the way up. I thought Ernie ought to come to the meeting, seeing we were going through his own fields, but he wouldn't stir.'

'Just wanted to tot up his accounts?'

'Said he wasn't going out today.'

'Has he got flu?'

'Ernie's poorly. That's plain. Never seen a young fellow in such a taking.'

Mr Gauntlett found Ernie Dunch's reason for not turning up excessively funny, then, pulling himself together, resumed his more usual style of ironical gravity.

'Seems Ernie went out after dark last night to shoot rabbits from the Land Rover.'

Rabbit-shooting from a Land Rover at night was a recognized sport. The car was driven slowly over the grass, headlights full on, the rabbits, mesmerized by the glare of the lamps, scuttling across the broad shaft of light. The driver would then pull up, take his gun, and pick them off in this field of fire.

'Did he have an accident? Tractors are always turning over, but I'd have thought a Land Rover ought to be all right for any reasonable sort of field.'

'No, not an accident, Mr Jenkins. I'll tell you what Ernie said, just as he said it. He passed through several o' these fields, till he got just about, I'd judge, where we are now, or a bit further. He was coming up to the start o' the meadow where The Fingers lie, so Ernie said, in sight o' the elder copse—and what do you think Ernie saw there, Mr Jenkins?'

'The Devil himself.'

'Not far short o' that, according to Ernie.'

Again Mr Gauntlett found difficulty in keeping back his laughter.

'What happened?'

'Ernie hadn't had no luck with the rabbits so far. There didn't seem none o' them about. Then, as soon as he drove into the big meadow, he noticed a nasty light round The Fingers. It seemed to come in flashes like summer lightning.'

'Nasty?'

'That's what Ernie called it.'

'Probably was summer lightning. We've had quite a bit of that. Or his own headlights reflected on something.'

'He said he was sure it wasn't the car's lamps, or the moonlight. Unearthly, he said. It didn't seem a natural light.'

'When did he see the Devil?'

'Four o' them there were.'

'Four devils? What form did they take?'

'Dancing in and out o' the elder trees, and between the Stones, it looked like, turning shoulder to shoulder t'ords each other, taking hold o'arms, shaking their heads from side to side.'

'How did he know they were devils?'

'They had horns.'

'He probably saw some horned sheep. There are a flock of them round about here.'

'It was horns like deer. High ones.'

157

'How were they dressed?'

'They weren't dressed, 'cording to Ernie.'

'They were naked?'

'Ernie swears they were naked as the day they were born
—if they were human, and were born.'

'Men or women?'

'Ernie couldn't properly see.'

'Can't he tell?'

Mr Gauntlett gave up any attempt to restrain the hearti-
ness of his laughter. When that stopped he agreed that Ernie
Dunch's sophistication might well fall short of being able
to distinguish between the sexes.

'Appearing and disappearing they were, Ernie said, and
there might ha' been more than four, though he didn't stop
long to look. He figured there might ha' been two male,
and two female, at least, but sometimes it seemed more,
sometimes less, one of 'em a real awful one, but, such was
the state he was in hisself, he was uncertain o' the numbers.
Even in his own home, when he was telling the tale—Mrs
Dunch and me nigh him—Ernie began to shake. He said
he didn't go any nearer to The Fingers, once he saw what
he saw, just swivelled the Land Rover round as quick as
might be, and made for the farm. He said to me 'twas a
wonder he didn't turn the Land Rover the wrong way up
on the run back, banging through the tussocks o' grass and
furrows o' ploughland. His forewheel did catch in one rut,
but he managed to right the wheel again. Mrs Dunch says
he was more dead than alive, when he got back. She says
she never saw him like that before. Ernie swears he don't
know how he did it.'

'He thought they were supernatural beings?'

'I don't know what Ernie thought—that the Devil had
come to take him away.'

'They must have been some jokers.'

'You tell Ernie Dunch they were jokers, Mr Jenkins.'

158

'If they'd been the genuine ghosts of The Fingers there'd only have been two of them.'

'Ernie may have seen double. He wasn't at all positive about the numbers. All he was positive about was that he wouldn't go up there again that night for a thousand pounds.'

'This happened last night as ever is?'

'St John's Eve.'

Mr Gauntlett, always an artist in effects, mentioned the date quite quietly.

'So it was.'

'Mrs Dunch reminded Ernie o' that herself.'

'What did Mrs Dunch think?'

'Told Ernie it was the last time she'd let him out after dark with the Land Rover. She said she'd never spent such a night. Every time the young owls hooted, Ernie would give a great jump in the bed.'

'What do you think yourself, Mr Gauntlett?'

Mr Gauntlett shook his head. He was not going to commit himself, however much prepared to laugh at Ernie Dunch about such a matter.

'Ernie looked done up. That's true enough. Not at all hisself.'

'Would you be prepared to visit The Devil's Fingers, Mr Gauntlett, say at midnight on Hallowe'en?'

Mr Gauntlett looked sly.

'Don't know about Hallowe'en, when it might be chilly, but I wouldn't say I'd not been on that same down on a summer night as a lad—nor all that far from The Fingers —and never took no harm from it.'

Mr Gauntlett smiled in reminiscence.

'You must have struck a quiet night, Mr Gauntlett.'

'Well, it were pretty quiet some o' the time. Some o' the time it were very quiet.'

Mr Gauntlett did not enlarge on the memory. It sounded

a pleasant enough one. At that moment Mr Tudor appeared beside us. I don't think Mr Gauntlett had more to say, either about Ernie Dunch's experiences at The Devil's Fingers, or his own in the same neighbourhood. He now transferred his attention to Mr Tudor. Mr Tudor either wanted to ask Mr Gauntlett's advice, as a local sage of some standing, or the two of them had been hatching a plot, before the meeting, which now required to be carried a stage further. They moved off together towards the easterly fork of the ridge. I pushed on alone.

This final field, plough when Isobel and I had visited the place several years before, was now rough pasture. In their individual efforts to obtain an overall picture of what would be the effect on the landscape of the various proposals, the assembled company had become increasingly spread out. Several were studying maps, making notes as they tried to estimate the position of proposed new constructions and plantations represented by the markers with their different coloured flags. Mrs Salter, pruning-hook under one arm, writing in a little book, was furthest in advance. Now, she fell back with the rest to gain perspective. I found myself alone in that part of the field. Over to the east, the direction where Mr Gauntlett and Mr Tudor had disappeared together, lay the workings of the quarry scheduled by its owners for expansion. High chutes, sloping steeply down from small cabins that looked like the turrets of watchtowers, rose out of an untidy jumble of corrugated iron sheds and lofty mounds of crushed limestone. The sun, still shining between dark clouds that had blown up, caught the reflection on the windscreens of rows of parked cars and trucks. To the west, over by Ernie Dunch's farm, still more clouds were drifting up, in confirmation of knowledgeable forecasts that the day would end in rain.

The scene in the fields round about resembled a TEWT —Tactical Exercise Without Troops—such as were held in the army, groups of figures poring over maps, writing in notebooks, gazing out over the countryside. My own guilty feelings, on such occasions, came back to me, those sudden awarenesses at military exercises of the kind that, instead of properly concentrating on tactical features, I was musing on pictorial or historical aspects of the landscape; what the place had seen in the past; how certain painters would deal with its physical features. That was just what was happening now. Instead of trying to comprehend in a practical manner the quarrymen's proposals, I was concentrating on The Devil's Fingers themselves.

The elder thicket was flowering, blossom like hoar frost, a faint sprinkling of brownish red, powdered over the green and white ivy-strangled tree-trunks, gnarled and twisted, as in an Arthur Rackham goblin-haunted illustration. In winter, the Stones would have been visible from this point. Now they were hidden by the ragged untidy elders. The trees might well have been cleared away, leaving The Fingers on the skyline. Possibly the quasi-magical repute attributed to elderberries—the mysterious bleedings of which Mr Gauntlett spoke—had something to do with their preservation.

I was mistaken in supposing Mrs Salter the foremost of our party, that none of the others had pressed so far as the elder thicket. That was what I had decided to do myself, a small luxury, before bending the mind to practical problems. Somebody else from the morning's expedition must have had the same idea; got well ahead at the start, then moved on at high speed across the big field. Now he was slowly returning towards the rest of us. I did not know him by sight. The dark suit probably meant an official. Most of the other representatives of local authorities had moved off to the right and left by now, or withdrawn again some way to the rear. As this figure emerged from the elder trees, advanced down the hill, I felt pretty sure he had not been among those collected earlier at the stile. He must be a stray visitor, a tourist, even professional archaeologist, who had hoped to avoid sightseers by picking a comparatively early hour to visit the monument. Usually there was no one to be seen for miles, except possibly a farmer herding cows or driving a tractor. This man could not have chosen a worse morning for having the place to himself.

He did seem a little taken aback by the crowd of people fanned out across the landscape, the markers on the higher ground, their coloured flags looking like little pockets of resistance in a battle. He paused, contemplated the scene, then continued to walk swiftly, almost painfully, down the slope. There was something dazed, stunned, about his demeanour. The dark suit, bald head, spectacles, looked for some reason fantastically out of place in these surroundings, notwithstanding the fact that others present were bespectacled, bald, dark-suited.

'Russell?'

'Hi, Nicholas.'

Gwinnett was far less astonished than myself. In fact he did not seem surprised at all. He was carrying under his arm what looked like a large black notebook, equipment that had at first assimilated him with other note-takers in the fields round about.

'I was told you live near here, Nicholas.'

'Fairly near.'

'What's going on?'

He managed to establish a situation in which I, rather than he, found it necessary to give an explanation for being on that spot at that moment. I tried to summarize briefly for him the problem of the quarry and The Devil's Fingers. Gwinnett nodded. He made some technically abstruse comment on quarrying. In spite of outward calmness he was not looking at all well. This was very noticeable at close quarters. Gwinnett's appearance was ghastly, as if he had drunk too much, been up all night, or—on further inspection—slept on the ground in his clothes. The dark suit was covered in dust and scraps of grass. His shoes, too, were caked with mud. He brought with him even greater disquiet than usual; a general sense of insecurity increased by the skies above becoming all at once increasingly dark.

'Have you been visiting The Devil's Fingers?'

'Yeah.'

'You're staying near here?'

'Not far.'

'With friends?'

'No.'

He named an inn at a small town a few miles distant. It appeared from what he said that he was alone there.

'I didn't know you were interested in prehistoric stuff—or has this something to do with your Jacobean dramatists?'

Gwinnett, as was often his habit, did not answer at once. He seemed to be examining his own case, either for a clue as to what had indeed happened to him, or, already knowing that, in an effort to decide how much to reveal.

'I've lost my way. Just now I came up the same path, as well as I could remember it. I don't know how to get down to the road from here.'

'You've been to The Devil's Fingers before?'

'We came up on foot last night. I couldn't sleep when I got back. I thought I'd drive out here again. Make more notes on the spot. It's because I'm tired I've forgotten the path down, I guess.'

'You've got a car with you?'

'It's parked in a gully off the road. Beside some old cars that have been dumped there. I took the steep path up the hill. It stops after a while. That's why I can't find the place.'

'You were here last night?'

'Some of the night.'

His manner was odd even for Gwinnett. He talked like a man in a dream. It occurred to me that he was recovering from a drug. The suspicion was as likely to be unfounded as earlier ones, in Venice, that he was a homosexual, or a reclaimed drunk.

'Were you one of the party dancing round The Devil's Fingers last night?'

Gwinnett laughed aloud at that. He did not often laugh. To do so was the measure of the state he was in. His laughter was the reverse of reassuring.

'Why? Were they seen? How do you know about that?'

'They were seen.'

'I wasn't one of the dancers. I was there.'

'What the hell was going on?'

'The stag-mask dance.'

'Who was performing?'

'Scorp Murtlock and his crowd.'

'Are they at your pub too?'

'They're on their own. In a caravan. Those taking part in the rites travelled together. Scorp thought that necessary. I met them near here. We came up to the place together.'

'Who were the rest of the party?'

'Ken Widmerpool, two girls—Fiona and Rusty—a boy called Barnabas.'

'Was Widmerpool in charge?'

'No, Scorp was in charge. That was what the row was about.'

'There was a row?'

Gwinnett puckered up his face, as if he was not sure he had spoken correctly. Then he confirmed there had been a row. A bad row, he said. Its details still seemed unclear in his mind.

'Did Widmerpool dance?'

'When the rite required that.'

'Naked?'

'Some of the time.'

'Why only some of the time?'

'Ken was mostly recording.'

'How do you mean—recording?'

'Sound and pictures. It was a shame things went wrong. I guess that was bound to happen between those two.'

The flashes of light seen by Ernie Dunch were now explained. Gwinnett seemed to find the operation, in which he had himself been anyway to some extent engaged, less out of the ordinary, less regrettable, than the fact that some untoward incident had marred the proceedings.

'Russell, what was all this about? Why were you there? Why was Widmerpool there? I can just understand Murtlock and his crew going on in that sort of way—one's reading about such things every day in the paper—but what on earth were you and Widmerpool playing at?'

Gwinnett's features took on an expression part obstinate, part bewildered. It was a look he had assumed before, when asked to be more explicit about something he had said or done. No doubt his present state added to this impression of being half stunned, a condition genuinely present; if not the result of a drug, then fatigue allied to enormously heightened nervous tension. Again, seeming to consider how best to justify his own standpoint, he did not answer for a moment or two.

'Gibson Delavacquerie said you'd seen something of the Widmerpool set-up, the commune, or whatever he runs. He said Murtlock had joined up with it. Murtlock seems to have taken over.'

Delavacquerie's name appeared for some reason to bring relief to Gwinnett. His manner became a trifle less tense.

'I like Delavacquerie.'

'You probably know he's abroad at the moment.'

'He told me he was going. I talked to him about seeing

Ken Widmerpool again, but I didn't tell Delavacquerie the whole story. When Ken sent me a letter after the Magnus Donners Prize presentation last year I said I just didn't have time, which was true. Anyhow I wasn't that anxious to see him. I thought he'd forget about it this time, though I may have mentioned I was coming over again. I don't know how he found out I was in London. I hadn't told anyone here I was coming over. I only was in touch with Gibson after I arrived. Then someone called me up, and said he was speaking for Ken, who had a young friend— and master—whom he wanted me to meet.'

'Master?'

'It was Scorp himself telephoning, I guess. I hadn't met him then. That was how it started. While he was speaking —and I've wondered whether Scorp didn't somehow put the idea in my head—it came to me in a flash that I'd often thought these weirdos linked up with the early seventeenth-century gothicism I was writing about. Here was an opportunity not to throw away. I was right.'

'It was worth it?'

'Sure.'

This was much the way Gwinnett had talked of his Trapnel researches.

'As soon as I went down there, I knew my hunch was right. Ken was altogether different from the man he had been the year before. He was crazy about Scorp, and Scorp's ideas. It was Scorp's wish that I should be present at the rites they were planning. A summoning. Scorp thought my being there might even make better vibrations, if I didn't take part.'

Gwinnett stopped. He passed his hand over a face of light yellowish colour. He looked uncommonly ill.

'Scorp said these rites can't be performed with any hope of success, if those taking part are in a normal state of mind and body. I haven't had anything to eat or drink myself now for thirty-six hours. I didn't want to miss the chance of a lifetime, to see played out in the flesh all the things I'd been going over and over in my mind for months—like Tourneur's scene in the charnel house.'

'What were they trying to do?'

'The idea was to summon up a dead man called Trelawney.'

'How far did they get?'

Gwinnett gave a slight shudder. He was detached, yet far from calm, perhaps no more than his normal state, now aggravated by near collapse.

'They got no further than the fight between Ken and Scorp.'

Gwinnett's use of these abbreviated first-names gave a certain additional grotesqueness to what was already a sufficiently grotesque narrative.

'Did they have a scrap during the rite?'

'In the middle of it.'

'The horned dance?'

'No—during the sexual invocations that followed.'

'What did those consist of?'

'Scorp said that—among the ones taking part in the rite—they should have been all with all, each with each, within the sacred circle. I was a short way apart. Not in the circle. Scorp thought that best.'

Gwinnett again put up his hand to his head. He looked as if he might faint. Then he seemed to recover himself. Heavy spots of rain were beginning to fall.

'Did everyone in the circle achieve sexual relations with everyone else?'

'If they could.'

'Were they all up to it?'

'Only Scorp.'

'He must be a remarkable young man.'

'It wasn't for pleasure. This was an invocation. Scorp was

the summoner. He said it would have been far more likely to be successful had it been four times four.'

'Not Widmerpool?'

'That was the quarrel.'

'What was?'

'It had something to do with the union of opposites. I don't know enough about the rite to say exactly what happened. Ken was gashed with a knife. That was part of the ritual, but it got out of hand. There was some sort of struggle for power. After a while Scorp and the others managed to revive Ken. By then it was too late to complete the rites. Scorp said the ceremony must be abandoned. It wasn't easy to get Ken back over the fields, and down the hill. As well as doing the recording—it was all wrecked when he fell—he'd been concentrating the will. He'd been giving it all he had. He wasn't left with much will to get back to the caravan.'

'And they just let you take notes?'

'Scorp didn't mind that. He even urged me to.'

Gwinnett spoke as if that permission surprised him as much as it might surprise anyone else. He took the black notebook from under his arm, and began to turn its pages. They were full of small spidery handwriting.

'Listen to this. When I first went to Ken Widmerpool's place, and met Scorp, I was reminded of something I read not long before in one of the plays by Beaumont and Fletcher I'd been studying. I couldn't remember just what the passage said. When I got back I hunted it up, and wrote the lines down.'

Gwinnett's hand shook a little while he held the notebook in front of him, but he managed to read out what was written there.

'Take heed! this is your mother's scorpion,
That carries stings ev'n in his tears, whose soul

Is a rank poison thorough; touch not at him;
If you do, you're gone, if you'd twenty lives.
I knew him for a roguish boy
When he would poison dogs, and keep tame toads;
He lay with his mother, and infected her,
And now she begs i' th' hospital, with a patch
Of velvet where her nose stood, like the queen of spades,
And all her teeth in her purse. The devil and
This fellow are so near, 'tis not yet known
Which is the ev'ler animal.'

'Scorpio Murtlock to the life.'
'He did shed tears during the rite. They poured down his cheeks. That was just before he gashed Ken.'
'The familiar contemporary slur of our own day gains force of imagery in additionally giving your mother a dose.'
'The kid in the play was the prototype maybe. Scorp's in the same league.'
'The girl called Fiona is a niece of ours.'
Gwinnett seemed taken aback at that. The information must have started him off on a new train of thought.
'I don't know how that nice kid got mixed up with that kind of stuff. Rusty's another matter. She's just a tramp.'
He brushed some of the mud from his sleeve. He appeared to feel quite strongly on the subject of Fiona, at the same time was unwilling to say more about her. That was like him.
'I have to get back. I just wanted to make a few notes on the spot. I've done that. They'll be useful. How do I find where I've parked, Nicholas?'
'We'll go as far as the top of the hill, and have a look round. You'll probably be able to recognize the country better from there. Why don't you have a sleep at your pub, then come over to us for lunch?'
'No, I'll sleep for an hour or two, if I can, then get back

to London. I want to write while it's all in my mind, but I've got to have my books handy too.'

He made a movement with his shoulders, and gave a sort of groan, as if that had been painful. He was not at all well. I was rather relieved that he had refused an invitation to lunch. It would not have been an easy meal to sit through. We walked up the field together in silence. Round about the circle of elder trees the grass had been heavily trodden down. Rain was descending quite hard now. Gwinnett's story had distracted attention from the weather. The men with flags were beginning to pack up, the inspecting party massing together again, on the way back to their cars; a few hardy individuals, Mrs Salter, for instance, continuing to talk with the quarry representatives, or make notes. Gwinnett and I reached the summit of the rise.

'Have a look from here.'

The far side sloped down to the waters from which The Fingers drank, when at midnight the cock crew. The Stones would probably need an extra drink after all that had happened during the past twelve hours. I did not mention the legend of their drinking to Gwinnett. It might seem a small matter, after whatever he himself had witnessed up there. We stood side by side on the edge of the hill. Fields and hedges stretched away in front; a few scattered farms; clumps of trees; telegraph poles; a pylon; far distant bluish uplands. The roofs of the small town, where Gwinnett was staying, were just visible in rainy haze. Main roads, hard to pick out in light diminished by heavy cloud, were marked from time to time by the passage of a lorry. Gwinnett stared for some seconds towards the country spread before us, rather than looking immediately below for his recent place of ascent. He pointed.

'There they are.'

He spoke in his usual low voice, quite dispassionately. A long way off, where two hedges met at a right angle, what might be the shape of a yellow caravan stood in the corner of a field. The sight of it seemed to cheer Gwinnett a little, convince him that he had not dreamt the whole experience. Now he was able to turn his attention to the land below, from which he had first approached The Fingers. While rain continued to fall he established his bearings.

'That was the path.'

He pointed down to a sharp decline in the ground, not far from where we stood. Away below to the left, in a hollow overgrown with yet more elder, thick in thistles and ragwort, two or three abandoned cars were slowly falling to pieces. They must have been driven in there, and dumped, from a nearby grass lane. Gwinnett's vehicle, not visible from where we stood, was somewhere beyond these. He raised his hand in farewell. I did the same.

'See you in London perhaps?'

'I'll be having to work hard through the summer and fall.'

The answer seemed to indicate a wish to be left alone. That was understandable after all the things he had by now tolerated from the presence of other people. He edged unsteadily down the incline towards the brook. Rain was pouring so hard that I did not wait to see him negotiate its breadth, shallow and muddy, but too wide to jump with convenience. Probably he waded through. That would not have added much to the general disarray of his clothing. There was a flicker of forked lightning, a clatter of thunder. The whole atmosphere quivered with fluxes of electricity, discernible running through one's limbs. At the same time the rain itself greatly abated, diminishing to a few drops that continued to fall. The lightning flickered again, this time across the whole sky. I hurried to rejoin the rest of the party, hastening away like an army in full retreat. In the big field I noticed the ruts, where Ernie Dunch had so violently reversed the Land Rover. They were now filled with water. Mr Goldney, of the archaeological society, collar turned up, hands in pockets, appeared. He was half running, but slowed up, supposing I was looking for something.

'No weather to search for flints. I once picked up a piece of Samian ware not far from here. It's an interesting little site. Not up to The Whispering Knights, where I was last month. That's an altogether grander affair. Still, we have to be grateful for what we have in our own neighbourhood.'

'Why is it called The Whispering Knights? I've heard the name, but never been there.'

'During a battle some knights were standing apart, plotting against their king. A witch passed, and turned them into stone for their treachery.'

'Perhaps a witch will be waiting at the stile, and do the same to the quarry directors. Then we'll have a second monument up here.'

Mr Goldney did not reply. He looked rather prim, shocked at so malign a concept, or unwilling to countenance light words on the subject of folklore. Rain had possibly soaked him past the threshold of small-talk. Mr Tudor, in company with Mrs Salter, both very wet, joined us. Mr Tudor showed signs of a tempered optimism so far as to the outcome of the meeting.

'The Advisory Committee will have to get together again, Mr Goldney. Will Thursday at the same hour suit you? There's the correspondence with the Alkali Inspector we ought to go through again in relation to new points raised in consequence of today's meeting.'

'That's all right for me, Mr Tudor, and I'd like to bring up haulage problems.'

Mrs Salter sliced at a bramble with her pruning-hook.

'Even Mr Gollop admits haulage problems. At first he was evasive. I wouldn't have that.'

Isobel, after a final word with Mr Todman, caught us up.

'Who was the man you were talking to on the ridge?'

'I'll tell you about it on the way home.'

'You looked a very strange couple silhouetted against the skyline.'

'We were.'

'A bit sinister.'

'Your instincts are correct.'

The company scattered to their cars. Mr Gauntlett, an elderly woodland sprite untroubled by rain—if anything, finding refreshment in a downpour—disappeared on foot along a green lane. The rest of us drove away. The meeting had been a success in spite of the weather. Its consequence, assisted by the findings of the Advisory Committee, and the individual activities of Mr Tudor, was that a Government Enquiry was ordered by the Ministry. To have brought that about was a step in the right direction, even if the findings of such an Enquiry must always be unpredictable. That was emphasized by Mr Gauntlett, when I met him some weeks later, out with his gun, and the labrador that had replaced Daisy.

'Ah. We shall see what we shall see.'

He made no further reference to nocturnal horned dancers round about The Devil's Fingers. Neither did I, though their image haunted the mind. It was not quite the scene portrayed by Poussin, even if elements of the Seasons' dance were suggested in a perverted form; not least by Widmerpool, perhaps naked, doing the recording. From what Gwinnett had said, a battle of wills seemed to be in progress. If, having decided that material things were vain, Widmerpool had turned to the harnessing of quite other forces, it looked as if he were losing ground in rivalry with a younger man. Perhaps the contest should be thought of— if Widmerpool were Orlando—as one of Orlando's frequent struggles with wizards. Or—since the myth was in every respect upsidedown—was Murtlock even Widmerpool's Astolpho, playing him false?

I did not see Delavacquerie again until the early autumn. I wanted to hear his opinion about Gwinnett's inclusion in the rites at The Devil's Fingers. As someone belonging to a younger generation than my own, coming from a different hemisphere, a poet with practical knowledge of the business world, who possessed personal acquaintance with several of the individuals concerned in an episode that took a fairly high place for horror, as well as extravagance, Delavacquerie's objective comment would be of interest. For one reason or another—I, too, was away for a month or more—we did not meet; nor did I hear anything further of Gwinnett himself, or his associates of that night.

When a meeting with Delavacquerie took place he announced at once that he was feeling depressed. That was not uncommon. It was usually the result of being put out about his own business routine, or simply from lack of time to 'write'. He did not look well, poor states of health always darkening his complexion. I thought it more than possible that the trip with Polly Duport had not been a success; projected marriage decided against, or shelved. On the principle of not playing out aces at the start of the game, I did not immediately attack the subject of The Devil's Fingers. Then Delavacquerie himself launched into an altogether unforeseen aspect of the same sequence of circumstances.

'Look, I'm in rather a mess at the moment. Not a mess so much as a tangle. I'd like to speak about it. Do you mind? That's more to clear my own head than to ask advice. You may be able to advise too. Can you stand my talking a lot about my own affairs?'

'Easily.'

'I'll start from the beginning. That is always best. My own situation. The fact that I like it over here, but England isn't

174

my country. I haven't got a country. I'm rootless. I'm not grumbling about being rootless, especially these days. It even has advantages. At the same time certain problems are raised too.'

'You've spoken of all this on earlier occasions. Did going home bring it back in an acute form?'

Delavacquerie dismissed that notion with a violent gesture.

'I know I've talked of all this before. It's quite true. Perhaps I am over-obsessed by it. I am just repeating the fact as a foundation to what I am going to say, a reminder to myself that I'm never sure how much I understand people over here. Their reactions often seem to me different from my own, and from those of the people I was brought up with. Quite different. I've written poems about all this.'

'I've read them.'

Delavacquerie stopped for a moment. He seemed to be deciding the form in which some complicated statement should be made. He began again.

'I spoke to you once, I remember, of my son, Etienne.'

'You said he'd had some sort of thing for our niece, Fiona, which had been broken off, probably on account of that young man, Murtlock. I'm in a position to tell you more about all that—'

'Hold it for the moment.'

'My additions to the story are of a fantastic and outrageous kind.'

'Never mind. I don't doubt what you say. I just want to put my own case first. That is best. We'll come to what you know later—and I'm sure it will help me to hear it, even if I've heard some of it already. But I was speaking of Etienne. He has been doing well. He got a scholarship, which has taken him to America. By then he had found a new girl. She's a nice girl. It seems fairly serious. They keep up a regular correspondence.'

'How does he like the States?'

'All right.'

Whether or not Etienne liked the US did not seem to be the point. Delavacquerie paused again. He laughed rather uncomfortably.

'When Fiona was about the place, with Etienne, I noticed that I was getting interested in the girl myself. It wasn't more than that. I wasn't in love. Not in the slightest. Just interested. You will have had sufficient experience of such things to know what I am talking about—appreciate the differentiation I draw.'

'Of course.'

'I examined myself carefully in that connexion at the time. I found it possible to issue an absolutely clean bill of health, temperature, pulse, blood pressure, above all heart, all quite normal. I didn't even particularly want to sleep with her, though I might have tried to do so, had the situation been other than it was. The point I want to make is that the situation was not in the least like that of *The Humorous Lieutenant*, the King trying to seduce his son's girlfriend, as soon as the son himself was out of the way.'

'No love potions lying about.'

'You never know when you're not going to drink one by mistake, but in this case I had not done so.'

'May I ask a question?'

'Questions might clarify my own position. I welcome them. All I wish to curtail, for the moment, is competing narrative, until I've finished my own.'

'How was this feeling of interest in Fiona related to your other more permanent commitment?'

'To Polly? But, of course. That is just what I meant. How shall I put it? If, as I said, the case had been other, the possibility of a temporary run around might not have been altogether ruled out. You understand what I mean?'

'Keeping it quiet from Polly?'

'I suppose so.'

'Would Fiona herself have been prepared for a temporary run around—I mean had the situation, as you put it, been quite other?'

'Who can say? You never know till you try. Besides, if things had been different, they would have been totally different. That is something that perhaps only those—like ourselves—engaged in the arrangement of words fully understand. The smallest alteration in a poem, or a novel, can change its whole emphasis, whole meaning. The same is true of any given situation in life too, though few are aware of that. It was because things were as they were, that the *amitié* was formed. Perhaps that *amitié* would never have been established had we met somewhere quite fortuitously.'

'I see what you mean.'

'Then—as I told you—Etienne's thing with Fiona blew over. She went off with Murtlock, whether immediately, I'm not sure, but she went off. Passed entirely out of Etienne's life, and, naturally, out of mine too. I was rather glad. For one thing I preferred what existed already to remain altogether undisturbed. It suited me. It suited my work. I forgot about Fiona. Even the interest—interest, as opposed to love—proved to have been of the most transient order.'

I wholly accepted Delavacquerie's picture. Everything in connexion with it carried conviction—several different varieties of conviction. I could not at all guess where his story was going to lead. Inwardly, I flattered myself that my own narration, when I was allowed to unfold it, would cap anything he could produce.

'I told you, before I went away, that Gwinnett was going to see Widmerpool. That visit took place.'

'I know. You haven't heard my story yet. I've seen Gwinnett since he told you that.'

'I myself have not seen Gwinnett, but keep your story just a moment longer. Gwinnett, in fact, seems to have disappeared, perhaps left London. Murtlock, on the other hand, has been in touch with me.'

'Did he appear in person, wearing his robes?'

'He sent a message through Fiona.'

'I see.'

'Fiona arrived on my doorstep one evening. She knew the flat from her Etienne days.'

Delavacquerie lived in the Islington part of the world, not far from where Trapnel had occasionally camped out in one form or another. I had never seen Delavacquerie on his own ground.

'This without warning?'

'No, she called me up first, saying she had something to tell me. I asked her in for a drink. I had forgotten that none of them drink, owing to the rules of the cult, but she came at drinks time of day.'

I thought—as it turned out quite mistakenly—that I saw how things were shaping.

'May I interpolate another question?'

'Permission is given.'

'You remain still living single in your flat?'

Delavacquerie laughed.

'You mean did the combined trip to the Antilles have any concrete result? Well, purely administratively, it was decided that Polly and I would remain in our separate establishments, anyway for a short time longer, on account of various not at all interesting pressures in our professional lives. Does that answer the substance of your enquiry?'

'Yes. That was what I wanted to know. A further query. Had Fiona more or less invented an excuse for coming to see you again?'

Delavacquerie smiled at that idea. It seemed to please him, but he shook his head. On the face of it, the suggestion was reasonable enough. If Delavacquerie had taken what he called an interest in Fiona, when she had frequented the house, she herself was likely to be at least aware of something of the sort in the air, an *amitié*, to use his own term. She could have decided later, if only as a caprice, that she might experiment with his feelings, see how far things would go. Delavacquerie stuck to his uncompromising denial.

'No, she was sent by Murtlock all right. I'm satisfied as to that. Murtlock's motive for wanting to get into communication with me was an odd one. Not a particularly pleasant one.'

'He is not a particularly pleasant young man.'

'Nevertheless people are attracted to him.'

'Certainly.'

'They come under his influence. They may not even like him when they do so. They may not even be in love with him—naturally they could be in love with him without liking him. My first thought was that Fiona was in love with Murtlock. I'm not sure now that's correct. On the other hand, she's certainly under Murtlock's influence.'

It sounded a little as if Delavacquerie was explaining all this to himself, rather than to me, establishing confidence by an opportunity of speaking his hopes aloud. He had, after all, more or less suggested that as his aim, when he broached all this.

'Does Murtlock hope to rope you into his cult? Surely not? That would be too much.'

'It wasn't me he was after. It was Gwinnett.'

'They met, I suppose, when Gwinnett went down to see Widmerpool.'

'That hadn't happened, when Fiona came to see me.'

'Murtlock knew about Gwinnett already.'

'It appears that Gwinnett has won quite a name for himself in occult circles—if that is what they should be called—by having allegedly taken part in an act of great magical significance—in modern times almost making magical history.'

'You mean—'

'By release of sexual energy in literally necromantic circumstances—if we are to accept Gwinnett did that—in short, direct contact with the dead. In performing a negative expression of sex, carried to its logical conclusions, Gwinnett took part in the most inspired rite of Murtlock's cult.'

'I knew that, according to Murtlock doctrine, pleasure was excluded. There is no reason to suppose Gwinnett himself believed that.'

'You are right. Such an attitude seems even to have shocked Gwinnett. At the same time he felt that, as a scholar, he should study this available form of the gothic image of mortality. I do not think Gwinnett exactly expected that the theme would be, so to speak, played back to himself by Murtlock when he paid his visit to Widmerpool. I understand that the reason for Murtlock's interest in him was never put—the metaphor is appropriate—in cold blood. How much Gwinnett himself guessed, I do not know.'

'You learnt all this from Fiona?'

'Yes.'

'Is it time to tell my story yet?'

Delavacquerie laughed. He looked at me rather hard.

'You knew some of this already—I mean in connexion with Fiona?'

'As it happens, yes.'

He hesitated, perhaps more tormented than he would admit to himself.

'Let me say one thing more. What I have been talking about is not quite so simple as the way I've told it. There is another side too. You imply that you know for a fact that Fiona was involved—physically involved—in some of these highly distasteful goings-on. Do you know more, Nicholas, than that she has been for quite a long time a member of the cult, therefore they would inevitably come her way?'

'Yes. I do know more.'

'Involved without love—even in the many heteroclite forms of that unhappy verb.'

'Yes.'

'My first thought—when Fiona came to me with Murtlock's message that he wanted to know Gwinnett's whereabouts—was to have nothing to do with the whole business. That was more on grounds of taste than morals. As Emily Brightman is always pointing out, they are so often hopelessly confused by unintelligent people.'

'Murtlock knew Gwinnett was in England?'

'He'd already found that out somehow.'

'He finds out a lot. I'm surprised, having got so far, he hadn't traced Gwinnett's whereabouts.'

'He may, in any case, have preferred a more tortuous approach. I felt it an imposition on the part of this young visionary—whatever his claims as a magician—to force his abracadabras on an American scholar, engaged over here on research of a serious kind, however idiosyncratic Gwinnett's own sexual tastes may be. Would you agree?'

'Besides, as you've said, so far as we know, Gwinnett pursues these for pleasure, rather than magical advancement.'

'Exactly. Love and Literature should rank before Sorcery and Power. There was, however, an additional aspect. That was why I was not speaking with absolute truth when I denied that Fiona was in some degree playing her own game, when she came to see me. On the other hand, that possibility did not possess quite the flattering slant you implied.'

'She told you in so many words why Murtlock wanted to meet Gwinnett?'

'Certainly. No embarrassments at all about that. More so

regarding the ulterior motive for her visit. That emerged while we were talking. The fact was that Fiona was getting tired—more than that, absolutely desperate—about the life she has been living for a long time now.'

'That's good news.'

'Of course.'

Delavacquerie paused again. He did not sound quite so enthusiastic about Fiona cutting adrift from Murtlockism as might have been expected. The chronological sequence of when these things happened—Fiona come to Delavacquerie, Gwinnett gone to visit Murtlock and Widmerpool, the period between—was not very clear to me. I was also uncertain as to Delavacquerie's present feelings about Fiona. Whatever she had said to him did not appear to have affected her doings at The Devil's Fingers. I fully believed what Delavacquerie had described as his attitude towards Fiona as his son's girlfriend; I believed, more or less, that he later put her from his mind; but this new Fiona incarnation remained undefined. It was quite another matter. Also there was Polly Duport in the background. More must be explained. When he spoke again it was in an altogether detached tone.

'Fiona more or less broke down while we were talking. Even then she was unwilling to say she would give up the whole thing. This was at our first meeting.'

'There were subsequent ones?'

'Several. Murtlock wouldn't accept no for an answer, so far as Gwinnett's whereabouts were concerned.'

'You had refused to reveal them?'

'Yes.'

'That showed firmness.'

'Firmness, in any sphere, is ultimately the only thing anyone respects. Murtlock seems to have foreseen a refusal at first. Either that, or he enjoyed linking Fiona and myself in a kind of game.'

'He would be capable of both.'

'His instincts told him that he could force Gwinnett's address out of me, sooner or later, through Fiona herself. Murtlock, as you know by now, is exceedingly cunning in getting what he wants. He was well aware that Fiona felt that he, Scorpio Murtlock, must in some manner release her, personally, from his domination—give her leave to go, before she herself, of her own volition, could escape the net.'

'All she had to do, in plain fact, was to walk out.'

'That is just what Fiona could not bring herself to do. Murtlock knew that perfectly. He knew she must have some sort of legal dismissal from his service, one afforded by himself.'

'An honourable discharge?'

'Even a dishonourable one, I think—since all abandoning of himself and the cult must be wrong—but it had to come from Murtlock. It was no good arguing with her. That was how she felt. We talked it over exhaustively—and exhaustingly—during various meetings.'

Delavacquerie seemed to have established a more effective relationship with Fiona than any up-to-date achieved by her own family.

'So what happened?'

'In the end I revealed Gwinnett's sleazy hotel. The price of that was that Fiona should be free to leave. Even then Murtlock would not allow her to go immediately. He said she could only go when she had taken part in a ceremony that included the presence of Gwinnett.'

'So it was through you, in a sense, that Gwinnett went to see Widmerpool. He said it was because he wanted to observe gothic doings done in a gothic way.'

'That was true too. It was a bit of luck for Murtlock—unless he bewitched Gwinnett too, put the idea into his head. I prefer to think it luck. No doubt he always has luck.

Those people do. Once I had told Murtlock where to find Gwinnett, Gwinnett himself decided there was a good reason to fall in with what Murtlock wanted all along the line.'

'Where's Fiona now? Has she got away from Murtlock yet?'

Delavacquerie looked for a moment a little discomposed.

'As a matter of fact Fiona's living in the flat—not living with me, I mean—but it was somewhere to go. In fact it seemed the only way out. She didn't want to have to live with her parents—obviously she could, for a time anyway, if she felt like doing that—and, if she set up on her own, there was danger that Murtlock might begin to pester her again. A spell of being absolutely free from Murtlock would give a chance to build up some resistance, as against a disease. There's no one in Etienne's room. It was her own suggestion. As you can imagine, she's rather off sex for the moment.'

'I see.'

That was untrue. I did not in the least see; so far as seeing might be held to imply some sort of understanding of what was really taking place. A complicated situation appeared merely to be accumulating additional complicated factors. Delavacquerie himself evidently accepted the inadequacy of this acknowledgment in relation to problems involved. He seemed to expect no more.

'When I say we talked things over, that isn't exactly true either. Fiona doesn't talk things over. She's incapable of doing that. That's partly her trouble. One of the reasons why it was better for her to be in the flat was that it offered some hope of finding out what she was really thinking.'

He abruptly stopped speaking of Fiona.

'Now tell me your story.'

To describe what had happened at The Devil's Fingers, now that Fiona was living under Delavacquerie's roof, was an altogether different affair from doing so in the manner that the story had first rehearsed itself to my mind. Then, planning its telling, there had been no reason to suppose her more than, at best, a sentimental memory; if—which might be quite mistaken—I had been right in suspecting him a little taken with her, when, in connexion with his son, Delavacquerie had first spoken Fiona's name. Nevertheless, there was no glossing over the incident at The Devil's Fingers. It had, in any case, been narrated by Gwinnett with his accustomed reticences, and, after all, Delavacquerie knew from Fiona herself more or less what had been happening. That was only a specific instance, though, for various reasons, an exceptional one. If he felt additional dismay on hearing of that night's doings, he showed nothing. His chief interest was directed to the fact that Gwinnett had been present in person at the rites. This specific intervention of Gwinnett had been unknown to him. He had also supposed anything of the sort to have been, more or less as a matter of course, enacted at whatever premises Widmerpool provided.

'How does Fiona occupy herself in London?'

'Odd jobs.'

'Has she gone back to her journalism?'

'Not exactly that. She has been doing bits of research. I myself was able to put some of that in her way. She's quite efficient.'

'Her parents always alleged she could work hard if she liked.'

One saw that in a certain sense Fiona had worked hard placating Murtlock. Delavacquerie looked a little embarrassed again.

'It seems that Fiona revealed some of her plans about leaving the cult to Gwinnett, when he was himself in touch with them. Gwinnett suggested that—if she managed to kick free from Murtlock—Fiona should help him in some of the seventeenth-century donkey-work with the Jacobean dramatists. I hadn't quite realized—'

Delavacquerie did not finish the sentence. I suppose he meant he had not grasped the extent to which Gwinnett, too, had been concerned in Fiona's ritual activities. Evidently she herself had softpedalled the Devil's Fingers incident, as such. He ended off a little lamely.

'Living at my place is as convenient as any other for that sort of work.'

I expressed agreement. Delavacquerie thought for a moment.

'I may add that having Fiona in the flat has inevitably buggered up my other arrangements.'

'Polly Duport?'

He laughed rather unhappily, but gave no details.

6

When, in the early spring of the following year, an invitation arrived for the wedding of our nephew, Sebastian Cutts, to a girl called Clare Akworth, I decided at once to attend. Isobel would almost certainly have gone in any case. Considerations touched on earlier—pressures of work, pressures of indolence—could have kept me away. Negative attitudes were counteracted by an unexpected aspect of the ceremony. The reception was to take place at Stourwater. Several factors combined to explain that choice of setting. Not only had the bride been educated at the girls' school which had occupied the Castle now for more than thirty years, but her grandfather was one of the school's governing body. The church service was to be held in a village not far away, where Clare Akworth's mother, a widow, had settled, when her husband died in his late thirties. Mrs Akworth's cottage had, I believe, been chosen in the first instance with an eye to the daughter's schooling, for which her father-in-law was thought to have assumed responsibility. Anyway, the Stourwater premises had been made available during a holiday period, offering a prospect that Moreland might have regarded as almost alarmingly nostalgic in possibilities.

That was not all, where conjuring up the past was concerned. In this same field of reminiscences, the bride's grandfather—no doubt the main influence in putting Stourwater thus on view—also sustained a personal rôle, even if an infinitely trivial one. In short, I could not pretend freedom from all curiosity as to what Sir Bertram Akworth now looked like. This interest had nothing to do with his being a governor of a well reputed school for girls, nor with the long catalogue of company directorships and committee memberships (ranging from Independent Television to the Diocesan Synod), which followed his name in *Who's Who*. On the contrary, Sir Bertram Akworth was memorable in my mind solely on account of the fact that, as a schoolboy, he had sent a note of an amatory nature to a younger boy (my near contemporary, later friend, Peter Templer), been reported by Widmerpool to the authorities for this unlicensed act; in consequence, sacked.

The incident had aroused a certain amount of rather heartless laughter at the time by the incongruity of a suggestion (Stringham's, I think) that an element of jealousy on Widmerpool's part was not to be ruled out. Templer's Akworth (Widmerpool's Akworth, if you prefer), a boy several years older than myself, was known to me only by sight. I doubt if we ever spoke together. Like Widmerpool himself, unremarkable at work or games, Akworth had a sallow emaciated face, and kept himself to himself on the whole, his most prominent outward characteristic being an unusually raucous voice. These minor traits assumed a sinister significance in my eyes, when, not without horror, I heard of his expulsion. The dispatch of the note, in due course, took on a less diabolical aspect, as sophistication increased, and, during the period when Stringham, Templer, and I used all to mess together, Stringham would sometimes (never in front of Templer) joke about the incident, which shed for me its earlier aura of fiendish depravity.

In later life, as indicated, Akworth (knighted for various

public services and benefactions) had atoned for this adolescent lapse by a career of almost sanctified respectability. From where we were sitting, rather far at the back of the church—in a pew with Isobel's eldest sister, Frederica, and her husband, Dicky Umfraville—Sir Bertram Akworth was out of view. One would be able to take a look at him later, during the reception. It was unexpected that Umfraville had turned up. He was close on eighty now, rather deaf, walking with a stick. On occasions like this, if dragged to them by Frederica, he could be irritable. Today he was in the best of spirits, keeping up a running fire of comment before the service began. I had no idea how he had been induced to attend the wedding. Perhaps he himself had insisted on coming. He reported a hangover. Its origins could have had something to do with his presence.

'Rare for me these days. One of those hangovers like sheet lightning. Sudden flashes round the head at irregular intervals. Not at all unpleasant.'

The comparison recalled that morning at The Devil's Fingers, when lightning had raced round the sky. The Government Enquiry had taken place, and, to the satisfaction of those concerned with the preservation of the site, judgment had been against further quarry development in the area of the Stones. Our meeting there was the last time I had seen Gwinnett. He had never got in touch. I left it at that. Delavacquerie spoke of him occasionally, but, for one reason or another—not on account of any shift in relationship—our luncheons together had been less frequent. Fiona was still lodging at his flat when we last met. Without too closely setting limits to what was meant by what Delavacquerie himself called a 'heteroclite verb', my impression was that he could be called in love with her. He never spoke of Fiona unless asked, the situation no less enigmatic than his association with Matilda years before.

Matilda Donners had died. She had told Delavacquerie

that she was not returning to London after the end of the summer. He had assumed her to mean that she had decided to live in the country or abroad. When questioned as to her plans Matilda had been evasive. Only after her death was it clear that she must have known what was going to happen. That was like Matilda. She had always been mistress of her own life. The organ began playing a voluntary. Frederica attempted to check Umfraville's chatter, which was becoming louder.

'Do be quiet, darling. The whole congregation don't want to hear about your hangovers.'

'What?'

'Speak more quietly.'

Umfraville indicated that he could not hear what his wife was talking about, but said no more for the moment. He was not alone in taking part in murmured conversation, the bride's grandmother, a small jolly woman, also conversing animatedly with relations in the pew behind that in which she sat. Umfraville began again.

'Who's the handsome lady next to the one in a funny hat?'

'The one in the hat, who's talking a lot, like you, is Lady Akworth. The one you mean is the bride's mother.'

'What about her?'

'She was called Jamieson—one of the innumerable Ardglass ramifications, not a close relation—her husband was in Shell or BP, and caught a tropical disease in Africa that killed him.'

That seemed to satisfy Umfraville for the moment. He closed his eyes, showing signs of nodding off to sleep. Sebastian Cutts, the bridegroom, tall, sandy-haired like his father, also shared Roddy's now ended political ambitions. He and his brother, Jonathan, resembled their father, too, in delivering a flow of information, and figures, about their respective computers and art sales. Hard work at his computers had not engrossed Sebastian Cutts to the exclusion of what was judged—by his own generation—as a not less than ample succession of love affairs; a backlog of ex-girlfriends Clare Akworth was thought well able to dispose of. An only child, she had been working as typist-secretary in an advertising firm. Her pleasing *beauté de singe*—the phrase Umfraville's—was of a type calculated to raise the ghost of Sir Magnus Donners in the Stourwater corridors. Perhaps it had done so, when she was a school-girl. Her spell at Stourwater had been later than that of the Quiggin twins (recently much publicized in connexion with *Toilet Paper*, a newly founded 'underground' maga-zine), both withdrawn from the school before Clare Akworth's arrival there. Umfraville, coming-to suddenly, showed signs of impatience.

'Buck up. Get cracking. We can't sit here all day. Ah, here she is.'

The congregation rose. Clare Akworth, who had an excellent figure, came gracefully up the aisle on the arm of her uncle, Rupert Akworth, one of her father's several brothers. He was employed in the rival firm of fine arts auctioneers to that of Jonathan Cutts. There were several small children in attendance. I did not know which families they represented. The best-man was Jeremy Warminster, the bridegroom's first-cousin. Junior Research Fellow in Science at my own former college, Jeremy Warminster was a young man of severe good looks, offhand manner, reputation for brilliance at whatever was his own form of biological studies. A throwback to his great-great-uncle, the so-called Chemist-Earl (specialist in marsh gases, though more renowned in family myth for contributions to the deodorization of sewage), Jeremy had always known exactly what he wanted to do. This firmness of purpose, engrained seriousness, allied to an abrupt way of talking, made him rather a daunting young man. His plan, not yet accomplished, was to turn Thrubworth into an institution for scientific research, while he himself continued to occupy the wing of the house converted into a flat by his uncle and predecessor. Jeremy Warminster's mother, stepbrother and stepsister (children of the drunken Lagos businessman, Collins, long deceased), had lived at Thrubworth until his coming of age. Then Veronica Tolland moved to London, which she had always preferred. Her Collins offspring were now married, with children of their own; Angus, a journalist, specializing in industrial relations; Iris, wife of an architect, her husband one of the extensive Vowchurch family.

There was no address at the wedding service, but—an unexpected bonus—Sir Bertram Akworth read the Lesson. This gave an excellent opportunity to study his bearing in later life. White hair, a small moustache, had neither much changed the appearance, so far as remembered from the days when Templer had aroused his passions. In failing to acquire a great deal of outward distinction, he resembled Sir Magnus Donners, a man of wider abilities in the same line. Sir Bertram Akworth showed, anyway at long range, no sign of projecting Sir Magnus's air of being nevertheless a little disturbing. Sir Bertram, still spare, sallow, rather gloomy, looked ordinary enough. Before he began to read he glanced round the church, as if to make sure all was arranged in a manner to be approved. Possibly he himself had decided that his own reading of the Lesson should be alternative to an address. The passage, one often chosen for such occasions, was from Corinthians. As the voice began to rasp through the church, the memory of the schoolboy Akworth (not yet Sir Bertram) came perceptibly back.

'Though I speak with the tongues of men and of angels, and have not charity, I am become as sounding brass, or a tinkling cymbal. And though I have the gift of prophecy, and understand all mysteries, and all knowledge; and though I have all faith, so that I could remove mountains, and have not charity, I am nothing. And though I bestow all my goods to feed the poor, and though I give my body to be burned, and have not charity, it profiteth me nothing.'

The reference to sounding brass was appropriate, recalling a sole personal memory of the reader, the rebuke administered by our housemaster, his nerves always tried by pupils with strident voices.

'Don't shout, Akworth.' Le Bas had said. 'It's a bad habit of yours, especially when answering a question. Try to speak more quietly.'

The habit remained. It seemed to have been no handicap in Sir Bertram's subsequent career. At one of the closing sentences of the Lesson he hardened the pitch of the utterance. It rang through the nave.

'For now we see through a glass, darkly; but then face to face.'

Giving a final glance round the congregation, he returned to his seat. The striking image of seeing through a glass darkly again brought thoughts of The Devil's Fingers. Fiona did not appear to be present in the church. She might well have decided to skip the service, just turn up at the reception. In the light of her newly organized life she was unlikely to forgo altogether her brother's wedding. So far as I knew she was still living at Delavacquerie's flat, their relationship no less undefined. Her parents were united in agreeing that, whatever the situation, it was preferable to the previous one. The impression was that Roddy and Susan Cutts, perhaps deliberately, had known little enough about the Murtlock period too. The handout issued by them now was that their daughter had taken a room in an Islington flat that belonged to a man who worked, respectably enough, in Donners-Brebner. Poets not playing much part in Cutts life, Delavacquerie's business side was more emphasized than the poetic; potential emotional ties with

Fiona not envisaged, more probably ignored. Delavacquerie was after all considerably older than their daughter; though, it had to be admitted, so too had been the handsome married electrician. The Wedding March struck up. For some minutes the congregation was penned in while photographers operated at the church door. Outside, we walked with Veronica Tolland towards the car park.

'Are your kids here? Angus couldn't get away either. He had to cover a strike. Iris will be at the reception. Fancy fetching up at Stourwater again. I used to go on visitors' day when I was a child. The park's open to the public now. My father's job was in the local town. I expect I've often said that—also I was at school with Matilda Donners, when she was a little girl called Betty Updike. Did you hear she'd died?'

'Apparently been ill for some time. I didn't know that. I always liked Matilda.'

'She made quite a career for herself. I don't know half the people here. Who's the good-looking black girl with the young Huntercombes. I know—she's wife of Jocelyn Fettiplace-Jones. His mother was an Akworth. How glad I am I live in London now.'

Like Ted Jeavons, Veronica had taken on the workings of a world rather different from that of her earlier life, without ever in the least wanting to be part. She had always regarded that world, not without a certain enjoyment, from the outside. Now she felt free of it all, except on occasions such as this one, which she liked to attend. In spite of such inherent sentiments, Veronica had come by now to look more than a little like a conventional dowager on the stage.

'See you later.'

The immediate vision of Stourwater, in thin vaporous April sunshine, was altogether unchanged. On the higher ground, in the shadows of huge contorted oaks, sheep still grazed. Down in the hollow lay the Castle; keep; turrets;

moat; narrow causeway across the water, leading to the main gate with double portcullis. All seemed built out of cardboard. Its realities had in any case belonged more to the days of Sir Magnus Donners, rather than to the later Middle Ages, when the Castle's history had been obscure. The anachronistic black swans were gone from the greenish waters of the moat. A large noticeboard directed to a car park. Round about the Castle itself playing fields came into view.

'What games would they be?'

'Net-ball, hockey, I suppose.'

We parked, then crossed the causeway on foot. The reception was taking place in the Great Hall, now the school's Assembly Room. Armoured horsemen no longer guarded the door. Forms had been pushed back against the walls, a long table for refreshments set across the far end. In place of Sir Magnus's Old Masters—several of doubtful authenticity according to Smethyck, and others with a taste for picture attribution—hung reproductions of the better known French Impressionists. We joined the queue, a long one, formed by guests waiting to meet bride and bridegroom. The two families had turned out in force. There must have been a hundred or more guests at least. We took a place far back in the line, working our way up slowly, as Roddy, relic of his parliamentary days, liked to talk for a minute or two to everyone he knew personally. When at last we found ourselves greeting the newly married pair, their closer relations in support, I felt this no moment to remind Sir Bertram Akworth that we had been at school together. There would in any case have been no opportunity. Susan Cutts drew us aside.

'Come away from them all for a moment. There's something I must tell you both.'

Leaving her husband to undertake whatever formalities were required, Susan was evidently impatient to reveal some piece of news, good or ill was not clear, which greatly excited her.

'Have you heard about Fiona?'

'No, what?'

One was prepared for anything. My first thought was that Fiona had returned to Murtlock and the cult.

'She's married.'

I thought I saw how things had at last fallen out.

'To Gibson Delavacquerie?'

Susan looked puzzled by the question. The name did not seem to convey anything to her, certainly not that of their daughter's new husband. Susan's words plainly stated that Fiona possessed a husband.

'You mean her landlord? No, not him. What could have made you think that, Nick?'

So far from Susan considering Delavacquerie to rate as a potential suitor, she was momentarily put off her stride at the very strangeness of such a proposition. Any emotional undercurrents of the Delavacquerie association must have completely passed by the Cutts parents, unless Susan was doing a superb piece of acting, which was most unlikely.

'No—it's an American. I believe you know him, Nick? He's called Russell Gwinnett.'

Roddy, disengaging himself from the last guest for whom he felt any serious responsibility at the moment, was unable to keep away from all share in imparting such news.

'Wasn't there some sort of contretemps years ago about Gwinnett? I believe there was. That fellow Widmerpool was mixed up with it, I have an idea. I used to come across Widmerpool sometimes in the House. Not too bad a fellow, even if he was on the other side. He's sunk without a trace, if ever a man did. I can't remember exactly what happened. Gwinnett seems a nice chap. He's a bit older than Fiona, of course, but I don't see why that should matter.'

Susan agreed heartily.

'In his forties. I always liked older men myself. Anyway they're married, so there it is.'

'When did this happen?'

'Yesterday, actually.'

'No warning?'

'You can imagine what it was like to be told this, with Sebastian's wedding taking place the following day.'

'They just turned up man and wife?'

'Fiona brought Mr Gwinnett—I suppose I should call him Russell now—along to see us the same afternoon. She seems very pleased about it. That's the great thing. They both do. He doesn't talk much, but I never mind that with people.'

'Have they gone off on a honeymoon?'

'They're just going to do a short drive round England, then Russell has to go back to America. He's got a little car he dashes about in all over the country, doing his research. He's a don at an American university, as you probably know. They're coming to the reception. Fiona suggested they should do that herself. Wasn't it sweet of her? They haven't arrived yet. At least I haven't seen them.'

Susan, in spite of determined cheerfulness, was showing signs of nervous strain. That was not to be wondered at. I mentioned—less from snobbish reasons than avoidance of cross-questioning about Gwinnett in other directions—that he was collaterally descended from one of the Signers of the Declaration of Independence. Roddy showed interest. At least he was deflected from closer enquiry into the subject of what exactly had happened to connect his new son-in-law with Widmerpool.

'Is he indeed? I must say I took to Russell at first sight. I'd like to have a talk with him about the coming Presidential election, and a lot of other American matters too.'

'I wish Evangeline were still here,' said Susan. 'She might

know something about the Gwinnetts. We'll talk about it all later. I'll have to go back and do my stuff now. There are some more people arriving... darling, how sweet of you to come... lovely to see you both...'

There was no time to contemplate further Fiona's marriage to Gwinnett, beyond making the reflection that, if he had done some dubious things in his time, so too had she. Leaving the threshold of the reception, we moved in among the crowd that filled the Great Hall. Most of the guests had chosen to wear conventional wedding garments, some of the younger ones letting themselves go, either with variations on these, or trappings that approximated to fancy dress. The children, of whom there was quite a large collection, scuffled about gaily, the whole assemblage making a lively foreground to the mediaeval setting. Hugo, Norah, and Blanche Tolland had all turned up, Norah grumbling about the superabundance of Alford relations present.

'Susie was always very thick with the Alford cousins. I hardly knew any of them. They look a seedy lot, large red faces and snub noses.'

'I find them charming,' said Hugo. 'Look here, what's all this about Fiona marrying an American? The last thing I heard was that she had given up all those odd friends of hers Norah was once so keen on, and was working hard at something or other in Islington.'

Norah was not prepared to be saddled with an admiration for Murtlock.

'I wasn't keen on Fiona's last lot of friends. I've been saying for ages she's hung about much too long doing that sort of thing. If she wants to get married, I'm glad it's an American. It will give her the chance of a new kind of life, if she goes to live there. Somebody said you knew him, Nick?'

'Yes, I know him.'

There was no point in trying to explain Gwinnett to Norah. In any case, given the most favourable circumstances, I was not sure I could explain him to anyone, including myself. The attempt was not demanded, because we were joined by Umfraville, carrying his rubber-tipped stick in one hand, a very full glass of champagne in the other. As prelude to an impersonation of some sort, he raised the glass.

> 'Here's to the wings of love,
> May they never lose a feather,
> Till your little shoes, and my big boots,
> Stand outside the door together.'

Hugo held up a hand.

'We don't want a scandal, Dicky, after all these years as brothers-in-law.'

Before Umfraville could further elaborate whatever form of comic turn contemplated, his own attention was taken up by a grey-haired lady touching his arm.

'Hullo, Dicky.'

Umfraville clearly possessed not the least idea who was accosting him. The lady, smartly dressed, though by no means young, might at the same time have been ten years short of Umfraville's age. She was tall, pale, distinguished in appearance, very sad.

'I'm Flavia.'

'Flavia.'

Carefully balancing his stick and champagne, Umfraville embraced her.

'How horrid of you not to recognize me.'

Umfraville swept that aside.

'Flavia, this is an altogether unexpected delight. Does your presence at our nephew's wedding mean that you and I are now related—in consequence of the marriage of these young people? How much I hope that, Flavia.'

The grey-haired lady—Stringham's sister—laughed a rather tinkly laugh.

'Dicky, you haven't changed at all.'

Flavia Wisebite—it was to be assumed she still bore the name of her American second husband, Harrison Wisebite (like Veronica Tolland's first, alcoholic, long departed)—laughed again tremulously. Her own affiliations with Umfraville dated back to infinitely distant days; Kenya, the Happy Valley, surroundings where, according to Umfraville himself—he had emphasized with a certain complacency his own caddishness in revealing the information—he had been the first to seduce her. That possibility was more credible than Umfraville's follow-up, that he (rather than the reprehensible Cosmo Flitton, married to Flavia not long after) could be true father of Flavia's daughter, Pamela. Pamela Flitton, it might be thought, carried all the marks of being Cosmo Flitton's daughter. Age had done little or nothing to impair Umfraville's capacities for routine banter, if he happened to be in the right mood. He continued to press the possibility of a remote family tie emerging from the Cutts/Akworth union that would connect Flavia Wisebite with himself.

'Bride or bridegroom? Come on, Flavia. I want to be able to introduce you as my little cousin.'

'No good, Dicky. I'm not a blood relation. I'm Clare Akworth's godmother. Her mother's a dear friend of mine. We live in cottages almost next door to each other, practically in walking distance of Stourwater.'

Flavia Wisebite began to narrate her past history to Umfraville in her rapid trembling voice; how nervous diseases had prostrated her, she had been in and out of hospital, was now cured. In spite of that assurance she still seemed in a highly nervous state. Umfraville, less tough in certain respects than in his younger days, was beginning to look rather upset himself at all this. No doubt he felt sorry for Flavia, but had reached a time of life when, if he came to a wedding, he hoped not to be harassed by having poured into his ears the troubles of a former mistress. His face became quite drawn as he listened. I should have been willing to escape myself, scarcely knowing her, and feeling in no way responsible. Before withdrawal were possible, Umfraville manoeuvred me into the conversation. Flavia Wisebite at once recalled the sole occasion when we had met in the past.

'It was when Dicky was first engaged to your sister-in-law, Frederica. You drove over from Aldershot to Frederica's house during the war. I was there with poor Robert, just before he was killed. I'm a contemporary of Frederica's, you know. We came out at the same time. I remember you talking about my brother, Charles.'

She began to speak disjointedly of Stringham. She was, I thought, perhaps a little mad now. As one gets older, one gets increasingly used to encountering this development in friends and acquaintances; causing periods of self-examination in a similar connexion. Seeing that Flavia and I had something in common to talk about together, Umfraville slipped away. Out of the corner of my eye I saw him stumping across the room on his stick to have a further word with the bride. Flavia Wisebite rambled on.

'Charles was never sent into the world to make old bones, of course I always knew that, but how sad that he should have died as he did, how sad. He was a hero, of course, but what difference does that make, when you're dead?'

She seemed to require an answer to that question. It was hard to offer one free from sententiousness. I made no attempt to do so.

'I suppose it makes a difference the way a few people remember you.'

That seemed to satisfy her.

'Yes, yes. Like Robert.'

'Yes. Robert too.'

She appeared to have been made quite happy by this justifiable, if unoriginal conclusion. Oddly enough, when at Frederica's, Flavia Wisebite had spoken almost disparagingly of her brother's determination, in face of poor health, to join the army. This canonization of Stringham after death had something of her daughter Pamela's way of remembering dead lovers. Now, in a somewhat similar manner, Flavia began to talk of Umfraville with affection, though she had hardly noticed him at Frederica's. Then, of course, she had been involved with Robert Tolland. Even so, the enthusiasm with which she went on about Kenya, how amusing Umfraville had been there, how much her father had liked him, was an illustration of the way human relationships fluctuate, without any action taking place; Umfraville, from being entirely disregarded, now occupying a prominent place in Flavia Wisebite's personal myth. Without warning, she switched to Pamela.

'Did you ever meet my daughter?'

'Yes. I knew Pamela.'

I was about to say that I knew Pamela well, then saw that, in Pamela Flitton's case, that might imply closer affiliations than had ever in fact existed. It was a needless adjustment of phrase. Her mother had certainly long ceased to worry, if she had ever done so, about her daughter's affairs, with whom she had, or had not, slept. Perhaps, in her own state of health, Flavia had been scarcely aware of all that. In any case something else in relation to Pamela was now on her mind.

'She died too.'

'Yes.'

'She married that dreadful man—Widmerpool.'

For the first time it occurred to me as strange, abnormally strange, that Flavia Wisebite had never, so far as I knew, played anything like an active rôle in her capacity as Widmerpool's mother-in-law. In fact I now saw that, without formulating the idea at all clearly in my mind, I had always supposed Flavia to have died. Whatever the reason—chiefly no doubt the interludes in hospitals and nursing-homes— she seemed to have sidestepped the scandals that had enveloped her daughter's name; not least Pamela's unhappy end. If that had been her mother's deliberate intention, she had been remarkably successful in keeping out of the way.

'Did you know Widmerpool?'

'Yes. I know him. I've known him for years.'

'I said *did* you know him. Nobody could know him now.'

'How do you mean?'

I did not grasp immediately the implication that Widmerpool had become literally impossible to know.

'You can't have heard what's happened to him. He's gone out of his mind. He lives with a crowd of dreadful people, most of them quite young, who wear extraordinary clothes, and do the most horrible, horrible things. They are quite near here.'

It was true that Widmerpool's mother's cottage had been only a mile or two from Stourwater.

'I did know he'd become rather odd. I'd forgotten he was in this neighbourhood.'

'I see them out running quite often.'

In the light of the cult's habits there was nothing particularly extraordinary in Flavia Wisebite catching sight of them at their exercises from time to time. During the period of working for Sir Magnus Donners, Widmerpool had often spoken of his good fortune in having his mother's cottage— later enlarged by himself—so close to the Castle.

'Sometimes they're in blue garments, sometimes hardly any clothes at all. I've been told they do wear absolutely nothing, stark naked, when they go out in the middle of the night in summer. They do all sorts of *revolting* things. I wonder it's allowed. But then everything is allowed now.'

Flavia Wisebite grimaced.

'I try not to look at them, if they come running in off a sideroad. When I see them in the distance I go off up a turning.'

'Is Widmerpool head of the cult?'

'How should I know? I thought he was. Didn't he start it? As soon as Pamela married him, he began his horrible goings-on, though they weren't quite like what he does nowadays. Why did she do it? How could she? Find the most horrible man on earth, and then marry him? She always had to have her own way. It was quite enough that everyone agreed that Widmerpool was awful, hideous, monstrous. She just wanted to show that she didn't care in the least what anyone said. She was the same as a child. Absolutely wilful. Nobody could control her.'

No doubt there was much truth in what her mother said. I remembered Pamela Flitton, as a child bridesmaid, being sick in the font at Stringham's wedding. One of the children had made a good deal of noise at the ceremony just attended, but nothing so drastic as that. Flavia's daughter had always been in a class by herself from her earliest days. A girl like Fiona was no real competitor.

'Because Pam didn't always go for unattractive people. When she was a little girl she fell madly in love with Charles—you know the way children do—at the time he was drinking too much. The amount he drank in those days was terrible. Pam didn't see him often because of that. Still, Charles was always fond of her, very nice to her, whenever he came to see us, which wasn't often. Charles left Pam his things, not much, hardly anything by then. Pam never made a will, of course, so Widmerpool must have got whatever there was. The Modigliani drawing. Pam loved that. I wonder what happened to it. I suppose that awful Widmerpool sold it.'

Flavia Wisebite took a small folded pocket handkerchief

from her bag. She lightly dabbed her eyes. It was the precise gesture her mother had used, another memory of Stringham's marriage to Peggy Stepney; Peggy Klein, as she had been for years now. Mrs Foxe's tears had been more prolonged on that occasion, lasting intermittently throughout the whole service. Flavia's were quickly over. She returned the handkerchief to the bag. I did not know what to say. Where could one begin? Stringham's past? Pamela's past? Flavia's own past? These were extensive and delicate themes to set out on; Widmerpool's present, even less approachable. There was no need to say anything at all. Flavia Wisebite, in the manner of persons of her sort, had suddenly recovered herself. She was perfectly all right again. Now she spoke once more in her tremulous social voice.

'Isn't Clare Akworth a sweet girl?'

'I don't really know her. She looks very attractive.'

'I'm so proud to be her godmother. He's a charming young man too. He told me all about his computers. It was far above my head, I'm afraid. I'm sure they'll be very happy. I never was, but I'm sure they will be. So nice to have met again.'

Smiling goodbye, she disappeared into the crowd. In its own particular way the encounter had been disturbing. I was glad it was over. One of its side effects was a sense of temporary inability to chat with other guests, most of them, unless relations, from their age unknown to me. Flavia Wisebite had diminished exuberance for seeking out members of an older generation, whom one had not seen for some time, hearing their news, listening to their troubles. In that line, Flavia Wisebite herself was enough for one day. She had also in some way infected me with her own sense of disorientation. I required to recover. The idea suggested itself to slip away from the reception for a few minutes, find release in wandering through the corridors and galleries of the Castle. After all, that was really why I had come here. There was the dining-room, for example, draped with the tapestries of the Seven Deadly Sins, the little library or study, drawings and small oils between bookshelves, where Barnby's portrait of the waitress from Casanova's Chinese Restaurant had hung. A side door seemed the most convenient exit from the party. Rupert Akworth, the bride's uncle, who had given her away, saw me about to leave.

'The gents? Down the stairs on the left. Rather classy.'

'Thanks.'

The Stourwater passages had by now acquired the smell common to all schools: furniture polish: disinfectant: fumes of unambitious cooking. I found the little library—now a schoolroom hung with maps—which Sir Magnus had entered with such dramatic effect that he seemed to have been watching for his guests' arrival through a peephole in the far door (concealed with dummy books), the night we had come over with the Morelands to dinner at the Castle. One of the pictures in this room had been another Barnby, an oil sketch of the model Conchita, described by Moreland as 'antithesis of the pavement artist's traditional representation of a loaf of bread, captioned *Easy to Draw but Hard to Get.*'

After striking one or two false trails, I came at last to the dining-room of the Seven Deadly Sins. Rows of tables indicated that its function remained unchanged, though the Sins no longer exemplified their graphic warning to those who ate there. The fine chimneypiece, decorated with nymphs and satyrs—no doubt installed by Sir Magnus to harmonize with the tapestries—had been allowed to remain as adjunct to school meals. Above this hung a large reproduction of an Annigoni portrait of the Queen. Here, scene of the luncheon where I had first met Jean Templer after her marriage to Duport; later, of the great impersonation of the Sins themselves, recorded in the photographs shown by

Matilda, were more pungent memories. I stood for a moment by the door, reconstructing some of these past incidents in the mind. While I was doing so, a man and a girl entered the dining-room from the far end. They were holding hands. Without abandoning this clasp, they advanced up the room. If wedding guests, like quite a few others present at the reception, neither had dressed up much for the occasion.

'Hullo, Fiona—hullo, Russell.'

Gwinnett offered the hand that was not holding Fiona's.

'Hullo, Nicholas.'

'Congratulations.'

'You've heard.'

'Yes.'

Gwinnett gave one of his rare smiles. I kissed Fiona, who accepted with good grace this tribute to her marriage. She, too, looked pleased. Her dress still swept the ground—as on the crayfishing afternoon, the last time I had actually set eyes on her—but her breast no longer bore the legend HARMONY. In her disengaged hand she carried a large straw hat trimmed with multicoloured flowers. A considerable cleaning up, positive remodelling, had taken place in Fiona's general style. No doubt much of that was owed to Delavacquerie. Gwinnett had surmounted the sober suit of the Magnus Donners dinner with a thin strip of bow tie. His head seemed to have been newly shaved.

'Have you both just arrived?'

'A side door outside was open. We thought we might look around before meeting the family. Is the Castle thirteenth or early fourteenth-century? I'd say that was the date. The machicolations might be later. What's its history?'

Gwinnett had shown architectural interests in Venice.

'Not much history, I think. Sir Magnus Donners, who owned it, had some story about a mediaeval lord of Stourwater, whose daughter drowned herself in the moat for love of a monk.'

Halfway through the sentence I saw that tradition was one preferably to have remained unrepeated in the circumstances. Sir Magnus had narrated the tale to Prince Theodoric the day the Walpole-Wilsons had taken me to luncheon here. I added quickly that the room we were in had once contained some remarkable tapestries depicting the Seven Deadly Sins. That seemed scarcely an improvement as a topic. Fiona may have felt the same, as she enquired about the wedding.

'How did Sebastian stand up to it?'

'Very well. Let's return to them, and drink some champagne.'

Fiona looked questioningly at Gwinnett, as she used to look at Murtlock for a decision; perhaps had so looked at Delavacquerie, before relinquishing him.

'Do you want to see them all yet?'

'Whatever you say.'

I supposed they would prefer to remain alone together.

'I'm going to continue my exploration of the Castle for a short time, then I'll see you later at the reception.'

Fiona did not seem anxious to face her relations yet.

'We'll come with you. You can show us round. I'd like to see a bit more of it. Wouldn't you, Rus?'

'I don't know the place at all well. I was here absolutely years ago, and only went into a few rooms then.'

'Never mind.'

The three of us set off together.

'I'm glad I wasn't at school here.'

Stourwater was one of the educational establishments Fiona had never sampled. The new rôle of young married woman seemed to come with complete ease to her. There could be no doubt that she liked exceptional types. Gwinnett's attraction to Fiona was less easy to classify. A faint train of thought was perceptible so far as Pamela Widmerpool was concerned, though Fiona had neither Pamela's looks, nor force of character. The impact of Pamela might even have jolted Gwinnett into an entirely different emotional channel, his former inhibitions cured once and for all. That was not impossible.

'Sir Magnus Donners once took some of his guests down to the so-called dungeons, but I'm not sure I can find them.'

Gwinnett pricked up his ears.

'The dungeons? Let's see them. I'd like to look over the dungeons.'

Fiona agreed.

'Me, too. Do have a try to find them.'

They did not cease to hold hands, while several rooms and passages were traversed. Structural alterations had taken place in the course of adapting the Castle to the needs of a school. The head of the staircase leading to these lower regions, where the alleged dungeons were on view—knowledgable people said they were merely storerooms—could not be found. Several doors were locked. Then a low door, a postern, brought us out into a small courtyard, a side of the Castle unenclosed by moat. Here school outbuildings had been added. Beyond this open space lay playing fields, a wooden pavilion, some seats. Further off were the trees of the park. Gwinnett surveyed the courtyard.

'This near building might have been a brewhouse. The brickwork looks Tudor.'

Fiona turned towards the fields.

'At least I'll never have to play hockey again.'

'Did you hate games?'

'I used to long to die, playing hockey on winter afternoons.'

Gwinnett gave up examining the supposed brewhouse. We moved towards the open.

'In the ball-courts of the Aztecs a game was played of which scarcely anything is known, except that the captain of the winning side is believed to have been made a human sacrifice.'

Gwinnett said that rather pedantically.

'The rule would certainly add to the excitement of a cup-tie or test match.'

'Another feature was that, when a goal was scored—a very rare event—all the clothes and jewellery of the spectators were forfeit to the players.'

'Less good. An incitement to rowdyism.'

'I think they both sound excellent rules,' said Fiona. 'Nothing I'd have liked better than to execute the captain, and I never watched any games, if I could help it, so they wouldn't have got my gear.'

Gwinnett would have liked to remain serious, but gave way to her mood. Marriage seemed already to have loosened up both of them. Further discussion of Aztec sport was brought to an end by something happening on the far side of the hockey-field, which distracted attention. Beyond the field a path led through the park. Along this path, some way off, a party of persons was slowly running. They might well have been the Aztec team, doubling up to play a sacrificial contest. There were about a dozen of them approaching, mostly dressed in blue, trotting in a leisurely way, knees high, across the park. Fiona, naturally enough, grasped at once the identity of this straggling body. I don't know how soon Gwinnett also took that in. Probably at once too. The strange thing was that, before comprehending the meaning of what was taking place, I thought for a second of childhood, of Dr Trelawney and his young disciples.

'Look! Look!'

Fiona was displaying great excitement. By that time I, too, had understood the scene.

'It's them all right.'

Fiona tried to discern something.

'Is *he* there?'

She spoke with a certain apprehension. Obviously she meant Murtlock. No one answered her. Gwinnett seemed interested. He watched the runners. Fiona examined them intently too.

'No—he's not there. I'm sure he's not there. But I can see Barnabas.'

There were at least a dozen of them, perhaps more. Not all wore the robes or tunic of the cult, some almost in rags. Both sexes were represented, the average age appeared to be early twenties. The only two older persons were much older. One of them, Widmerpool, was leading the pack. He wore the blue robe. The other elderly man lacked a robe. Dressed in a red sweater and trousers, greybearded, dishevelled, incredibly filthy in appearance even from far-off, this one was by a long way the last of the runners. Fiona was thrilled.

'He's not there. Let's talk to them. Let's talk to Barnabas.'

'OK.'

Gwinnett said that quite warmly, as if he too would enjoy the encounter.

'You don't mind?'

'Not at all.'

She turned towards the runners, and shouted.

'Barnabas! Barnabas!'

At the sound of Fiona's voice, the pace set by Widmerpool became even more sluggish, some of the party slowing up to the extent of not running at all. These last stood staring in our direction, as if we, rather than they, were the odd figures on the landscape. That may well have seemed so to them. Fiona cried out again.

'Come and talk to us, Barnabas.'

Widmerpool was the last to stop running. He had to walk back some little way to where the rest had drawn up. He was evidently in charge. If the run were to be interrupted, he might have been supposed the correct individual to be hailed by Fiona. I was not sure what her attitude towards him had been when herself a member of the cult. No doubt he was a figure to be taken very much into account, but, if only from his age, having no such grip as Murtlock on her imagination. It was unlikely she would ever have made our presence known had Murtlock been sighted among the runners. Now, behaving like a girl seeing old schoolfriends again, some of the pleasure coming from their being still at a school from which she had herself escaped, Fiona began to walk across the field to meet them. Gwinnett followed. It was not clear whether he was indifferent to the reunion, wanting only to humour his bride, or still felt curiosity as what this encounter might bring forth. The runners, Henderson foremost among them, strayed across the grass towards us, the elderly man with the tangled beard remaining well to the rear.

'How are you, Barnabas?'

Henderson looked as if a far more ascetic life had been imposed on him since crayfishing days. His face was pale and thinner. He had removed the moustache, and taken to wire spectacles. The sight of Fiona greatly cheered him. She began to explain what was happening at Stourwater.

'Sebastian's wedding reception is going on here this afternoon. Chuck told me he was going to come to it. Chuck knows Clare Akworth.'

I did not grasp the significance of that, nor hear Henderson's answer. The sight of Widmerpool at close quarters absorbed all my attention. Although I knew he had by now been more or less entangled with the cult for the best part of two years, was accustomed to take part in its esoteric rites, in all respects identified himself with this new mode of life—as The Devil's Fingers showed—the spectacle of him wearing a blue robe was nevertheless a startling one. Flavia Wisebite had been justified in the account she had given, so far as that went. The image immediately brought to mind was one not thought of for years; the picture, reproduced in colour, that used to hang in the flat Widmerpool shared with his mother in his early London days. It had been called *The Omnipresent*. Three blue-robed figures respectively knelt, stood with bowed head, gazed heavenward with extended hands, all poised on the brink of a precipice. It was a long time ago. I may have remembered the scene incorrectly. Nevertheless it was these figures Widmerpool conjured up, as he advanced towards me.

'Nicholas?'

When he spoke, within a second, that impression was altered. What had momentarily given him something never achieved before, a kind of suitability, almost dignity, dwindled to no more than a man gone into the garden wearing a blue dressing-gown. It was largely the clothes that had outraged Flavia Wisebite, but, in the end, it was not this kind of bathrobe that made the strong impression —any more than with Murtlock—it was the man himself. Widmerpool looked ill, desperate, worn out. The extreme debility of his appearance brought one up short. The low neckband of the garment he wore revealed a scar that ran from somewhere below the neck to the upper part of one cheek; possibly the gash inflicted on the night of The Devil's Fingers ceremony. In this physical state it was surprising that he was able to run at all, even at the slow pace he himself had been setting. No doubt the determination always shown to go through with anything he took up, carry on to the furthest limit of his capacity, was as painfully exercised in the activities to which he had latterly given himself, as in any undertakings of earlier life.

'Hullo.'

His manner was as changed as his costume. He sounded altogether bemused. He stood there limply, haunted in expression, glancing from time to time at Fiona and Gwinnett, though not speaking to either. So far as could be seen, Fiona was introducing her husband to these former

213

associates; Henderson, the young ones, all crowding round.
There was a hum of chatter. The filthy grey-beard hung
about in the background. Widmerpool seemed to make an
effort to pull himself together.

'Why are you wearing a tailcoat?'

'A wedding is taking place. I'm one of the guests.'

'A wedding's taking place in Stourwater?'

'Yes.'

'But—but the Chief's dead, isn't he?'

Sir Magnus Donners, in days when Widmerpool worked
for him, had always been referred to by subordinates as
the Chief. Widmerpool put the question in an uncertain
puzzled voice that seemed to indicate loss of memory more
damaging than reasonably to be associated with a man of
his age.

'He died some little while ago—close on twenty years.'

'Of course he did, of course. Extraordinary that I should
have doubted for a moment that the Chief had passed over.
A mistaken term escaped me too. I shall do penance for
that. At our age transmutations take place all the time. Yes,
yes.'

Widmerpool gazed round again. Perhaps more to steady
himself than because he had not already recognized Gwinnett, he suddenly held up a hand in Murtlock's benedic-
tional manner.

'It is Professor Gwinnett—to use an absurd prefix?'

'It is, Lord Widmerpool.'

Gwinnett smiled faintly, without the least friendliness.
That was hardly surprising in the circumstances.

'Not Lord, not Lord—Ken, Ken.'

Gwinnett withdrew his smile.

'You came to see us about a year ago?'

'Yes.'

Fiona turned from the group with which she had been
talking. Perhaps she wanted to impress on Widmerpool her

ownership of Gwinnett; anyway now absolute separation from the cult, whatever her taste for still hobnobbing with its members.

'Russell and I have have just got married, Ken.'

'Married?'

The way Widmerpool spoke the word was hard to define. It might have been horror; it might, on the other hand, have aroused in his mind some infinitely complicated chain of ideas as to what Fiona meant by using such a term. Fiona may also have wished to shock by stating that she had taken so conventional a step. Acceptance of the fact that she gave the word its normal face value seemed to sink into Widmerpool's head only slowly. Not unnaturally, in the light of what he had just been told about a wedding taking place in the Castle, he mistook the implications.

'You've just been married at Stourwater, Fiona?'

He looked more astounded than ever. Fiona laughed derisively. I think she intended to make fun of him, now that she was free from any possible reprisals. Even Gwinnett smiled at the question.

'No, it's my brother's wedding.'

Taking Gwinnett's arm, Fiona turned back to her younger acquaintances. Widmerpool reverted to the subject of Sir Magnus Donners. It seemed to trouble him.

'Extraordinary I should not only have forgotten about Donners, but used that erroneous formula, there being no death, only transition, blending, synthesis, mutation—just as there are no marriages, except mystic marriages. Marriages that transcend the boundaries of awareness, the unmanifest solutions of Harmony, galvanized by meditation and appropriate rites, the source of all Power—rather than the lethal manufacture of tensions as constructed in these very surroundings today.'

Widmerpool's observations on such matters were suddenly interrupted by a burst of singing. The notes, thin and quavering, possessed something of Flavia Wisebite's conversational tones, mysteriously transmuted to music, weird, eerie, not at all unpleasant all the same. They came from the other elderly man, the bearded one, who had still moved no nearer to join the rest of the group.

> 'Open now the crystal fountain,
> Whence the healing stream doth flow:
> Let the fire and cloudy pillar
> Lead me all my journey through.'

Widmerpool started violently. It was as if someone had touched him with a red-hot iron. Then he recovered himself, was about to go on talking.

'Who is that singing?'

'Take no notice. He's all right, if left alone. He finds Harmony in singing that sort of thing.'

The bearded man stood a little way apart, hands clasped, eyes uplifted. He had hardly more hair on his head than Gwinnett. Something about the singing suggested he had absolutely no teeth. It crossed my mind that the old red high-necked sweater he wore, over torn corduroy trousers, might have been passed on by Widmerpool himself. The beard was matted and grubby, his feet bare and horrible. Entirely self-occupied, he took no notice at all of what was otherwise going on. What he chose to sing altogether distracted my attention from Widmerpool's discourse on death and marriage. The strains brought back the early days of the war. It was the hymn my Regiment used to sing on the line of march. The chant seemed to disturb Widmerpool, irritate, upset him. His expression became more agonized than ever.

'Don't you remember the men singing that on route marches?'

'Singing what?'

Widmerpool, himself on the staff of the Division of which my Battalion had been one of the units, might not have heard the motif so often as I, but the tune could hardly have passed entirely unnoticed, even by someone so uninterested in human behaviour.

'Who is he?'

'One of us.'

Widmerpool had to be pressed for an answer. He was prepared to agree that I might have heard the verse sung before.

'True, true. He's a man I apparently ran across in the army. Somebody brought him along to us. He'd been a dropout for years—before people knew about an alternative lifestyle—and was at the end of his tether. We thought he was going to pass over. When he got better, Scorp took a fancy to him. At the time he came to us, I didn't remember seeing him before. Didn't recognize him at all. Then one day Bith brought it all up himself.'

'Bith?'

'He's named Bithel. I seem to have known him in the army. Through no fault of my own, it seems I had something to do with his leaving the army. Many people would have been grateful for that. Scorp likes Bith. Thinks he contributes to Harmony. I expect he does. Scorp is usually right about that sort of thing.'

Widmerpool sighed.

'But I know Bithel too. I knew all about him in those days. He commanded the Mobile Laundry. Don't you remember?'

Widmerpool looked blank. While he had been speaking these words, his thoughts were evidently far away. He was almost talking to himself. If he had forgotten about the death of Sir Magnus Donners, he could well have forgotten about Bithel; even the fact that he and I had soldiered together. In any case the matter did not interest him so far as Bithel was concerned. He was evidently thinking of himself, overcome now with self-pity.

'When Scorp found out that I'd had to tell Bith he must leave the army—leave the Mobile Laundry, you say—Scorp made me do penance. What happened had been duty—what I then quite wrongly thought duty to be—and wasn't at all my fault. I must have been told by those above me that I'd got to tell Bith he had to go. I tried to explain that to Scorp. He said—he'd got the story from Bith, of course—that I acted without Harmony, and must make amends, mystical amends. He was right, of course. Scorp made me ... made me ...'

Widmerpool's voice trailed away. He shuddered violently, at the same time swallowing several times. His eyes filled with tears. Whatever Murtlock had made him do as penance for relieving Bithel of his commission was too horrific to be spoken aloud by Widmerpool himself, even though he had brought the matter up, still brooded on it. I was decidedly glad not to be told. One's capacity for hearing about ghastly doings lessens with age. At least this showed that Murtlock had taken over complete command. Even thinking about the retribution visited on him had brought Widmerpool to near collapse. In fact he looked much as he had described Bithel, when—not at all unjustly so far as the actual sentence went—the alternatives of court martial, or acceptance of a report declaring Bithel unsuitable for retention as an officer were put before him. This was the incident to which Greening had referred. It may well have been true —as Greening had said—that Widmerpool had talked in a callous manner later in the Mess about Bithel breaking down. Certainly he had spoken of it to me.

'Bithel's one of your community?'

'For a year or more now.'

Again Widmerpool answered as if his thoughts were elsewhere. Bithel continued to stand apart, smiling and muttering to himself, apparently quite happy. His demeanour was not unlike what it had been in the army after he had drunk a good deal. Fiona left the group with which she had been talking, and came up to Widmerpool.

'Look, Ken, I want you all to look in on my brother's wedding party for a minute or two. Barnabas's old boyfriend, Chuck, is there, and rows of people Barnabas knows. You must come. Just for a moment. Scorp always said that Harmony, in one form, was to be widely known.'

It looked very much as if marriage had caused Fiona to revert, from the gloom of recent years, to the more carefree style of her rampageous schoolgirl stage. Widmerpool made an attempt to avoid the question by taking a general line of disapproval.

'You went away, Fiona. You left us. You abandoned Harmony.'

The others, uneasy perhaps, but certainly tempted, now began to crowd round. Fiona continued her efforts to persuade Widmerpool, who was plainly uncertain how the suggestion should be correctly handled. It seemed to daze him. Possibly he was not without all curiosity to enter Stourwater again himself. Bithel began to sing once more.

'From every dark nook they press forward to meet me,
I lift up my eyes to the tall leafy dome.
And others are there looking downward to greet me,
The ashgrove, the ashgrove, alone is my home.'

At this, Fiona abandoned Widmerpool, and made for Bithel. Bithel seemed all at once to recognize her for the first time. He held his arms above his head. Fiona said something to him, then taking his hand, led him towards the rest of the group.

'Come along all of you. Bith's coming, if no one else is.'

Widmerpool's powers of decision were finally put out of

action by the inclusion of Bithel in an already apparently insoluble situation. It could well be that one of his responsibilities was to keep an eye on Bithel, probably easy enough out on a run, quite another matter in what was now promised. He made a final effort to impose discipline.

'Remember, no drink.'

'All right,' said Fiona. 'How do we find our way?'

The last question was addressed to myself. It was a disconcerting one. I was not particularly anxious to take on the responsibility of leading this mob into the wedding reception. If Fiona wanted to present them all to her brother and his bride that was her own affair. She must do it herself. Apart from other considerations, such as uncertainty how they would behave, was the very real possibility that I might not be able to find the way back to the Great Hall by the path we came. Some of them might easily get left behind in the Stourwater corridors. This last probability suggested an alternative route to the reception.

'The easiest would be to walk round to the front of the Castle. You follow the banks of the moat, then cross the causeway, and straight ahead.'

Fiona looked uncertain for a moment. Gwinnett, either because he saw the tactical advantages of such an approach, or simply speaking his own wish, gave support to this direction.

'I'd like to do that. We haven't seen the double-portcullised gateway yet.'

Fiona concurred. Her chief desire seemed to be to transfer her former friends of the cult to the party the quickest possible way. This was no doubt intended as a double-edged tease; on the one hand, aimed at her relations; on the other, at Murtlock. That was how things looked.

'All right. This way. Come along, Bith.'

They set off; Fiona, Gwinnett, Henderson, Bithel, all in the first wave. Widmerpool lagged behind. He had been taken by surprise, unable to make up his mind, incapable of a plan. If I did not wish to appear at the head of the column, there was no alternative to walking with him. This also solved for the moment the question of Bithel; whether or not to draw his attention to our former acquaintance. We strolled along side by side, Widmerpool now apparently resigned to looking in on the reception. It could be true, as Fiona had hinted, that Murtlock encouraged his people to show themselves, from time to time, in unlikely places. This might not be Widmerpool's main worry so much as Bithel. Widmerpool's own words now gave some confirmation to that. He was still speaking more or less to himself.

'I daresay it's all right if we don't stay too long. People can see Harmony in action. Bith, in my opinion, has never achieved much Harmony—still slips away and drinks, when he can lay hands on any money—and I must be sure to keep an eye on him where we're going. The others are all right. One glass doesn't matter for Bith—Scorp recognizes that. He says it won't necessarily make bad vibrations in Bith's individual validation. He's a special case. Scorp thinks a lot of Bith. Says he has remarkable mystic powers inherent in him. Still, I mustn't let him out of my sight. I'm in charge of today's mystical exercises, and Scorp will hold me responsible. Who are the couple going through these meaningless formulas today?'

Widmerpool asked the last question in a more coherent tone.

'Fiona's brother, Sebastian Cutts, and a girl called Clare Akworth.'

Widmerpool winced, much as he had done when Bithel had first begun to sing.

'Akworth?'

'Akworth.'

He began to stammer.

'Like ... like ...'

He did not finish the question. His face went the dull red colour its skin sometimes took on under stress. I knew, of course, what he meant. At least I thought I knew. As it turned out, I knew less than I supposed. In any case there was no point in pretending ignorance of the essence of the enquiry. The obvious assumption was that, even after half a century, Widmerpool was unwilling to be confronted with Akworth, if there were any danger of such a thing. This was only the second occasion, so far as I could remember, when the Akworth matter had ever cropped up between us. The first had been when we had not long left school, and were both learning French with the Leroy family at La Grenadière.

'The name is spelt like the boy who was at school with us. In fact the bride is that Akworth's granddaughter.'

'Granddaughter of Bertram Akworth?'

'Yes.'

'Is he still—still on this side?'

'Who?'

'Bertram Akworth.'

'If you mean is he still alive, he's actually at the wedding. He read the Lesson in church.'

'He's—at Stourwater?'

'If you're coming to the reception you'll see him.'

Widmerpool stopped abruptly. I had hoped for that. It looked as if he might now decide not to enter the Castle at all. His absence would make one less potentially unwelcome addition to the wedding party; in fact remove what was probably the least assimilable factor. The young people were likely to mix easily enough with their own contemporaries. At worst Bithel would pass out. He could be put in the cloakroom, until time came to take him away. That sort of thing should easily be dealt with on premises as large as Stourwater. Widmerpool was another matter. Not only would his appearance in a blue robe attract—owing to his age—undue attention, but his nervous condition might assume some inconvenient form. With any luck, now he knew Akworth would be present, he would make for home right away. Instead of doing so Widmerpool began to babble disconnectedly.

'I've know Bertram Akworth for years . . . years . . . We were on the board of the same bank together—until he and Farebrother got me off it, between them. Farebrother always had it in for me. So did Akworth. It was natural enough.'

It was certainly natural enough in Akworth's case; even if surprising that Widmerpool recognized the fact. A moment's thought ought to have made it obvious that Widmerpool and Sir Bertram Akworth were certain to encounter each other in the City. It seemed to have been more than occasional acquaintance, indeed looking as if they had been engaged in a running fight all their lives. This prolonged duel added to the drama of the original story. If I had known about it, I should have been more than ever convinced that this cross-questioning on Widmerpool's part was aimed at avoiding a meeting with his schoolboy victim and commercial rival. That was a dire misjudgment. On the contrary, Widmerpool was filled with an inspired fervour, carried away with delighted agitation, at the prospect of a face-to-face confrontation.

'Bertram Akworth will be there? He will actually be present? It can't be true. This is an opportunity I have been longing for. I behaved to Akworth in a way I now know to be not wrong—so-called right and wrong being illusory concepts—but what must be deplored as transcendentally discordant, mystically in error, in short, contrary to Harmony. In those days I was only a boy—a simple boy at that—who knew nothing of such experiences as cohabiting with the Elements, as a means of training the will. Moreover, I should have encouraged any breaking of the rules, struck a blow for, rather than against, rebellion, aided the subversion of that detestable thing law and order, as commonly understood. In those days—my schoolboy years —I had already dedicated myself to so-called reason, so-called practical affairs. I allowed no—at least very little— unfettered play of those animal forces that free the spirit, though later I began to understand the way, for example, that nakedness removes impediments of all sorts. Besides, if the universe is to be subjected to his will, a man must develop his female nature as well as the male—without lessening his own masculinity—I knew nothing of that...but Akworth...long misunderstood...should make amends ...as with Bith...though not...not...'

Again Widmerpool tailed off, unable to bring himself to mention whatever Murtlock had made him act out in relation to the Bithel penance. What he said about Sir Bertram Akworth was most disturbing. A far more threatening situation than before had now suddenly come into being. It was one thing for Fiona, the bridegroom's sister, to bring into her brother's wedding party a crowd of young persons, curious specimens perhaps, but, not long before, closely associated with herself. It was quite another to allow the occasion to be one for Widmerpool to give rein to an ambition—apparently become obsessive with him—that he should make some sort of an apology to a lifelong business antagonist, grandfather of the bride, the boy he had caused to be sacked from school half a century earlier. In his present mood Widmerpool was capable of exploring in public, in much the same manner that he had been expatiating on them to me, all the mystical implications of Sir Bertram Akworth's youthful desires.

'If the matter of reporting Akworth has never come up in the years you've been meeting him, doesn't it seem wiser to leave things at that now? It might even be preferable not to go to the reception?'

Widmerpool was not listening.

'Amazing how long it took me to understand the ritual

side of sex. Although I never enjoyed sex much myself, I'd always supposed you were meant to enjoy it. Now I know better. I see now that, even when I was young, I was reaching out for the ritual side, to the exclusion of enjoyment. In objecting to Akworth's conduct, I was displaying an attitude I later took up in my own mind in relation to Donners and his irregular practices. He, too, may have had his own instinctive reactions in the same field. In those days I knew nothing of the Dionysiac necessities. They were revealed to me all but too late. If Donners was aware of such needs earlier than myself, he fell altogether short in combining them with transcendental meditation, or mystical exercises of a physical kind, other than sexual.'

Widmerpool, absorbed with the case of Sir Magnus, shook his head. By this time we were crossing the causeway, about to pass under the portcullised gate, through which Fiona's vanguard had already disappeared. Either to catch up with the rest of his company, or from impatience to make contact with Sir Bertram Akworth, Widmerpool pressed forward. This urgency on his part impelled his own entry into the Great Hall well ahead of myself, something I was anxious to manoeuvre, but had seen no way of bringing about. Widmerpool was lost in the crowd by the time I came through the doorway. Caroline Lovell—a niece of ours, married to a soldier called Thwaites—was standing just by. She began some sort of conversation before it was possible to estimate the effect of Fiona's additions to the party. We talked for a minute or two.

'Is Alan here?'

Caroline said her husband, having just been posted to Northern Ireland, had been unable to come to the wedding. She looked worried, but was prevented from saying more of this by Jonathan Cutts, who joined us, and began to speak of the Sleaford Veronese—as it once had been—a favourite subject of Caroline's father, Chips Lovell. The *Iphigenia* had come on the market again, handled by Jonathan's firm, and achieved a record price. Neither Jonathan Cutts nor Caroline seemed to have noticed the incursion of Fiona's friends from the cult; confirming the impression that, once within the lofty dimly lit limits of the Great Hall, they had quickly merged with other less than conventionally clad guests. Certainly there was no clearcut isolation of the group. For a second I caught a glimpse of Bithel; a moment later he disappeared. He had been surrounded by a circle of laughing young men. By this time a fair amount of champagne had been drunk. Widmerpool was nowhere to be seen. No doubt he was searching for Sir Bertram Akworth, but Sir Bertram, too, had disappeared for the moment. I asked Caroline where he had gone.

'There was a hitch about the car to take Sebastian and Clare to the airport. Sir Bertram's making some new arrangement, somebody said.'

Flavia Wisebite appeared again at my elbow.

'Have you seen who's just come in?'

'Do you mean Fiona Cutts and her former crowd?'

'Widmerpool.'

She was overcome with indignation, her face dead white.

'The dreadful man is wandering about the room in his loathsome clothes. What could have made them invite him? Young people will do anything these days. I'm sure it wasn't Clare's choice. She's such a sweet girl. Sebastian seemed a nice young man too. Surely he can't have asked Widmerpool? Do you think his father—who used to be an MP—had to have Widmerpool for political reasons. That's a possibility.'

'Widmerpool and his lot were brought in by Fiona Cutts, Sebastian's sister.'

'Fiona brought them? I see. Now I understand. Do you know who Fiona Cutts has just married—who my goddaughter, little Clare, is going to have for a brother-in-law?

An American called Gwinnett. I don't expect you've even heard of him. I have. I know a great deal about Mr Gwinnett. It's all too dreadful to say. Dreadful. Dreadful.'

Gwinnett, in sight on the far side of the room, was talking in a comparatively animated manner to his new in-laws. Behind them, in a corner, Jeremy Warminster had made contact with one of the prettier girls of the cult, whether or not for the first time was hard to judge. The two of them seemed already on easy terms with each other. A husband and wife, introduced as Colonel and Mrs Alford-Green, came up to speak with Flavia Wisebite. Their friendship seemed to date back to very ancient days, when Flavia had still been married to Cosmo Flitton. Colonel Alford-Green was evidently a retired regular soldier. While they were talking Sir Bertram Akworth reappeared. Hailing the Alford-Greens in his loud harsh voice, he greeted Flavia, too, as one already well known to him.

'How are you, Rosamund, how are you, Gerald? How nice to see old friends like you both, and Flavia here today. The honeymoon car broke down. All is now fixed. I've seen to it. No cause for panic.'

'We thought you read the Lesson very well, Bertram.'

'You did, Rosamund? Thank you very much. I'm glad you thought I did it all right. You know I rather pride myself on my reading. It's a beautiful passage. A great favourite of mine. It was the one on the agenda anyway. A bit of luck. I was very glad. If I'd been asked, I'd certainly have chosen it.'

'When are you coming up to our part of the world again, Bertram?'

'I hope I shall one of these days. I very much hope I shall. You know how hard it is to get away. Is Reggie still joint-master?'

The question prompted a rather complicated account of some quarrel in which the local hunt had been involved for a long time. I was about to move away, when I became aware that Widmerpool was near by. In fact he was very close. He must have been wandering about in the crowd, looking for Sir Bertram. Now at last he had run him to ground. Sir Bertram had not yet seen him. He was much too engrossed with the foxhunting feuds of the Alford-Greens. Widmerpool began muttering to himself. Suddenly he spoke out.

'Bertram.'

Use of the christian name somehow surprised me; though obviously, if the two of them had come across each other as often as Widmerpool indicated, they would be on those sort of terms, however great their mutual dislike.

'Bertram.'

Widmerpool repeated the name. He spoke quite quietly, in an almost beseeching voice. Sir Bertram either did not hear the first appeal, or, more probably, decided that, whoever it was, he wanted to hear the end of the Alford-Greens' story, which treated of one of those rows between foxhunting people, which have a peculiar intensity of virulence. At the second summons, Sir Bertram turned. Plainly not recognizing an old business adversary under the blue robe Widmerpool wore, he did not seem more than a trifle taken aback at what might quite reasonably have been regarded as an extraordinary spectacle of humanity. His face merely assumed an expression of rather self-consciously wry amusement; the tolerant good humour of a man of the world, who is prepared for anything in the circumstances of the moment in which he finds himself; in this case, unexpected guests invited by his granddaughter to her wedding.

Without making excessive claims for Sir Bertram's imperturbability, or good humour, one could see that it took more than an excited elderly man, not too clean and wearing a blue robe, socially to discompose him these days. Sir Bertram had not reached the position he had in his own world without achieving a smattering of what was afoot in an essentially disparate one. This particular instance happened to be considerably more than a sharp contrast, to be neutralized by tactful ingenuity, with his own way of life. In short, Sir Bertram Akworth became suddenly aware that he was contemplating Widmerpool. No doubt he had already heard rumours of Widmerpool's changed ways—probably associated in his mind more with treasonable contacts and equivocal financial dealings—but, a man not given to imaginative reconstructions, Sir Bertram was not altogether prepared for the reality now set before him. Enlightenment caused a series of violent emotions—deep hatred the most definable—to pass swiftly across his sallow cadaverous features; reactions gone in a split second, recovery all but instantaneous.

'Kenneth, what are you up to?'

Sir Bertram spoke calmly. There was no time for him to say more. Instead of answering an undoubtedly rhetorical question—even if some sort of explanation were required, conventionally speaking, for thus arriving unasked at a party—Widmerpool, in terms of ritual of another kind, went straight to the point; if repentance were to be expressed in physical form. While Sir Bertram Akworth stood, eyebrows slightly raised, a rather fixed expression of humorous enquiry imposed on his features, like that of a reasonably talented amateur actor, Widmerpool, without the slightest warning, knelt before him; then bent forward, lowering his face almost to the parquet.

This description of what Widmerpool did suggests, in fact, something much more immediate, more outwardly astounding, than the act seemed at the time. I should myself have been completely at a loss to know what Widmerpool was at, if he had not expressed only a short time before his intention of making some sort of an apology about what had happened at school. Even so, when Widmerpool went down on all fours in utter self-abasement, I supposed at first that he was searching for something he had dropped on the floor. That was almost certainly the explanation that offered itself to those standing round about who witnessed the scene at close quarters. Of these last no one, so far as I knew, had ever heard of the incident from which the action stemmed. Even had they been familiar with it, the complexity of Widmerpool's declared attitude towards social revolt, ritual sex, mystical repentance, was likely to be lost on them, as it was lost, collectively and separately, on Sir Bertram Akworth himself.

If quite other events had not at that moment intervened, Widmerpool's innate perseverance, his unsnubbableness, might at last have made his motives clear to the object of this melodramatic self-condemnation. As things fell out, two happenings diminished the force of the act—in any case for the moment generally misunderstood—to almost nothing, altogether removing possibility of its meaning being driven home. The first of these interpolations, not more than a matter of routine, was the reappearance of bride and bridegroom, who had retired a short time before to put on their going-away clothes. This entry naturally caused a stir among the guests, distracting the attention of those even in the immediate Widmerpool area of the Great Hall. The second occurrence, individual, distressing, even more calculated in its own way to cause concentration on itself, was prefigured by a sort of low gasp from Flavia Wisebite.

'Oh . . . Oh . . .'

She must have moved up quite close to Widmerpool, possibly with the object of making some sort of a contact, in order to express in her own words, personally, the detestation she felt for himself and all his works. If that were the end she had in view, Widmerpool's own unexpected obeisance to Sir Bertram Akworth had taken her completely by surprise. It seemed later that, when Widmerpool went down on his knees, Flavia Wisebite, brought up short in her advance, had fallen almost on top of his crouching body. This caused considerable localized commotion among guests in that part of the room; by this time beginning to empty in preparation for seeing off the newly married pair. Sir Bertram Akworth and Colonel Alford-Green, who were the nearest to the place of her collapse, with help from several others, managed to get Flavia to one of the forms by the wall. Finally, at the suggestion of Sir Bertram, she was borne away to the school's sickroom. Perhaps someone lifted Widmerpool from the floor too. When I next looked in that direction he was gone. Isobel came up.

'Are we going out to see them off? Did somebody faint near where you were standing?'

'Widmerpool's mother-in-law.'

'What do you mean?'

'Flavia Wisebite.'

'Is she here?'

'Her son-in-law is a subject she feels strongly about.'

Outside, farewells were taking place round the bridal car. Whatever the mishap, the vehicle had been repaired or replaced. Sir Bertram Akworth came across the causeway. He looked rather flustered. Somebody asked about Flavia Wisebite.

'Not at all well, I'm afraid.'

'Where is she?'

'Being looked after by the school's skeleton staff. We've rung for a doctor.'

Absurdly, the phrase made me think of the opening inscription of *Death's-head Swordsman*, conjured up a picture of the dead ministering to the dead, which would have appealed to Gwinnett. He and Fiona, once more hand in hand, moved away now that the car had driven off, crossing the drive to continue their examination of the exterior features of the Castle. Having gone to some trouble to bring her former associates to the wedding reception, Fiona seemed now to have lost interest in them. As usual, bride and bridegroom departed, there was a certain sense of anticlimax. Some of the guests continued to stand about in small groups, chatting to friends and relations; others were going off to look for their cars. The members of the cult were, most of them, standing, rather apart from the wedding guests, in a small forlorn circle, which included Widmerpool. Looking somewhat distraught, he was now at least upright, apparently haranguing his young companions; either explaining the significance of his own prostration before Sir Bertram Akworth, or merely taking the first steps in rounding up the crew, preparatory to setting out on the homeward run.

'To hell with all that.'

The voice, shrill, unconsenting, sounded like that of Barnabas Henderson. It appeared that he was arguing with Widmerpool. One of the wedding guests, a long-haired beefy young man in a grey tailcoat, was standing beside Henderson. Both these last two were in a state of some excitement. So was Widmerpool. It was at first not possible to hear what was being said, though Widmerpool was evidently speaking in an admonitory manner. The young man in the tailcoat, whose muscles were bursting from its contours, was becoming angry.

'Barnabas wants to get out. That's all about it.'

Henderson must have been asserting that intention too. Widmerpool was inaudible. His voice was more measured than theirs, possibly advised that things should be thought over before any such step be taken. Henderson almost shrieked.

'Not now I've found Chuck again. I'm going right away. Chuck will put me up at his place.'

Clearly a wrangle of some magnitude was in progress.

The big young man, who spoke in scathing cockney when addressing Widmerpool, snatched Henderson by the arm, walking him across to the side of the drive where Fiona and Gwinnett stood discussing the Castle. I felt no particular interest in the row. It was no affair of mine. Isobel, with Frederica and Norah, were chatting with Alford cousins. They would be some little time dishing up family news. I strolled towards the moat. As I did so, Widmerpool's tones sounded desperately.

'I forbid it.'

Since the days of Sir Magnus, the waterlilies had greatly increased in volume. If not eradicated, they would soon cover the whole surface of the stagnant water. On the far side, placed rather low in the wall near the main gate, was a small window, scarcely more than an arrow-slit, probably sited for observation purposes. A frantic face appeared at this opening for a moment, then was instantly withdrawn. The features could have been Bithel's. There was not time to make sure; only the upper half visible. It was just as likely I was mistaken, though Bithel was not among those standing round Widmerpool, nor, apparently, elsewhere on the drive. He might have decided to make his own way home. Some of the cult, possibly Bithel among them, were straying about in the neighbourhood of the Castle, because a blue robe was visible at some distance from where I stood. Its wearer was crossing one of the playing-fields. This was likely to be a straggler returning to the main body for the homeward journey.

Watching the approaching figure, I was reminded of a remark made by Moreland ages before. It related to one of those childhood memories we sometimes found in common. This particular recollection had referred to an incident in *The Pilgrim's Progress* that had stuck in both our minds. Moreland said that, after his aunt read the book aloud to him as a child, he could never, even after he was grown-up, watch a lone figure draw nearer across a field, without thinking this was Apollyon come to contend with him. From the moment of first hearing that passage read aloud—assisted by a lively portrayal of the fiend in an illustration, realistically depicting his goat's horns, bat's wings, lion's claws, lizard's legs—the terror of that image, bursting out from an otherwise at moments prosy narrative, had embedded itself for all time in the imagination. I, too, as a child, had been riveted by the vividness of Apollyon's advance across the quiet meadow. Now, surveying the personage in the blue robe picking his way slowly, almost delicately, over the grass of the hockey-field, I felt for some reason that, if ever the arrival of Apollyon was imminent, the moment was this one. That had nothing to do with the blue robe, such costume, as I have said before, if it made any difference to Murtlock at all, softened the edge of whatever caused his personality to be a disturbing one. Henderson must have seen Murtlock too. His high squeak became a positive shout.

'Look—he's coming!'

Fiona seemed a little frightened herself. She appeared to be giving Henderson moral support by what she was saying. For the moment, while doing that, she had relinquished Gwinnett's hand. Now she took hold of it again. Murtlock continued his slow relentless progress. As this descent upon them of their leader became known among the cult—such of them as were present on the drive—a sense of trepidation was noticeable, not least in the case of Widmerpool. Abandoning the group he appeared to have been exhorting, he crossed the drive to where Henderson was standing with Fiona and Gwinnett. Widmerpool began a muttered conversation, first with Henderson, then with Fiona.

'So much the better.'

Fiona spoke with what was evidently deliberate loudness. At the same time she turned to glance in the direction of

Murtlock. He had somewhat quickened his pace for the last lap, reaching the gravel of the drive. Small pockets of ordinary wedding guests still stood about chatting. Most of these were some distance away from the point where Murtlock would have to decide whether he made for the bulk of his followers, or for the splinter group represented by Widmerpool and Henderson. There was no special reason why the run-of-the-mill guests, having accepted the blue-robed intruders as an integral part of the wedding reception, should suppose Murtlock anything but an offshoot of the original body. Of the two groups—the one huddled together, robed or otherwise; the other, consisting of Widmerpool, Henderson, Fiona, Gwinnett, together with the beefy young man called Chuck—Murtlock made unhesitatingly for the second. He stopped a yard or two away, uttering his greeting gently, the tone not much more than a murmur, well below the pitch of everyday speech. I heard it because I had moved closer. It was possible to ignore squabbles between Widmerpool and Henderson; Murtlock had that about him to fire interest.

'The Essence of the All is the Godhead of the True.'

Only Widmerpool answered, even then very feebly.

'The Visions of Visions heals the Blindness of Sight—and, Scorp, there is—'

Murtlock, disregarding the others, held up a hand towards Widmerpool to command silence. There was a moment's pause. When Murtlock answered, it was sharply, and in an altogether unliturgical manner.

'Why are you here?'

Widmerpool faltered. There was another long pause. Murtlock spoke again.

'You do not know?'

This time Murtlock's question was delivered in an almost amused tone. Widmerpool made great effort to utter. He had gone an awful colour, almost mauve.

235

'There is an explanation, Scorp. All can be accounted for. We met Fiona. She asked us in. I saw an opportunity to take part in an active rite of penitence, a piece of ritual discipline, painful to myself, of the sort you most recommend. You will approve, Scorp. I'm sure you will approve, when I tell you about it.'

After saying that, Widmerpool began to mumble distractedly. Murtlock turned away from him. Without troubling to give further attention to whatever Widmerpool was attempting to explain, he fixed his eyes on Henderson, who began to tremble violently. Fiona let go of Gwinnett's hand. She stepped forward.

'Barnabas is leaving you. He's staying here with Chuck.'

'He is?'

'Aren't you, Barnabas?'

Henderson, still shaking perceptibly, managed to confirm that.

'I'm going back with Chuck.'

'You are, Barnabas?'

'Yes.'

'I hope you will be happier together than you were before you came to us.'

Murtlock smiled benevolently. He seemed in the best of humours. Only Widmerpool gave the impression of angering him. The defection of Henderson appeared not to worry him in the least. His reply to Fiona, too, had been in the jocular tone he had sometimes used on the crayfishing afternoon; though it was clear that Murtlock had moved a long way, in terms of power, since that period. Perhaps he had learnt something from Widmerpool, while at the same time subduing him.

'A mystical sister has been lost, and gained. You are not alone in abandoning us, Fiona. Rusty, too, has returned to Soho.'

Fiona did not answer. She looked rather angry. Her

236

general air was a shade more grown-up than formerly. Murtlock turned to Gwinnett.

'Was not the Unicorn tamed by a Virgin?'

Gwinnett did not answer either. Had he wished to do so, in itself unlikely, there was no time. At that moment Widmerpool seemed to lose all control. He came tottering forward towards Murtlock.

'Scorp, I'm leaving too. I can't stand it any longer. You and the others need not be disturbed. I'll find somewhere else to live. I won't need much of the money.'

Apparently lacking breath to continue, he stopped, standing there panting. Murtlock's demeanour underwent a complete change. He dropped altogether the sneering bantering manner he had been using intermittently. Now he was angry again; not merely angry, furious, consumed with cold rage. For a second he did not speak, while Widmerpool ran on about Harmony.

'No.'

Murtlock cut Widmerpool short. Chuck, not at all interested in the strangeness of this duel of wills, put a protective arm round Henderson. He may have thought his friend in danger of capitulating, now that Murtlock was so enraged. That passion in Murtlock was not without its own horror.

'Come on, Barnabas. No point in hanging about. Let's be getting back.'

After Henderson had spoken some sort of farewell to Fiona, he went off with Chuck towards the cars. Murtlock took no notice of this withdrawal. His attention was entirely concentrated on Widmerpool, who, avoiding the eyes Murtlock fixed on him, continued to beg for release.

'Where could you go?'

Widmerpool made a gesture to signify that was no problem, but seemed unable to think of a spoken reply.

'No.'

'Scorp...'

'No.'

Murtlock repeated the negative in a dead toneless voice. Widmerpool was unable to speak. He stood there stupefied. Murtlock came closer. This conflict—in which Widmerpool, too, was evidently showing a certain amount of passive will power—was brought to an end by the re-entry of an actor forgotten in the course of rapid movement of events. The sound of singing came from the gates of the Castle.

> 'When I tread the verge of Jordan,
> Bid my anxious fears subside,
> Death of Death and hell's destruction,
> Land me safe on Canaan's side.'

Bithel was staggering across the causeway. His voice, high, quavering, much enhanced in volume by champagne, swelled on the spring air. Some sort of echo of the hymn was briefly taken up by another chant, possibly Umfraville's —he had served with the Welsh Guards—on the far side of the drive. Murtlock, as remarked earlier, was not in the least lacking in practical grasp. At a glance he took in the implications of this new situation.

'You allowed Bith to drink?'

'I—'

'What have I always said?'

'It was—'

'Lead the others back. I will manage Bith myself.'

This time Widmerpool made no demur. He accepted defeat. An unforeseen factor had put him in the wrong. He was beaten for the moment. The rest of the cult still stood in a glum group, no doubt contemplating trouble on return to base. Widmerpool beckoned to them. There was some giving of orders. A minute or two later Widmerpool, once more at the head of the pack, was leading the run home; a trot even slower than that employed when we first sighted them. Bithel had stopped half-way across the causeway. He was leaning over the parapet, staring down at the water-lilies of the moat. The possibility that he might be sick was not to be excluded. That idea may have crossed Murtlock's practical mind too, because a slight smile flickered across his face, altering its sternness only for a moment, as he strode towards the Castle. Some words were exchanged. Then they moved off together towards the playing-fields. Bithel could walk; if not very straight. Once he fell down. Murtlock waited until Bithel managed to pick himself up again, but made no effort to help. They disappeared from sight. Fiona came over to where I was standing.

'Will you be seeing Gibson?'

'I expect so.'

'I want you to give him a message from me.'

'Of course.'

'When Russell and I first knew each other, Rus lent me his copy of Middleton's *Plays*. It's got some of his own notes pencilled in. I can't find it, and must have left it at Gibson's flat. Could you get him to send the book on—airmail it—to Russell's college? Just address it to the English Department. We're not going to have any time at all when we get back to London.'

'You're going straight to America?'

'The following day.'

'No other messages for Gibson?'

'No, just the book.'

By the time I next saw Delavacquerie he was aware that Fiona was married to Gwinnett. I don't know whether he heard directly from her, or the news just got round. She appeared to have left the flat without warning, taking her belongings with her. He smiled rather grimly when I passed on the request to send the Middleton book to Gwinnett's college.

'As a matter of fact I read some of the plays myself in

consequence—*The Roaring Girle*, which Dekker also had a hand in. I enjoyed the thieves' cant. Listen to this:

> A gage of ben rom-bouse
> In a bousing ken of Rom-vile,
> Is benar than a caster,
> Peck, pennam, lay, or popler,
> Which we mill in deuse a vile.
> O I wud lib all the lightmans,
> O I wud lib all the darkmans
> By the salomon, under the ruffmans,
> By the saloman, in the hartmans,
> And scour the queer cramp ring,
> And couch till a palliard docked my dell,
> So my bousy nab might skew rom-bouse well.
> Avast to the pad, let us bing;
> Avast to the pad, let us bing.

Not bad, is it?'

'It all sounds very contemporary. What does it mean?'

'Roughly, that a quart of good wine in London is better than anything to be stolen in the country, and, as long as wine's to be drunk, it doesn't matter if you're in the stocks, while some heel is stuffing your tart—that's a palliard docking your dell. Owing to Gwinnett, I came across a good couplet in Tourneur too:

> Lust is a spirit, which whosoe'er doth raise,
> The next man that encounters boldly, lays.

There seems a foot too many in the first line. They may have elided those relatives in a different way at that period.'

'How does the thieves' slang poem come into the Middle-ton play?'

'The Roaring Girl sings it herself, with a character called

Tearcat. The Roaring Girl dresses like a man, smokes, carries a sword, fights duels. A narcissistic type, rather than specifically lesbian, one would say. At least there are no scenes where she dallies with her own sex.'

Delavacquerie's good memory, eye for things that were unusual, had certainly been useful to him as a PR-man; for which he also possessed the requisite toughness. What he said next was a side he much less often revealed. It suggested reflections on Fiona.

'It's odd how one gets acclimatized to other people's sexual experiences. At a younger age, they strike one so differently. For instance, during the war I knew a married woman—a captain's wife—who told me of her first seduction. She was seventeen or eighteen, and on the way to her art-school one morning. Running to catch a bus, she just missed it. Two men, cruising by in a car, laughed at her standing breathless on the pavement. They stopped and offered her a lift. When they dropped her at the art-school door, the one who wasn't driving asked if she'd dine with him later in the week. She agreed. They went to a road-house outside London. In the course of dinner—establishing his bonafides as *homme sérieux*—her host remarked that he had lived with one girl for two years. Telling the story to me, she commented that—in those days—she thought love was for ever. Anyway, the chap gave her dinner, they had a good deal to drink—which she wasn't used to—and, after-wards, went into the garden of the roadhouse where he had her in the shrubbery. When she got home, finding her knickers all over blood, she thought to herself: I've been a silly girl. That's what she told me.'

'What's the moral of all that?'

'There isn't one, except that the story used to haunt me. I don't quite know why. It seemed to start so well, and end so badly. Perhaps that's how well constructed stories ought to terminate.'

'She never saw the bloke again?'

'No. I don't think it really made a ha'p'orth of difference to her. All I say is that for a while the story haunted me.'

'You were in love with the heroine?'

'Naturally. In a way that wasn't the point, which is that, in due course, you find girls are really perfectly well able to look after themselves, most of them. Even allowing for the fact that *les chiens sont fidèles, mais pas aux chiennes*. To retain the metaphor—bring it up to date—in sexual matters, as in others, the dogs bark, the Caravelle takes off.'

I never knew what Delavacquerie really felt about the Fiona business. Afterwards I wondered whether the heroine of the story he had told was really his dead wife. As Canon Fenneau had observed, we go through life lacking understanding of many things, though I think the Canon inwardly made something of an exception of his own case, where knowledge was concerned. That, at least, was modestly implied in an article I came across later that year, in which he contrasted Chaldean Magic with the worship of Isis and Osiris.

7

BAD WEATHER, OTHER ODD JOBS, mere lack of energy, had all contributed to allowing the unlit bonfire, projected as a few hours' clearing and burning, to become an untidy pile of miscellaneous débris; laurel (cut down months before), briars, nettles, leaves, unsold rubbish from a jumble sale, on top of it all several quite large branches of oak and copper beech snapped off by the gales. In spite of fog, something calm, peaceful, communicative, about the afternoon suggested the time had come to end this too long survival. A livid sky could mean snow. That dense muffled feeling pervaded the air. The day was not cold for the season, but an autumnal spell of mild weather—short, though notably warm that year—was now over. It had given place to a continuous wind blowing from the west, dropped the night before, after bringing down a lot of leaves and the sizeable boughs. There was a great stillness everywhere, except for a monotonous thud-thud from the quarry; a persistent low rumble, like a faraway train making laborious headway along a rough stretch of track. White vapour, less thick over by Gauntlett's farm, where a few ghostly trees penetrated its mists, wholly obscured the quarry's limestone platforms and Assyrian rampart.

For kindling, I shoved twists of newspaper in at the base of the heap. At the moment of ignition, the match flared against capital letters of a headline displayed on the outward surface of one of these scraps of newsprint.

EDWARDIAN SYMBOLIST
SEASCAPE VOTARIES

The enigmatic antithesis topped an article read a week or two before. Even allowing for contemporary changes in art fashions, the critic's enthusiasm had then seemed surprising. After seeing the pictures, remembering the piece, I vaguely thought of glancing through the notice again, to see if I now felt more agreement with the opinions expressed. By then the newspaper had been thrown away, or disappeared among a heap of others; kept for such uses as lighting fires. A search, likely to be unfruitful, seemed scarcely worth the trouble. Now, inclination to read about what had been said of the exhibition—the two exhibitions— was reanimated. In any case the visit to the gallery had been rather an historic occasion; setting something of a seal on all sorts of past matters.

Lighting another screw of newspaper under the stack, I extracted a handful of crumpled up pages, and straightened them out. On the back of one of these was a paragraph reporting Quentin Shuckerly's end in New York (battered to death in Greenwich Village), while on a cultural mission of some kind. I tore out Edwardian Symbolist/Seascape Votaries, committing Shuckerly's obituary lines to their funeral pyre. The paper flared up, dry twigs began to crackle, damp weeds smouldered, smoke rose high into the white mists, merging into grey-blueness. The atmosphere was filled all at once with the heart-searing bonfire smell.

'...albeit his roots lie in Continental Symbolism, Deacon's art remains unique in itself. In certain moods he can recall Fernand Khnopff or Max Klinger, the Belgian's near-photographic technique observable in Deacon's semi-naturalistic treatment of more than one of his favourite renderings of Greek or Roman legend. In his genre pictures, the academic compliances of the Secession School of Vienna are given strong homosexual bias—even Deacon's sphinxes and chimaeras possessing solely male attributes—a fearless sexual candour that must have shocked the susceptibilities of his own generation, sadomasochist broodings in paint that grope towards the psychedelic . . .'

The writer of the critique, a young journalist, with already something of a name in art circles, had been less enthralled by the late Victorian seascapes, also on view at the gallery; though he drew attention to the fact that here too, as with the Deacons, an exciting revival had taken place of a type of painting long out of fashion with yesterday's art critics. He expressed his welcome of these aesthetic reinstatements; noting the fact that at least a few connoisseurs, undeterred by the narrow tastes of the day, had followed their own preference for straightforward marine subjects, painted in an unaffectedly naturalistic manner. Most of those on view at the gallery had come from a single collection. He praised the 'virtuosity' and 'tightness of finish' of *Gannets Nesting*, *The Needles: Schooner Aground*, *Angry Seas off Land's End*, all by different hands.

Although a card had arrived for a Private View at this gallery, a new one, these two exhibitions had run for at least a fortnight before I found opportunity to pay a visit. Returning to the newspaper article—having been to the gallery—I felt less surprise at the critic's warm responses, not only to the Deacons, but also to the Victorian seascapes. That was probably due, as much as anything else, to a desire to keep in the swim. There was also a sense of satisfaction in reading praise of Mr Deacon (to me he always remained 'Mr Deacon'), given by a responsible art critic; a young one at that. The last quality would have delighted Mr Deacon himself. He had once remarked that youth was the only valid criterion in any field. He himself never quite achieved a fusion of the physical and intellectual in propagating that view. Certainly the notice marked how far tastes had altered since the period—just after the second war—when I had watched four Deacons knocked down for a few pounds in a shabby saleroom between Euston Road and Camden Town. At the time, I had supposed those to be the last Deacons I should ever set eyes on. In a sense they were; the last of the old dispensation. The pictures on view at the Barnabas Henderson Gallery (the show specifically advertised as the Bosworth Deacon Centenary Exhibition) were not so much a Resurrection as a Second Coming.

If the rehabilitation of Mr Deacon's art had not in itself provided an overriding inducement to visit the exhibition, the name of the gallery—proving all curiosity was not at an end—would have gone a long way as an alternative inducement to do so. A single-page pamphlet, accompanying the Private View card, outlined the aims of this new picture firm, which had just come into being. They seemed admirable ones. The premises were in the neighbourhood of Berkeley Square. It was rather late in the afternoon when I finally reached the place, a newly painted exterior, the street in process of being rebuilt, the road up, several Georgian houses opposite looking as if they had been recently bombed. In the window of the Barnabas Henderson Gallery itself a poster proclaimed Mr Deacon's name in typography of a size, and fount, he would have approved, an aureole of favourable press notices pinned round about.

Within, I found myself surrounded by Deacon canvases assembled on an unprecedented scale; more Deacons than might be supposed even to have been painted, far less survived. The Victorian seascapes were segregated in a room beyond, but an arrow pointed to an extension of the Deacon Centenary Exhibition on the upper floor, which I decided to explore first. The red tag of a sale marked a high proportion of the pictures. Two of those so summarily dismissed at the

down-at-heel auction-rooms were immediately recognizable
from their black-and-gold Art Nouveau frames, Deacon-
designed to form part of the picture itself; a technique Mr
Deacon rather precariously supported by quoting two lines
from *Pericles*:

> In framing an artist, art hath thus decreed:
> To make some good, but others to exceed.

In the shabby saleroom this purpose of the frames had
been obscured by dirt and tarnished paint, which cleaning
and restoration now made clear. Light in pigment, some of
the canvases were huge in size, remembered subjects included Hellenic athletes painfully straining in some contest;
another (too grimy at the time to be properly appreciated),
a boy slave reproved by his toga-enveloped master, whose
dignified figure was not without all resemblance to Mr
Deacon himself in his palmy days. The show was stylish
in presentation. In fact Barnabas Henderson had done a
stupendous rescue job from the Valley of Lost Things; Mr
Deacon's Astolpho, or perhaps one of the well disposed
swans, fishing up his medallion for the Temple of Fame.
Henderson clearly knew his business. To have supposed
him the dim figure he had seemed, only a few months
earlier in the same year, under the Murtlock régime, was
an error of judgment. Since his self-manumission at
Stourwater the Private View card was the first I had heard
of him; nor was there any further news of Murtlock and
Widmerpool.

Even Mr Deacon's closest friends were accustomed to
smile tolerantly, behind his back, about his painting. The
few patrons had all faded away by the later stages of his
life, when he had exchanged an artist's career for an antique-
dealer's. All the same, in days when Barnby's studio was
above the antique shop, Barnby had remarked that, little as
he approved himself, Sickert had once put in a good word

for Mr Deacon's work. Looking round, more impressed than I should have been prepared to admit, I took heart from Sickert's judgment; at the same time trying to restore self-confidence as to an earlier scepticism by noting something undoubtedly less than satisfactory in the foreshortening of the slave boy's loins.

There was still no one about in the first ground floor room of the gallery when I returned there, the attendant's desk in the corner unoccupied. Through a door at the far end several persons, one of them in a wheel-chair, were to be seen perambulating among the Victorian seascapes. I had not at first noticed that one of the smaller pictures in this first room was *Boyhood of Cyrus*. Moving across to ascertain how closely, if at all, the palace in its background resembled the configurations of the local quarry, I was intercepted by Barnabas Henderson himself, who came hurrying up a flight of stairs leading from the basement. It was instantaneously apparent that he was a new man; no less renovated than the Deacon pictures on the walls. That was clear in a flash, a transformation not in the least due to adjustments in dress and personal appearance, also to be observed. He had slightly shortened his haircut, reverted to a suit, elegant in cut without being humdrum in style, wore a tie of similar mood. These, however different from a blue robe, were trivial modifications in relation to the general air of rebirth. There was a newly acquired briskness, even firmness of manner, sense of self-confidence amply restored.

'Oh, hullo, Nicholas. You received our card all right? I was afraid it might have gone astray, as you hadn't been in.'

'I couldn't get to the Private View.'

'I hope your wife will look in, too, before the Deacon show closes. I always remember how good she was about our turning up once with that awful man. I was quite ashamed at the time. We went crayfishing, do you remember? It was an unusual experience. I can't say I enjoyed it much. Still, I didn't enjoy anything much in the circumstances of what my life was then. I hope you like these pictures—and the ones in the next room too, which are by various painters. Bosworth Deacon is one of my own discoveries.'

'I used to know him.'

'Know whom?'

'Edgar Deacon.'

'Who was Edgar Deacon—a relation of Bosworth Deacon?'

'He was called Edgar. Bosworth was only his middle name.'

'No, no. Bosworth is the painter's name. Are you sure you aren't confusing your other Deacon man? Bosworth Deacon is a most remarkable artist. In his way unique. I can think of no other painter like him.'

Henderson, possibly with reason, was not in the least interested in whether or not I had known Mr Deacon. Perhaps it was not really a relevant subject; or rather seemed relevant only to myself. It was clear that Mr Deacon—born a hundred years before—seemed in Henderson's eyes a personage scarcely less remote in time than the kindly slave-master of the artist's own self-image.

'I saw you were making for *Boyhood of Cyrus*, one of Deacon's best. On the whole I prefer the smaller compositions. He's more at ease with figure relationships. Several of the critics picked out *Cyrus* in their notices. I sold it within an hour of the show opening.'

'The background looks rather like the quarry to be seen from our windows. You may have noticed it on your caravan visit?'

Henderson raised his eyebrows. They could have been plucked. The comparison of Mr Deacon's picture with the quarry landscape struck no chord. Henderson sold pictures, rather than pondered their extraneous imagery.

'Surely the palace in the distance represents Persepolis. It's symbolic.'

'Well Persepolis isn't unlike Battersea Power Station in silhouette. An industrial parallel is not excluded out of hand.'

Henderson did not reply. He pursed his lips a little. We were getting nowhere. The subject was better changed. Eleanor Walpole-Wilson had probably sold *Cyrus* after her parents died. When, in days of frequenting the house, I had once referred to 'their Deacon', she was all but unaware of its existence, hanging over the barometer in the hall.

'When I was young I sometimes dined with the people to whom *Boyhood of Cyrus* used to belong.'

At this information Henderson regarded me with keener interest.

'You knew Lord Aberavon?'

He was not incredulous; merely mildly surprised. One had to be grateful even for surprise.

'Not actually. Aberavon died five or six years before I was born. My hostess was his daughter. She owned the picture. Her husband was a diplomat called Walpole-Wilson.'

Henderson was no more prepared to allow that the Walpole-Wilsons had once possessed *Boyhood of Cyrus* than for Mr Deacon to have been commonly addressed as Edgar.

'The provenance of *Cyrus* has always been recognized as the Aberavon Collection. Several Aberavon pictures—by a variety of artists—have been coming on the market lately. They're usually good sellers. Aberavon was an erratic collector, but not an uninstructed one. Have you looked at *By the Will of Diocletian*? It hasn't found a buyer yet. Owing to being rather large for most people's accommodation these days it is very reasonably priced, if you're thinking of getting a Deacon yourself.'

'The younger of the two torturers is not unlike Scorpio Murtlock.'

This time Henderson reacted more favourably to extension of a picture's imaginative possibilities.

'Canon Fenneau said the same, when he was in here the other day. He's someone who knew Scorp when he was quite young. One of the few who can control him.'

'Where did you come across Fenneau?'

'Scorp once sent me with a message to him. Chuck and I sometimes go to his church. It was Canon Fenneau who told me that *By the Will of Diocletian* was painted during Bosworth Deacon's Roman Catholic period.'

'Do you ever hear of Murtlock now? Or Widmerpool?'

Henderson, facetiously, made the sign to keep off the Evil Eye.

'As a matter of fact I do once in a way. Somebody I knew there comes to see me on the quiet if he's in London. There's a thing I'm still interested in they've got in the house.'

'Would coming to see you not be allowed?'

'Of course not.'

Henderson might perhaps have said more on that subject had not Chuck appeared from the inner room. Chuck (perhaps also of seafaring origins) had some of the same burly working-class geniality—now adapted to the uses of the art world—that had once characterized Hugo Tolland's former partner, Sam.

'Can you come through for a moment, Barney? Mr Duport wants a word.'

Henderson indicated that he would be along in a moment. Towards Chuck, too, his manner had changed. Himself no longer a victim requiring rescue, Henderson had become something not much short of Mr Deacon's benign slave-owner. No doubt mutual relationship was carefully worked out in that connexion, Chuck showing no resentment at the readjustment. On the contrary, they seemed on the best of terms.

'There are some rather interesting people in the further room. The actress, Polly Duport, and her parents. Far the best of the Victorian marine painters show come from the Duport Collection. He's decided to sell now the going's good. He's quite right, I think. I expect you've seen Polly Duport in the Strindberg play. Super, I thought. She's an absolute saint too, the way she looks after her father. Wheels him round all the time in that chair. He's not at all easy. Can be very bad mannered, in fact. He was a businessman —in oil, I'm told—then had to retire on account of whatever's wrong with him. He'd always been interested in these Victorian seascapes, picked them up at one time or another for practically nothing. Now they're quite the thing. He comes in almost every day to see how they're selling.'

'I know Polly Duport—and her father.'

'Do you? But you won't know her mother, who's come with them this afternoon. She's lived most of her life in South America. She must be partly South American, I think. She looks like one of those sad Goya duchesses. She and Robert Duport, the owner of the Collection, have been separated for years, so Polly Duport told me, but have been seeing a good deal of each other lately. He's never brought her along before. She was married to a South American politician, who was killed by urban guerillas. That's why she came back to England.'

Henderson's explanation had taken so long that the people next door, tired of waiting, now moved into the room where we were talking; Duport's wheeled-chair pushed by his daughter. Her mother followed. Norman Chandler, who was directing the Strindberg production to which Henderson referred, was one of this party. Henderson was right about Jean. The metamorphosis, begun when the late Colonel Flores had been his country's military attaché in London at the end of the war, was complete.

She was now altogether transformed into a foreign lady of distinction. The phrase 'sad Goya duchess' did not at all overstate the case. Chandler gave a dramatic cry of satisfaction at seeing someone with whom he could exchange reminiscences of Mr Deacon.

'Nick, so you've come to see Edgar's pictures? Who'd ever have thought it? Do you remember when I sold him that statuette called *Truth unveiled by Time*? Barney and Chuck ought to have that on show here too. I wonder where it is now?'

Duport stirred in the wheel-chair. He looked a rather ghastly sight. All the same he recognized me at once, and let out a hoarse laugh.

'How the hell do you know he hasn't come to see my pictures, Norman, not these naked Roman queers? He probably loves the sea.'

He turned in my direction.

'I can't remember your name, because I can't remember anyone's name these days, including my own most of the time, but we were in Brussels together, looking after different fragments of the Belgian military machine.'

'We were indeed.'

I told Duport my name. Chandler hastened to make additional introductions.

'So you and Bob know each other, Nick, and I'm sure you've met Polly. This is her mother, Madame Flores—'

Jean smiled graciously. She held out the hand of a former near-dictator's lady—Carlos Flores cannot have been much short of dictator at the height of his power—a clasp, brief and light, not without a sense of power about it too. There could have been no doubt in the mind of an onlooker—Henderson, say, or Chuck—that Jean and I had met before. That was about the best you could say for past love. In fact Jean's former husband, whom I had never much liked, was appreciably less distant than she.

'I've gone down the drain since those Brussels days. It all started in the Middle East. Gyppy Tummy, then complications. Never got things properly right. Look at me now. Shunted round in a bathchair. Penny for the guy. That's how I feel. One of the things I remember about you is that you knew that château-bottled shit Widmerpool.'

Polly Duport patted her father's head in deprecation of such forcible metaphor. Duport's appearance certainly bore out an assertion that he was not at all well. There seemed scarcely room in the chair for his long legs, the knees thrust up at an uncomfortable angle. Spectacles much altered his appearance. His daughter looked much younger than her forties. Firmly dedicated—somebody said like a nun—to her profession, she was dressed with great simplicity, as if to emphasize an absolute detachment from anything at all like the popular idea of an actress. This was in contrast with Jean, who had acquired a dramatic luxuriousness of turnout, not at all hers as a girl. Polly had always greatly resembled her mother, but, their styles now so different, perhaps only someone like myself, who had known Jean in her young days, would notice much similarity. Duport was not in the least disposed to abandon the theme of Widmerpool, whom he regarded as having at one moment all but ruined him financially.

'Polly once saw Widmerpool knocked out by an American film star. I wish I'd been there to shake him by the hand.'

'He wasn't really knocked out, Papa. Only his specs broken. And Louis Glober wasn't a film star, though he looked like one.'

'It was something to break that bastard's glasses. I'd have castrated him too, if I'd ever had the chance. Not much to remove, I'd guess.'

Jean made a gesture to silence her former husband.

'How are you, Nick? You're looking well. Better than the time you and your wife came to a party we gave, when

Carlos was over here. Everybody in London was so utterly tired out at the end of the war. Do you remember our party? How is your wife? I liked her so much.'

'I was sorry to hear—'

Before Jean could answer, Duport, recognizing the imminence of condolences for the death of Colonel Flores, broke in again.

'Oh, don't worry about Carlos. Carlos didn't do too badly. Had the time of his life, when the going was good, then went out instantaneously. Lucky devil. I envy him like hell. Wish I'd met him. He always sounded the sort of bloke I like.'

Jean accepted that view.

'I've often said you'd both of you have got on very well together.'

Polly Duport, possibly lacking her parents' toughness in handling such matters, at the same reminded by them of emotional complications suffered by herself, turned the conversation in the direction of these.

'You know Gibson Delavacquerie, don't you?'

'Of course. I haven't seen him for a month or two. He said he was working very hard.'

'Gibson and I are getting married.'

'You are? How splendid. Best possible wishes.'

'He's got a new book of poems coming out. That's why he's gone into retirement as much as possible.'

She looked very pleased; at the same time a little sad. I wondered whether the poems had anything to do with the sadness. In any case there had been quite a bit of sadness to surmount. She had given this information in an aside, while her parents were laughing, with Chandler and the owners of the gallery, about some incident illustrated in one of the Deacons, to which Chandler was pointing. Now he turned to Polly and myself.

'Goodness, don't these bring Edgar back? Do you

remember his last birthday party when he fell down stairs at that awful dive, *The Brass Monkey*?'

'I wasn't there. I knew that was the final disaster.'

Duport stared round disapprovingly.

'I prefer my wind and waves. Smart of me to hang on to them all these years, wasn't it? That took some doing. Do you remember, Jean, how your brother, Peter, used to grumble about looking after my pictures for me, when I was in low water, and hadn't anywhere to put them. He hung them in the dining-room of that house he had at Maidenhead. He'd no pictures of his own to speak of—except that terrible Isbister of his old man—so I can't see what he was grousing at. I might easily have got rid of them, but was spry enough not to sell. They wouldn't have made a cent.'

Jean laughed.

'Poor Peter. Why should he keep your junk? You weren't in low water. You were running round with Bijou Ardglass.'

'Perhaps I was. One forgets these things. Poor Bijou too.'

'Do you remember the pictures in the dining-room, Nick? Peter's Maidenhead house was where we met.'

'And played planchette.'

'Yes—we played planchette.'

Duport, becoming suddenly tired, lay back in his chair. He gave a very faint groan. I felt I liked him better than I used. His daughter made a movement to leave.

'I think we'd better go home now, Papa.'

Duport sat up straight again.

'So we've only got one more to sell?'

Henderson agreed. Jean once more held out her hand. Fashion, decreeing one kissed almost everyone these days, might not unreasonably have brought that about had she kept herself less erect. It was thus avoided without prejudice to good manners.

'So nice to have met.'

'Yes, so nice.'

Polly Duport smiled goodbye. I told her how glad I was to hear about herself and Delavacquerie. She smiled again, but did not say anything. Chandler waved. Taking Henderson and Chuck each by an arm, he led them towards the door, evidently imparting an anecdote about Mr Deacon. Duport gave a nod, as he was wheeled away. I strolled round the marine painters. There was—as Jean had said— a vague memory of sea pictures, hung rather askew, on Templer's dining-room wall. Rather a job lot they had seemed to me that weekend. Even if other things had not been on my mind—that soft laugh of Jean's—Victorian seascapes would have made no great appeal.

'It's the bedroom next to yours. Give it half an hour. Don't be too long.'

The Needles: Schooner Aground was by no means without all merit. The painter had evidently seen the work of Bonington. I was less keen on *Angry Seas off Land's End*. Henderson returned.

'Polly Duport's sweet, isn't she? Don't you find her mother a little alarming? But then you'd met her before. She must have been very handsome when young. Let me show you that last remaining one of the Duport Collection. You might like to consider it yourself.'

He did so. There was no sale. Chuck reappeared.

'Time to close.'

Henderson looked at his watch.

'You were telling me you still had some line on the Murtlock/Widmerpool setup. I'd be most interested to hear more of what went on there.'

Chuck interposed.

'Do you want me to stay?'

Henderson hesitated.

'No thanks, Chuck. I'll deal with everything. Just do the usual, and go home. I'll follow on.'

Henderson seemed divided between wanting to tell his

story, and something else that appeared to weigh on his mind. Then he must have decided that telling the story would be sufficiently gratifying to make up for possible indiscretion in other directions.

'If you've got a moment, we could go down to the office.'

I said goodnight to Chuck, by then making preparations to leave. Henderson led the way down a spiral staircase to the basement. The narrow passages below were cluttered with more pictures, framed and unframed. We entered a small room filled with filing cabinets and presses for drawings. Henderson took up his position behind a desk. I chose an armchair of somewhat exotic design, of which there were two. Henderson now seemed to relish the idea of making a fairly elaborate narration. He had perhaps exhausted the extent of persons of his own age prepared to listen.

'When we all crashed Clare Akworth's wedding, did you notice an old fellow with us. He had a beard and a red sweater. It was him all the trouble was about at the end, so I heard. Chuck and I had gone off by then.'

'You mean Bithel?'

'You know about him? I was told Scorp had almost to carry him home. Bith was a drunk. Somebody sent him along to us when he was just about to freak out. Bith was the only man or woman I've ever seen Scorp behave in a decent way to. He pretty well saved Bith's life. Bith worshipped Scorp in return. When he got better, Bith did odd jobs about the place nobody else wanted to do. That was pretty useful. There was no one who liked household chores. There was another side too. Scorp said an aged man was required for certain rites. Bith didn't mind that. He didn't mind what he did.'

Henderson's face suggested that some of the acts Bithel had been required to perform were less than agreeable, bearing out Widmerpool's reluctance to detail his own experience in that line.

'Could he stand being allowed no alcohol?'

'That's the point. Bith found that a drag. It was just the knowledge he was being kept alive prevented him from packing it in—plus adoration for Scorp. From time to time Bith would get hold of a little money, and have a drink on the quiet. Scorp winked at that. He'd never have stood it from anyone else, unless for strictly ritual purposes. That was permitted, like getting high on whatever Scorp might sometimes decide to produce. I used to give Bith the price of a drink once in a while, so he'd do things for me. I'd got some money hidden away.'

'You weren't allowed money?'

'Scorp controlled all that. Most of them hadn't much anyway. I'd hidden some at the top of the house under the eaves. I'd been thinking about getting away for some time, but it wasn't so easy. Then seeing Chuck gave me the chance. If Chuck hadn't been working in the same firm as Clare Akworth—he's one of their drivers, and gives her lifts to the office—I might not be here. I might not even be alive, if she'd not invited Chuck to the wedding, and he hadn't always wanted to wear a grey tailcoat.'

Henderson looked absolutely serious when he said he might not have been alive. His manner had become even a little disconcerting in its seriousness.

'It's Bith who looks in to see me occasionally. Scorp sends him to London sometimes to do odd jobs. Perhaps with a message to Canon Fenneau, if a respectable link is needed. It is sometimes. Fenneau helped once about getting a girl who was having a baby into hospital. Scorp recognizes that Bith will arrive back drunk, but he just makes him do a small penance. There's a particular thing Widmerpool's got that I hope one of these days to get out of him. That's why I keep in touch with Bith. He isn't very coherent as a rule. That doesn't much matter. Do you ever hear anything of Fiona? She used to use Bith too.'

'Her mother got a letter from her the other day. Fiona seems all right. They're in the Middle West.'

The Cutts parents, 'good' as ever, never complained about hearing rarely from their daughter. Probably they took the view that no news was better than bad news.

'Scorp used to talk a lot about that American Fiona married.'

'In connexion with Fiona?'

'No, not at all. Scorp was angry when Fiona went away, but I don't think he foresaw she would end up with Gwinnett. It was Gwinnett's own potential powers that attracted Scorp.'

'Transcendental ones?'

'Yes.'

'What about Widmerpool? Did Murtlock think he possessed transcendental powers too?'

The question was put lightly, even ironically. Henderson chose to answer it seriously. Having now abandoned the cult, he was prepared to denounce Murtlock as an individual; he had been too long connected with its system and disciplines utterly to reject their foundations. That was the impression his manner suggested.

'Ken's transcendental gifts were not what Scorp valued him for. I doubt if he possessed any. Not like Gwinnett. It was Ken's will-power. Also, of course, the basic fact of being able to live in and around his house. Ken wanted to be head. I see now he never could have been. At first it seemed touch and go. At least I thought so. I was afraid Ken would take over. He picked up the doctrinal part so quickly. I was terrified.'

'Why terrified?'

Henderson looked surprise at being asked that.

'Because I was in love with Scorp. I wanted him at the head.'

'Is Widmerpool in love with Murtlock too?'

This time Henderson did not give a snap answer. He hesitated. When he spoke it was objectively, almost primly.

'I don't know. It was hard for me to judge. I thought everybody was in love with Scorp. I was jealous of them for that. Ken doesn't actively dislike girls. He'd watch them naked, whenever he could. He may like boys better now he's used to them.'

'You mean in sexual rites?'

'Or on runs.'

'You went for naked runs?'

'Not at all often. Very rarely. Sometimes the ritual required it. In spring or autumn we would have to wait for a fairly warm night. Even then it could be dreadful.'

'Before breakfast?'

'Breakfast—you don't suppose we had breakfast? It was usually about half-past four in the morning. Only about once a year.'

'Murtlock himself?'

'Of course.'

'Widmerpool too?'

'Why not?'

'Bithel?'

'No—not Bith. Bith was let off. He'd make up for it by the other things he had to do.'

'And Widmerpool took part in the sexual rites?'

'When he was able.'

'Didn't you meet anyone on your naked runs?'

'Not in the middle of the night. It wasn't often. Scorp took us along paths through the woods.'

'Murtlock had Widmerpool completely under control in the end?'

'Only after the arrival of Bith. That was the turning point. Ken hated Bith. There was no Harmony. No Harmony at all. That made Scorp angry. It made bad vibrations. He was quite right. It did. I won't tell you some of the things Scorp made them do together. I don't like to think of it.'

Henderson shuddered.

'Why didn't Widmerpool leave?'

'Where would he go? If he went, Scorp remained in possession of the house. There's no getting him out. Ken's believed to have bequeathed it to the cult anyway. He could have made it over already.'

'Was thought of the house what caused Widmerpool to change his mind at Stourwater?'

'It was Scorp's will-power. That's stronger than anything. You'd know, if you'd ever had to face it. He came to Chuck's flat, and tried to get me back. There was an awful scene. I don't know how I got through it. I was shaky for a fortnight after. I did somehow—with the help of Chuck.'

Henderson shuddered again.

'But what was the point of it all. What did—what does— Widmerpool expect to get out of it?'

Once more Henderson seemed surprised. He was prepared to accept that he himself might find the ways of Murtlock harsh, horrible, even murderous. The aim of the cult, if impossible to express in words, was to him an altogether understandable one.

'Ken was playing for high stakes, if he really became head. It's hard to explain. Of course I don't believe now, not in the least. But Scorp, for instance, where's he going to end? He might go anywhere. That's what Ken felt. Of course Ken was too old, apart from anything else.'

'A messiah?'

'If you like.'

A bell rang at some length from upstairs. It sounded as if someone was following that up by rattling on the front door. Henderson rose,

'What can that be? It's just possible ... Wait a moment. I'll go and see.'

When Henderson's voice sounded again, at the top of the spiral staircase, its note suggested unexpected satisfaction. Henderson himself seemed to be doing all the talking. At least no replies were audible from whomever he had let in. There was a crash, a pause, a great scrambling and stumbling on the stairs, several steps missed; then Bithel, closely piloted from behind by Henderson, arrived—almost fell down—in the office. The immediate conclusion seemed to be that, whatever gratified Henderson, was not the fact of Bithel having arrived sober. On the contrary, Bithel was in a state of extreme intoxication. He was clutching a brown-paper parcel. Henderson spoke formally, as if nothing were more natural than Bithel's state.

'Here's Bith. I thought it might be him, but I never guessed what he'd bring with him. He can't speak at present. Wait till he's unwrapped the parcel.'

Henderson made an unsuccessful effort to get hold of this. Bithel clung on. He was, as described, entirely speechless. If Bithel had seemed filthy at Stourwater, out in the open, he looked infinitely filthier enclosed within the narrow confines of the gallery's office. He smelt horrible. In the army he had admitted to an age in the late thirties, so now was at least seventy, if not more. He appeared a great deal older than that; some dreadful ancient, brought in from tramping the roads day in day out. A decaying push-teen, torn and grimy, covered patched corduroy trousers. This time his feet were in sandals.

'Sit down, Bith. When did you get to London? Pretty early I'd guess from your state. Let's have a look at the picture.'

Bithel, deposited in the other exotically designed arm-chair, evidently wanting desperately to make some statement, was literally unable to speak. What had at first seemed a mere state of drunkenness gave signs of being something more than that. Drink had at least brought no solace, none of the extreme garrulousness that had characterized Bithel's army toping. He conveyed the air of a man, whatever his innately broken-down state, who had been seriously upset. That might be the form Bithel's intoxication now took. Henderson was chiefly interested in the brown-paper parcel, trying to get it into his own hands, always failing. Then Bithel got a word out.

'Scotch.'

'Haven't you had enough?'

'Not . . . feeling . . . myself.'

'No, you're not your usual self, Bith, on a day off. All right. We'll see what can be done.'

Henderson, opening a cupboard, brought back to the desk a bottle and glasses.

'Now unwrap it. How did you manage? It wasn't theft? You're sure of that? I'm not going to handle it, if it's stolen. There must be evidence you were allowed to take it. That's absolutely definite.'

Bithel made a jerky movement of his shoulders, apparently indicating that nothing at all nefarious had taken place in regard to whatever was under discussion.

'All right, but why can't you say more? You're not usually like this, Bith. You've had much too much. What will Scorp do to you? Try and tell me about it.'

Bithel took a deep gulp, finishing off the reasonably generous shot of whisky Henderson had poured for him. He held out the glass for more. Henderson allowed him an individual replenishment. I attempted to explain to Bithel that we had been comrades-in-arms. It was hard to think of an incident that had not reflected some unhappy moment in his own military career; any happy ones almost certainly experienced at times he would have been too drunk to recall.

'Do you remember our Company Commander, Rowland Gwatkin?'

Bithel's eyes, damp and bleary, suddenly reacted.

> 'Fol-low, fol-low, we will fol-low Gwatkin—
> We will fol-low Gwatkin, everywhere he leads.'

Bithel sang the words gently. Their reference to romping round the Mess on Christmas night, following the Commanding Officer over tables and chairs, sideboards and sofas, must have been entirely lost on Henderson. In any case the Commanding Officer's name had been Davies. Now Colonel was evidently merged as a single entity with Gwatkin in Bithel's mind. Becoming more than ever impatient, Henderson once more tried to get hold of the parcel. Bithel demanded a third round before giving it up.

'Not before I see the picture—know how you got it.'

Bithel made a violent effort to give an explanation.

'Going to . . . be burnt.'

'Scorp wanted to burn it. You rescued it?'

Bithel's twitching face seemed to indicate that solution as near the mark.

'Does Ken know?'

This question threw Bithel into a paroxysm of coughing, followed by an awful dry retching. He seemed about to vomit, something not at all out of the question in experience of him. An alternative possibility was apoplexy. When this violent attack was at an end he got out a sentence.

'Lord Widmerpool's . . . dead.'

'What?'

Both Henderson and I exclaimed simultaneously.

'Murdered.'

Bithel's powers of speech made some sort of recovery now. He had contrived to articulate what was on his mind. This was when it became clear that nervous strain, at least as much as drink, was powerfully affecting him. In fact the whisky he had just drunk had undoubtedly pulled him together. At first his words, dramatically gasped out, aroused a picture of gun, knife, poison, length of lead piping.

Then one saw that Bithel was almost certainly speaking with exaggeration. Even so, some ritual—like the gash at The Devil's Fingers—might have gone too far; for example, misuse of a dangerous drug. Allowing for overstatement, I was not at all sure which was meant. Henderson, with closer knowledge of the circumstances, seemed to regard anything as possible. He had gone white in the face.

'Was he found dead? Has this just happened? Are the police in on it?'

'Scorp was responsible. You can't call it anything but murder. I'm not going back. I've left for good. I'm fond of Scorp—fonder than I've ever been of any boy—but he's gone too far. I'm not going back.'

'But what happened? You don't really mean murder?'

'What Scorp made him do.'

'Say what that was.'

The story came out only by degrees. Even in a slightly improved condition Bithel was not easy to follow. In his—comparatively speaking—less dilapidated days, Bithel's rambling narratives had been far from lucid. The events he had just been through seemed to have been enough to disturb anyone. They had, at the same time, to some degree galvanized him out of the state of brain-softening he had displayed at Stourwater. He kept on muttering to himself, his voice at times entirely dying away.

'Lord Widmerpool ought never to have gone. Wasn't fit. Wasn't in the least fit. It was murder. Nothing short.'

That the old Bithel—with his respect for the 'varsity man'—survived under the tangled beard and foul rags, was shown by dogged adherence to calling Widmerpool by a title he had himself renounced by word and deed; if never by official procedure. After a bout of breathlessness, Bithel now showed signs of falling asleep. Henderson prodded him with a paper-knife.

'What happened?'

Bithel opened his eyes. Henderson repeated the question.

'What happened about Ken?'

'We could all see Lord Widmerpool wasn't well. He hadn't been well for weeks. He was bloody ill, in fact. Not himself at all. He could hardly get up from the floor.'

I asked why Widmerpool was on the floor. Henderson explained that the cult did not use beds. Bithel groaned in confirmation of that.

'When Lord Widmerpool did get up he was all shaky. He wasn't fit, even though it was a warmish night last night. It was Scorp who insisted.'

'Was Widmerpool unwilling to go?'

Bithel looked at me as if he did not understand what I was talking about. Even if prepared to accept that we had served in the same regiment, could recognize the same songs or horseplay, he certainly had not the least personal recollection of a common knowledge of Widmerpool.

'Lord Widmerpool didn't object. He wanted to be in Harmony. He always wanted that. He took a moment to get properly awake. At first he could hardly stand, when he got up from the floor. All the same, he took his clothes off.'

'Why did he take his clothes off?'

Henderson explained that was the rite. He seemed to have fallen back into regarding what had gone forward as natural enough in the light of the ritual, a normal piece of cere-monial. Not only did he understand, he seemed a little carried away by the devotional aspects of the story.

'Scorp must have thought it would get too cold if use was not made of that late mild spell we've been having. He was right. The temperature dropped this afternoon. If he'd left it till tonight they'd never have been able to go out.'

'Do you mean they all went out on a naked run in the early hours of this morning?'

'Ken never wanted to be outdone in Harmony by Scorp.'

Henderson and Bithel agreed about that, Bithel almost showing animation.

'Didn't we all? Didn't we all? But I'm through. I'm bloody well through. I swear I am. If I go back, it won't be for long. I swear that. I can't stand it. I'll find somewhere else. I swear I will.'

Bithel rocked himself backwards and forwards.

'What happened on the run?'

'It was through the woods.'

'Scorp was leading of course. Did Ken feel ill when he got outside?'

'Lord Widmerpool seemed recovered at first, they said. There was a warm mist. It was cold enough, they told me, but not as bad as they thought it would be.'

'So they set off?'

'Then Lord Widmerpool shouted they weren't going fast enough.'

Henderson showed amazement at such a thing happening.

'Why should Ken have done that? It was never a race. The slow pace was to give a sense of Harmony. Scorp always made a point of that.'

'When Lord Widmerpool shouted, they said Scorp sounded very angry, and said no. They were going fast enough. To increase the speed would disrupt the Harmony. Lord Widmerpool didn't take any notice of Scorp.'

'That was unlike Ken.'

Bithel lay back, so far as doing so were possible, in the pop-art armchair. The Scotch had greatly revived him, calmed his immediate fears, enabled him to tell the story with a kind of objectivity.

'If Lord Widmerpool disagreed with Scorp he'd always say why. They quite often argued. Lord Widmerpool seemed to enjoy a tussle, then giving in, and being given a penance. Never knew such a man for penances.'

Abandoning his narrative, at the thought of Widmerpool's penances, Bithel sighed.

'Did Widmerpool increase his own speed?'

'Not at first, they told me. Then he began complaining again that they weren't running fast enough. He started to shout "I'm running, I'm running, I've got to keep it up." Everybody thought he was laughing, trying to get himself warm. After shouting out this for a while, he did increase his pace. Some of the others went faster too. Scorp wouldn't allow that. He ordered Lord Widmerpool to slow down, but of course he couldn't stop him. He was way on ahead by then. Somebody heard Lord Widmerpool shout "I'm leading, I'm leading now."'

'How did it end?'

'It was rather a twisty way through the woods. Nobody could see him, especially in the mist. When they came round a corner, out of the trees, he was lying just in the road.'

'Collapsed?'

'Dead.'

Bithel held out his glass for yet another refill. Henderson topped it up. There was quite a long silence.

'How did they carry the body back?'

'They managed somehow.'

'It must have been quite a way.'

'You bet.'

'What did Scorp say?'

Henderson's voice shook a little when he asked that. I felt disturbed myself. Bithel seemed glad to leave the more macabre side of the story, for its administrative elements.

'I was sent to London to ask Canon Fenneau what should be done.'

'That's why you came up?'

'I couldn't find Canon Fenneau till this afternoon. He wasn't too keen on being mixed up with it all. In the end he said he'd do what he could to help.'

269

'And the drawing?'

'Scorp said the first thing was for all Lord Widmerpool's things to be ritually burned. There wasn't much. You know there was hardly anything, Barnabas, except the picture you told me to try to get hold of, if ever Scorp, in one of his destructive moods, insisted on throwing it out. You said it was between the cupboard and the wall, bring it along, if you've half a chance. It looks like a rough scribble to me, but I'm sure it's the one you said. I hope it's the right picture, and you'll make me a nice bakshee for bringing it along. I got it off the fire without Scorp seeing, just as he was going to set everything alight with the ritual torch. I stuffed it away somewhere, and here it is. God, I'm tired. Bloody well done in. I haven't had any sleep since they got back at five this morning.'

Henderson snatched the parcel, and began to open it. Bithel lay still further back in the pop-art armchair. He closed his eyes. Henderson threw away the brown paper. He held the Modigliani drawing up in front of him. The glass of the frame was cracked in several places; the elongated nude no worse than a little crumpled. It had been executed with a few strokes running diagonally across the paper. The marvellous economy of line would help in making it hard to identify—if anybody bothered—as more than a Modigliani drawing of its own particular period. It was signed. In any case, no one was likely to worry. It had hung in Stringham's London flat in early days; then passed to Stringham's niece, Pamela Flitton; on Pamela's demise, to her husband, Widmerpool. Pictures had never been Widmerpool's strong point. For some reason he must have clung on to this one. It was odd that he had never sold it. Henderson, even at the period of his renunciation of such vanities as art, must have marked it down, as it lay about somewhere in the commune. Now the agent, even at secondhand, of its preservation, he deserved his prize. Bithel gave a terrible groan in his sleep.

He had begun to slip from the exotically shaped armchair; would soon reach the floor.

'I shall have to be going.'

'I'll come and let you out.'

'What will you do about Bithel?'

'I'll ring up Chuck. He'll lend a hand. Chuck won't be too pleased. He doesn't like Bith. This has happened before. We put him on the late train.'

'You'll send him back?'

'Of course. Where else can he go? He'll be all right.'

'Will Fenneau do the clearing up down there?'

'Everything he can. He's very good about that sort of thing. He understands. Now I know about it, I'll get in touch with him too.'

We said goodbye. Henderson was right about the temperature dropping. It was getting dark outside, and much colder. A snowflake fell. At first that seemed a chance descent. Now others followed in a leisurely way. The men taking up the road in front of the gallery were preparing to knock off work. Some of them were gathering round their fire-bucket.

The smell from my bonfire, its smoke perhaps fusing with one of the quarry's metallic odours drifting down through the silvery fog, now brought back that of the workmen's bucket of glowing coke, burning outside their shelter. For some reason one of Robert Burton's torrential passages from *The Anatomy of Melancholy* came to mind:

'I hear new news every day, and those ordinary rumours of war, plagues, fires, inundations, thefts, murders, massacres, meteors, comets, spectrums, prodigies, apparitions, of towns taken, cities besieged, in *France, Germany, Turkey, Persia, Poland, &c.*, daily musters and preparations, and suchlike, which these tempestuous times afford, battles fought, so many men slain, monomachies, shipwrecks, piracies, and sea-fights, peace, leagues, stratagems, and fresh alarms. A vast confusion of vows, wishes, actions, edicts, petitions, lawsuits, pleas, laws, proclamations, complaints, grievances, are daily brought to our ears. New books every day, pamphlets, currantoes, stories, whole catalogues of volumes of all sorts, new paradoxes, opinions, schisms, heresies, controversies in philosophy, religion, &c. Now come tidings of weddings, maskings, mummeries, entertainments, jubilees, embassies, tilts and tournaments, trophies, triumphs, revels, sports, plays: then again, as in a new shifted scene, treasons, cheating tricks, robberies, enormous villainies in all kinds, funerals, burials, deaths of Princes, new discoveries, expeditions; now comical then tragical matters. Today we hear of new Lords and officers created, to-morrow of some great men deposed, and then again of fresh honours conferred; one is let loose, another imprisoned, one purchaseth, another breaketh; he thrives, his neighbour turns bankrupt; now plenty, then again dearth and famine; one runs, another rides, wrangles, laughs, weeps, &c.'

The thudding sound from the quarry had declined now to no more than a gentle reverberation, infinitely remote. It ceased altogether at the long drawn wail of a hooter—the distant pounding of centaurs' hoofs dying away, as the last note of their conch trumpeted out over hyperborean seas. Even the formal measure of the Seasons seemed suspended in the wintry silence.

A Selected List of Classics Available from Mandarin

While every effort is made to keep prices low, it is sometimes necessary to increase prices at short notice. Mandarin Paperbacks reserves the right to show new retail prices on covers which may differ from those previously advertised in the text or elsewhere.

The prices shown below were correct at the time of going to press.

☐	7493 0325 5	**Cannery Row**	John Steinbeck	£3.50
☐	7493 0326 3	**East of Eden**	John Steinbeck	£4.99
☐	7493 0327 1	**Grapes of Wrath**	John Steinbeck	£3.50
☐	7493 0328 X	**Long Valley**	John Steinbeck	£3.50
☐	7493 0329 8	**Once There Was a War**	John Steinbeck	£3.99
☐	7493 0330 1	**The Pearl**	John Steinbeck	£2.50
☐	7493 0331 X	**To a God Unknown**	John Steinbeck	£3.50
☐	7493 0332 8	**Tortilla Flat**	John Steinbeck	£3.50
☐	7493 0333 6	**Travels with Charley**	John Steinbeck	£3.99
☐	7493 0334 4	**Log from Sea of Cortez**	John Steinbeck	£4.99
☐	7497 0194 3	**The Red Pony**	John Steinbeck	£2.50
☐	7493 0371 9	**The English Teacher**	R. K. Narayan	£3.99
☐	7493 0370 0	**The Financial Expert**	R. K. Narayan	£3.99
☐	7493 0305 0	**The Bachelor of Arts**	R. K. Narayan	£3.99
☐	7493 0304 2	**The Dark Room**	R. K. Narayan	£3.99
☐	7493 0461 8	**The Balkan Trilogy**	Olivia Manning	£7.99
☐	7493 0414 6	**A Town Like Alice**	Nevil Shute	£3.99
☐	7493 0408 1	**On the Beach**	Nevil Shute	£3.99
☐	7493 0341 7	**Requiem for a Wren**	Nevil Shute	£3.99
☐	7493 0413 8	**No Highway**	Nevil Shute	£3.99
☐	7493 0412 X	**Trustee from the Toolroom**	Nevil Shute	£3.99
☐	7493 0410 3	**Slide Rule**	Nevil Shute	£3.99

All these books are available at your bookshop or newsagent, or can be ordered direct from the publisher. Just tick the titles you want and fill in the form below.

Mandarin Paperbacks, Cash Sales Department, PO Box 11, Falmouth, Cornwall TR10 9EN.

Please send cheque or postal order, no currency, for purchase price quoted and allow the following for postage and packing:

UK — 80p for the first book, 20p for each additional book ordered to a maximum charge of £2.00.

BFPO — 80p for the first book, 20p for each additional book.

Overseas including Eire — £1.50 for the first book, £1.00 for the second and 30p for each additional book thereafter.

NAME (Block letters) ....

ADDRESS ....

....

....